THE DRUZE
in the Middle East

Their Faith, Leadership, Identity and Status

To

Shoshana,

Jehuda, Ofer, Ilan, Amir and Ro'i

THE DRUZE
in the Middle East

Their Faith, Leadership, Identity and Status

NISSIM DANA

sussex
ACADEMIC
PRESS

Brighton • Portland

2 4 6 8 10 9 7 5 3 1

First published 2003
in Great Britain by
SUSSEX ACADEMIC PRESS
PO Box 2950
Brighton BN2 5SP

and in the United States of America by
SUSSEX ACADEMIC PRESS
920 NE 58th Ave Suite 300
Portland, Oregon 97213-3786

British Library Cataloguing in Publication Data
A CIP catalogue record for this book is available from the British Library.

Library of Congress Cataloging-in-Publication Data
Dana, Nissim, 1938-
The Druze in the Middle East : their faith, leadership, identity and status / Nissim Dana.
p. cm.
Includes bibliographical references and index.
ISBN 1–903900–36–0
1. Druzes—Israel. 2. Druzes. I. Title.
DS113.72 .D364 2003
305.6'97105694—dc21
2003004320

Typeset and designed by G&G Editorial, Brighton
Printed by MPG Books Ltd, Bodmin, Cornwall
This book is printed on acid-free paper.

Contents

Maps, Illustrations and Documents

—

Maps

Illustrations and Documents

Jacket picture: *Shaykh Amīn Ṭarīf*, the Spiritual Leader of the Druze, dressed with a religious gown known as a 'Abā'a Muqallama

Arabic Original of the Laws of Personal Status in Lebanon and Israel *and* The Arabic Original of the Personal Status Laws of the Druze in Syria are detailed on pp. 155–84.

Foreword by Elyakim Rubinstein

Within the huge mosaic of ethnic communities and religious sects of the Middle East, one finds the Druze community (Banū Ma'rūf), which possesses unique characteristics so far as their religion, society, culture, and history. The Druze community is a religious denomination that differs from other religions in regard to its conception of monotheism; in its internal division of believers into 'wise men', or *'uqqāl*, who are the experts in the secrets of the Druze religion, and the lay people, or *juhhāl*, who are distant from it; and also in regard to religious strictures (*ta'ālīm*), which place emphasis on the obligation of internal solidarity as a fundamental of the faith and on the need for separation from surrounding religious faiths. Of special interest is the 'exemption' given to the *juhhāl* in regard to various religious obligations, an exemption based on the religious motif that when a child is born, his or her fate is born with them.

On the socio-cultural plane, this community is characterized by two striking elements: the woman has a special status that is without parallel in any other Middle Eastern religion. She is not exposed to the problems of bigamous marriages by her husband; her husband cannot force her to continue in the marriage against her will; and in principle, it is impossible to force her into a marriage with a partner she finds undesirable. The second prominent element characterizing the Druze people, in particular the *'uqqāl*, is their modesty of appearance and way of life: the Druze home is characterized by the absence of eye-striking elements; the Druze wedding is a very restrained affair; and the external appearance of the Druze man or Druze woman, radiating simplicity, generally earns respect.

On the national level, the Druzes are characterized by nonconformism: in contrast to the ever-growing wave of population groups demanding recognition as groups with a national uniqueness, and hence a demand to recognize their right to a certain territory as their homeland, the Druzes have no such nationalist territorial demands. They see themselves as an integral part of the population in whose midst they reside. In this context, it should be noted that Druze towns and villages are characterized by their separation – as far as possible – from a non-Druze environment and their being located in high places, making it easier to defend against any hostile party.

Similarly, in contrast to other religious groups that, whether fervently or resignedly, do allow a person of another religion to join them, the Druzes are utterly proscribed from accepting into their faith anyone not born to two Druze parents.

Let me add that the Druze community in the State of Israel has constituted a unique and prominent pillar within Israeli society. Although not large in numbers, it has played a significant role in major spheres of public life – politics, defense, and law-enforcement services, as well as other areas. It has over the years attained high levels in the public service. Israeli law recognizes the Druze denomination as having religious autonomy, with state religious courts. Personally, I have in my various capacities followed the development and progress of this community.

Of course, there are Druze communities elsewhere in the Middle East. Against this background there is, and there should be, great interest in the history and life of the Druze community in our part of the world. The present work by Dr. Nissim Dana is a welcome step in this direction.

Dr. Dana, whose principal field of expertise has to do with the religions and cultures of the peoples of the Middle East, has enriched us with this volume of basic and extensive information about the Banū Maʻrūf. It has opened more than just a porthole to a fascinating world that to a great extent has remained largely hidden and unknown to the general public.

My personal interest was especially, and naturally, drawn to the legal areas, which abound in the book: Druze laws dealing with family relations, their comparison with parallel enactments in Judaism and Islam, the status of the community in the three Middle East countries where the Druzes are concentrated, the religio-legal status of Druzes who leave the community and wish to convert, and more.

Dr. Dana's book constitutes an important document for anyone interested in religions in general, and in the religions and cultures of the Middle East, in particular – especially for anyone who wants to complement his or her knowledge of important issues connected with this highly interesting region.

Elyakim Rubinstein
Attorney-General, State of Israel

Preface

The world population of Druze (*banū ma'rūf* = the righteous people) today numbers fewer than one million souls. They live in three main concentrations: in Syria, Lebanon, and Israel.

Anyone who wants to know about Druze life faces a real difficulty: The Druze religion is the most important characteristic of this community, and any attempt to get to know the people without studying the foundations of their faith is seriously defective. Ironically, however, finding out about the Druze religion is almost a mission impossible, since this religion is a secret one.

Research and publications about this population are relatively sparse, but even the works that have been published are suspect so far as their reliability and approach are concerned. For the most part, Muslim researchers have tried to describe the Druze – unjustifiably – as co-religionists and, therefore, have highlighted commonalities shared by the two faiths, at times presenting a version of the "facts" that is distorted in order to fit their view that the Druze are Muslim-Arabs. On the other hand, the Druze, being an (almost) insignificant and persecuted minority among the Muslim population of the Middle East, have been unable to express themselves freely. Consequently, they have tried not to give prominence to those basic points that separated them from the Muslim majority. On this matter, they acted according to the principle of *taqiyya*, or self-preservation, permitting them to adjust their external behavior in accordance with the people and religion in whose midst they reside.

Four principal subjects of discussion have been selected: (1) faith, commandments, and the life-cycle; (2) spiritual leadership and community organization; (3) population, society, and identity in Israel; and (4) laws governing personal status.

Part I – *Faith, Commandments, and the Life-Cycle* – includes the principles of the Druze faith, its commandments, and its manifestations. It also discusses the relationship of the Druze faith toward non-Druze. Druze holidays, festivals, holy sites, and the life-cycle of a Druze individual are explained. I cite with pride the long and fruitful cooperation that I enjoyed with the late Labīb Abū Rukn, a member of the Druze Religious Appeals Court. Abū Rukn served as my spiritual teacher in matters of Druze faith and tradition.

Part II – *Spiritual Leadership and Community Organization* – surveys the history of the Druze leadership and the community status and organization of the Druze in Israel and in other Middle Eastern countries.

Part III – *Population, Society, and Identity in Israel* – surveys Druze settlement and their settlements in Israel, with particular attention to demographic statistics relating to the Druze population, and the impact of social and economic changes.

Research is presented that traces the attitude of the faithful toward those who have erred – that is, Druze who have converted. Updated statistics are presented on the Druze in Israel since the establishment of the state who have "strayed" from the path of their faith, who have opted out entirely, or who have returned to the fold.

Part IV – *Laws Governing Personal Status* – presents the principal Druze family laws and their implementation in practice in each of the three main concentrations of Druze in the Middle East. A comparison is made of Judaism, Islam, and the Druze religion in regard to these essential laws.

Finally, appendices contain the laws of personal status of the Druze, and their implementation, in original Arabic source.

Most of the book is based on new material, never before published. There are, though, chapters in this book that are based on information contained in two of my previous works, *The Druze: A Religious Community in Transition* (Turtledove Publishing, 1980) and *Ha-druzim* (Bar-Ilan University Press, 1998, Hebrew). Due acknowledgment and thanks are given to those publishers. Thanks are also due to A. M. Goldstein for his editorial and translation assistance.

The letter reproduced on page xv is a kind endorsement from the late Labīb Abū Rukn, a member of the Druze Religious Appeals Court, of an earlier book of mine, *The Druse: Community and Transition* (1974): "I express my complete admiration for the great effort and attention that you devoted to a study . . . on Druze tradition and the foundations of its faith, which is distinguished by its accuracy as well as esteem for this people and its secret principles."

Preparation of this volume was aided by a grant of the Academic College of Judea and Samaria in Ariel.

Nissim Dana
Haifa, September 2003

Scheme of Transliteration

Consonants

أ	a	ز	z	ق	q
ب	b	س	s	ك	k
ت	t	ش	sh	ل	l
ث	th	ص	s̲	م	m
ج	j	ض	d̲	ن	n
ح	h̲	ط	t̲	هـ	h
خ	kh	ظ	z̲	و	w
د	d	ع	‘	ي	y
ذ	dh	غ	gh		
ر	r	ف	f		

Short vowels

ـَ	a
ـُ	u
ـِ	i

Long vowels

ـَا	ā
اء	ā’
ىَ	a
ـؤ	ū
ـي	ī

Note: ـة a, final; at, in construct form.

Labīb Abū Rukn,
Judge of the Druze Court, Haifa

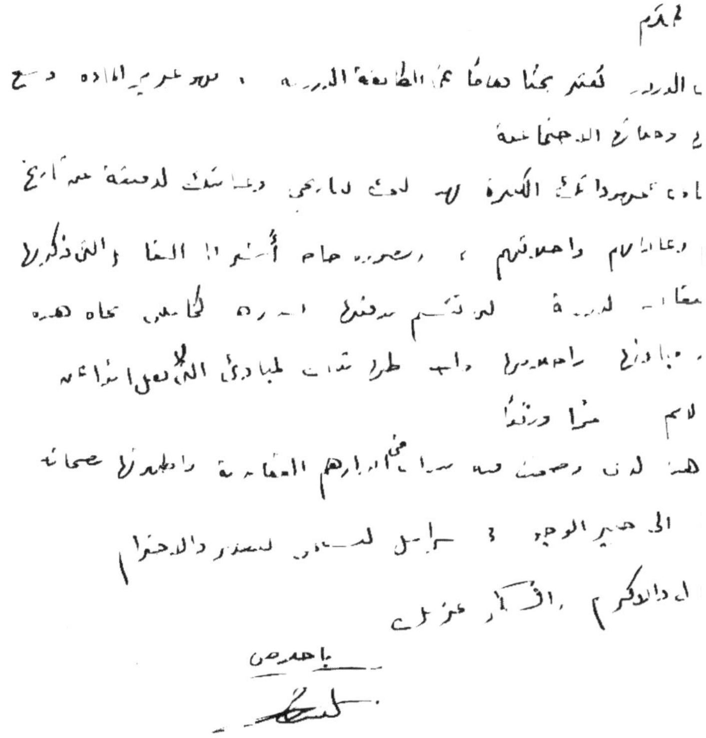
المحترم

[illegible] الدروز تعتبر بحثاً هاماً عن الطائفة الدرزية [illegible] المادة [illegible]

[illegible] الاجتماعية

[illegible] الكبيرة [illegible]

[illegible] أشعر [illegible] التي ذكرتها

[illegible] تجاه هذه

المبادئ [illegible] لمبادئ التي [illegible]

[illegible]

هذا [illegible] العقائدية [illegible]

الى [illegible] الاحترام

[illegible] والتكريم [illegible]

[illegible]

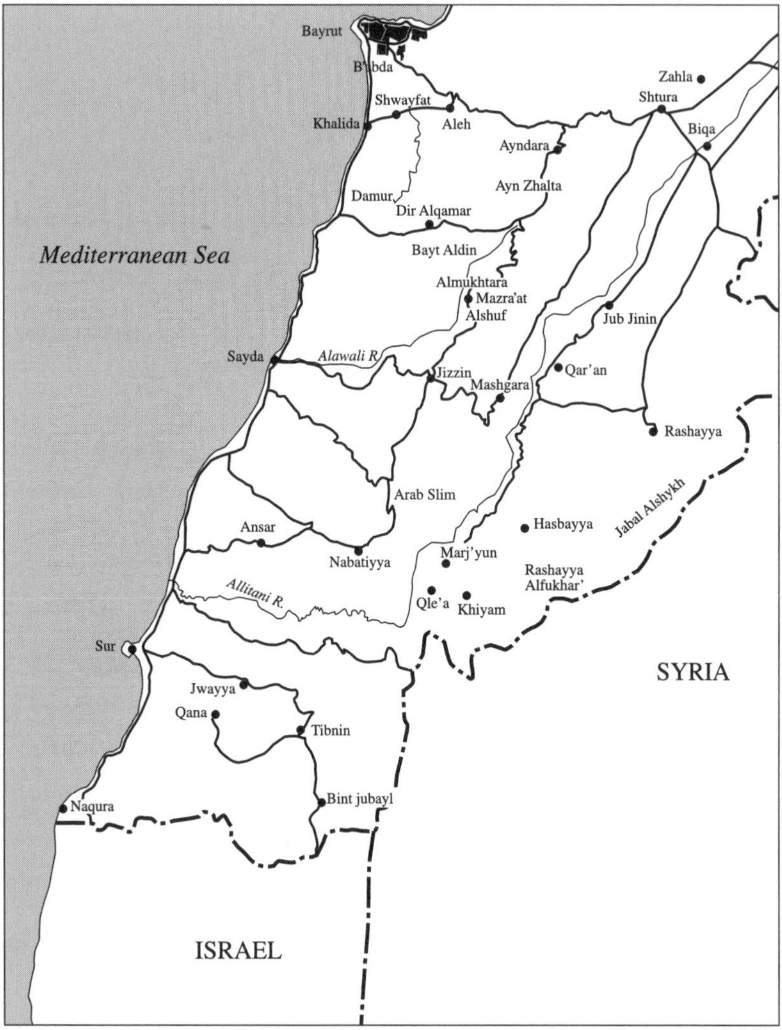

Druze Settlements in Lebanon

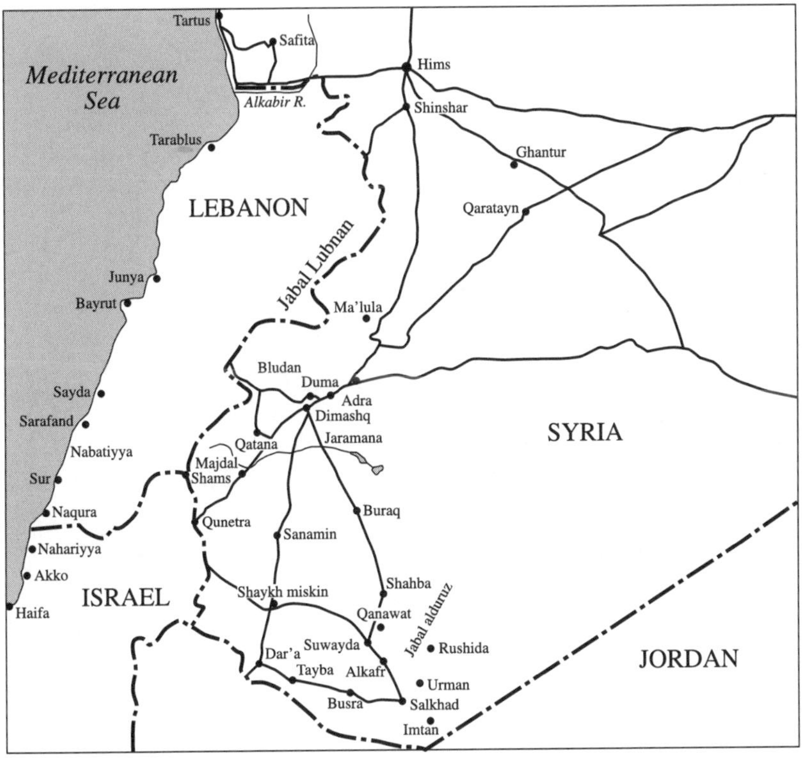

Druze Settlements in Syria

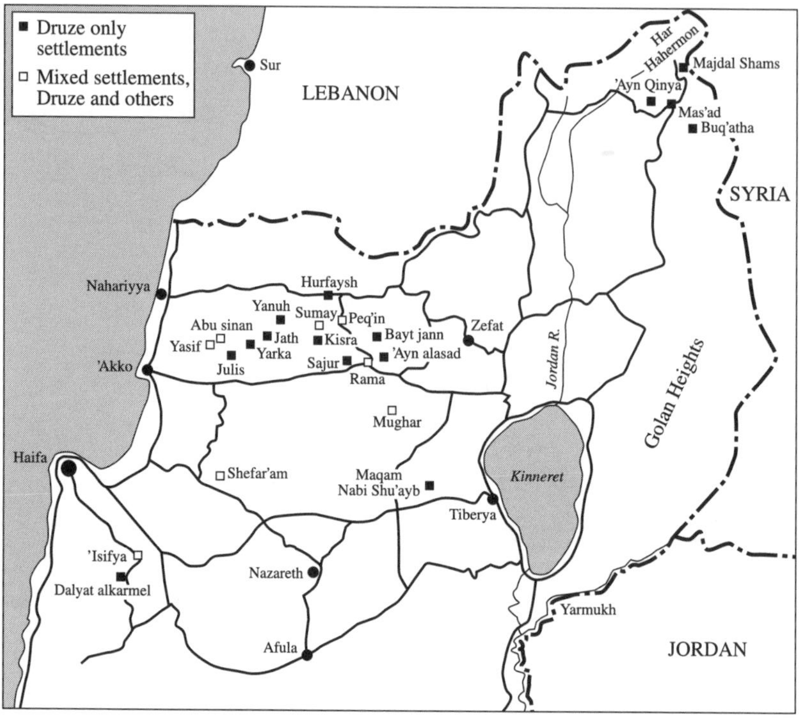

Druze Settlements in Northern Israel

Part I

Faith, Commandments, and the Life-Cycle

1

The Druze Faith and Its Believers

The Beginnings of the Sect

Khalīf Abū 'Alī al-Manṣūr al-'Azīz billāh, the 6th Egyptian Fatimid Khalīf, known also as al-Ḫākim bi-Amr Allāh, is the central figure of the Druze faith. According to Druze belief, God revealed himself several times before the eleventh century, when al-Ḫākim lived.[1] The religion is termed "a monotheistic religion" (*dīn al-tawḫīd*), its believers are called "those who proclaim oneness" (*muwaḫḫidūn*), and the last embodiment of the divine spirit was in al-Ḫākim.[2] Al-Ḫākim's "human" behavior was strange to many residents of Egypt at the time. Muslim historians of the period describe him as odd: an ascetic, a loner, extreme in his attitudes, and opposed to Muslims and Islam as well as to people of other religions who lived then in Egypt: Christians, Jews, and others.

Information about the beginnings of the new sect is vague. The following details are all that is known about al-Ḫākim, its central personage: In 1021, al-Ḫākim disappeared. No one knows for certain what happened to him. He was not yet 40. Ḫamza ibn 'Alī, one of the propagandists (*du'ā*) involved in propagating the belief that al-Ḫākim was a divine manifestation, claimed that al-Ḫākim disappeared from human sight as a sign of protest and to put believers to the test (*miḫna*). Non-Druze historians, in contrast, think that al-Ḫākim was assassinated, apparently by someone who disagreed with his way of life and behavior: a Muslim fanatic or even al-Ḫākim's sister, who was fifteen years older than her brother.

Spreading the word (*da'wa*) about al-Ḫākim, a topic we shall discuss in due course, was done by a team of propagandists. Two prominent propagandists who apparently came from Persia, were Ḫamza ibn 'Alī and Muḫammad ibn Ismā'īl al-Darazī, the latter known as Nashtakīn. Their preaching focused on the belief – to which al-Ḫākim gave his consent, at least silently – that he was the Creator himself, who was revealed to his believers as a human being.

Relations between Ḥamza and al-Darazī, however, were not good, especially because of the latter's repeated attempts to distort the contents of several religious "Epistles" in regard to the new faith.

Even al-Darazī's end is shrouded in mystery. There are those who say that the man was murdered in Cairo several years before al-Ḥākim's disappearance. Another version is that he died in Wādī al-Taym in Lebanon or perhaps at a location near Damascus. Common to all these versions is that al-Darazī's disappearance was connected with charges that he had committed wrong-doing: permitting sexual orgies, drinking alcohol, trying to undermine Ḥamza, and even a pretentious attempt to compare his status to that of al-Ḥākim. Because of these acts, believers considered al-Darazī a very negative figure, and it is common for believing Druze to use terms of derision whenever they mention al-Darazī's name.[3]

Ḥamza did not live long after al-Darazī disappeared. What is known is that he vanished about the same time as al-Ḥākim's disappearance. The Druze believe that Ḥamza's passing from the scene was also related to the "test" of the faithful in regard to their loyalty to the message of distinctiveness; and that even after he had disappeared, he continued secretly to send sermonizing epistles to a selected few of the faithful.

Al-Ḥākim's and Ḥamza's sudden exit left believers in Egypt in a difficult position, especially since their faith contradicted Islam, the religion of most of the people of that country. Even before the disappearance of these two, most of the propagators of the new faith had died,[4] and the leadership of the sect passed into the hands of one of the most important proponents of the religion, Abū al-Ḥasan Bahā' al-Dīn 'Alī ibn Aḥmad al-Samūqī. In the new circumstances, Bahā' al-Dīn moved the center of his activity from Egypt to Wādī al-Taym in Lebanon as well as to Syria and northern Palestine (*Bilād Ṣafad* – the land of Safed). Since then, members of this faith have concentrated in these areas. Druze who remained in Egypt were forced to give up their belief or to live undercover.

Rule of the Druze Emīrs

One of the most striking groups to respond to the call to join the Druze faith when it was still possible to do so (1017–43) was the Tanūkh tribe.[5] Members of this tribe, which originated in Iraq and over time located itself in Lebanon and Syria, occupied a prominent place in the Druze leadership in the first hundred years of its existence as a distinct community. Several times, in different places, they engaged in hostilities with the Crusaders, including assisting Ṣalāḥ al-Dīn al-Ayyūbī in overcoming the Crusaders at the Horns of Ḥiṯṯīn in 1187. Another battle in which they featured took place in 1260 in 'Ayn Jālūt. Members of the tribe also aided the Mamelukes in their war with the Tartars.

In the fifteenth century, the Tanūkhs reached the apex of their military strength and consolidation. Doubtless contributing to their standing – both religiously and as a community – was the personality and intensive activity of Shaykh Jamāl al-Dīn 'Abd Allāh al-Tanūkhī (1417–79), known as al-Amīr al-Sayyid.[6]

At the start of the era of the Ottoman Empire and the conclusion of Mameluke rule in the early sixteenth century, the Tanūkh tribe's status, which they had held for almost 500 years, diminished. Taking their place were the leaders of a competing Druze dynasty, the Ma'n tribe, who were allies of the Ottomans.[7] The head of the Ma'n tribe at this time was Fakhr al-Dīn al-Ma'nī I. He died in 1544. Because of Ottoman fears of Fakhr al-Dīn II's growing power, relations between the two went awry, and in 1635 he was murdered. Since his ascendancy in 1585, he had ruled most of the territory of Lebanon and parts of Syria and Palestine. His reign was characterized by wide-ranging economic activity that brought prosperity and security to the region, as well as by his granting complete freedom of religion to those of other faiths who lived under his rule. His special personality earned him a reputation for firmness and Druze pride.

The Ma'n leadership weakened toward the end of the seventeenth century, and the rule over the Shūf Mountains passed into the hands of the Shihāb family, seen by some researchers as a Muslim-Druze family.[8]

The eighteenth century saw the beginning of the Druze emigration from Mount Lebanon, where their population was mainly concentrated, to the Ḥawrān Mountain in Syria. It was from this period that the name *Jabal al-Durūz* (the Druze mountain) was transferred from Mount Lebanon to Ḥawrān. This concentration of Druze in the new area came about slowly but grew to be very large. The migration was caused by internal Druze wars, which were a continuation of the well-known dispute between the northern and southern tribes of Arabia – Qays and Yaman.[9] The Tanūkhs and the Shihābs were identified with the Qays, and the Ma'ns with the Yamans. One prominent battle between the warring factions took place at 'Ayn Dāra in the Shūf Mountains in 1711; the *casus belli* was the religious identity of the Shihābs. The Yamans were routed in this battle, which became known as *madhbaḥat* (the slaughter) of 'Ayn Dāra.

From this period on, the internal Druze rivalry took on a new composition: instead of the Qays–Yaman split, the Druze were now divided into Yazbaks (and later Arsalāns) and Junblāṯs, a division that has persisted to the present time.

The battle of 'Ayn Dāra in effect marked the beginning of the decline of Druze power in Lebanon. In addition to the reasons already listed – the emigration wave from Lebanon to Ḫawrān and the internal disputes – there are other important causes of this decline in power:

1 The Turks looked upon Druze autonomy in this region as an insult. Since Ottoman rule here was only symbolic, they made efforts to restrict this independence as far as possible. Among other things, they instigated disputes between the Druze and their Maronite Christian neighbors.
2 The feudal system that had characterized Druze society at the time began to fall apart.
3 Several members of the ruling Shihābs converted to Christianity in the mid-eighteenth century. These converts worked methodically to encourage Christian immigration to Lebanon in order to strengthen the family's economic status. They also strove to introduce Western European culture, particularly French culture, into this region. At the end of the process, the British were the ones who "adopted" the Druze, while the French strengthened their support of the Christians (the roots of this support had been planted much earlier).

The Druze in the Nineteenth Century

In October 1841, armed conflict between Druze and Maronite Christians crested, and an attempt was made to allocate separate regions of influence to each of the two populations: the area north of the Beirut–Damascus road was designated as the Maronite sector, under the leadership of a Maronite (of Druze origin, as it happened); and the area to the south was the Druze sector, headed by an Emīr of the Arsalān family. The experiment did not succeed, both because each sector included populations of the rival religion and because of inherent problems in the personalities of the appointed governors.

Another wave of hostilities flooded the region in 1845 and led to a visit by the Foreign Minister of the Ottoman Empire. Following this visit, several regional governors were replaced, inter-community advisory councils were set up, and other action was taken. For a short time, the waters remained calm.

The 1860s, however, saw the dam burst. The disturbances started with the murder of several Druze by Maronite villagers. The subsequent fighting led to serious damage: villages were destroyed and there were tens of

Leaders of the Druze Sect in Lebanon

The Druze in Lebanon are split into two groups: one headed by the Junblāṯ family and the other by the Arsalān family. In the picture, the author of this book sits next to Shaykh Majīd Arsalān, who served as Defense Minister in many Lebanese governments.

thousands of casualties, including dead on both sides. The agitation boiled over, affecting regions beyond the land of the cypresses. In general, the Druze gained the upper hand in these disturbances, but their battlefield victories were not translated into political success. The new ruling arrangements for the region were set under the influence of the European states that took part in the conflict. The various Christian sects received a more preferential status than did the Druze or other communities. A Christian governor was placed at the head of the new establishment. Following this arrangement, the violence was held in check until the outbreak of the First World War.

The Druze, as mentioned, had settled on the Ḫawrān Mountain (*Jabal al-Durūz*) in southern Syria at around the time of the battle of ʻAyn Dāra, and their strength in Lebanon lessened. The basis for this settlement was laid by Ḫamdān al-Ḫamdān, a Lebanese Druze who with his family had found refuge here from the internal conflicts afflicting his country. He was joined by others, and the Druze population on the mountain rapidly increased. Other points of Druze settlement were established, the most important of them being the town of Suwaydā'. Until the mid-nineteenth century, the Ḫamdān family were the undisputed leaders of the Druze in the area. During this period, Mount Druze had its share of clashes and its inhabitants even went to war both with the local Bedouins and with the Egyptian army. The latter tried to subdue the mountain dwellers in the course of its conquest of Palestine, Syria, and Lebanon. The Druze stood fast, exploiting the ground conditions and the desert character of the region.

From the mid-nineteenth century, another family gained ascendancy, the al-Aṯrash. The Ḫamdān family's star began to fade as the al-Aṯrash family made life more difficult for its brethren on the mountain. Under the leadership of the al-Aṯrash family, the Druze were forced to fight for their independence from the Ottomans, who tried again and again to subdue the mountain dwellers. In the First World War, it was only natural that the Druze would take part in the Arab revolt against the Ottomans, which was proclaimed in Ḫijāz in June 1916.

The Druze in the Twentieth Century

An ambivalent relationship prevailed between Turks and Druze in Syria prior to the war: friendship and closeness, on the one hand; suspicion and even hostility, on the other. There were Druze, led by Sulṭān (Pasha) al-Aṯrash, who inclined toward the British, an inclination that was openly expressed and that grew deeper as war drew closer. These Druze believed that they were ensuring for themselves a continuation of their autonomy in the Jabal (*Jabal al-Durūz*). There was, though, another Druze faction, also headed by members of the al-Aṯrash family, who wanted to strengthen ties with the French. The outstanding leader of this group was Salīm al-Aṯrash, who from 1914 served as a kind of ruler of the Jabal and whom the French finally appointed governor in 1921.

With the end of the First World War, Lebanon and Syria were included in the area of the French Mandate. Druze factions helped the French win control over the Ḫawrānī, and in exchange gained recognition of the independence of the Jabal and its declaration as one of the five states of the Levant subject to the Mandate of France.

In March 1921, an agreement was signed between the French authorities and the Druze leadership that granted the Jabal considerable autonomy. It was governed by a select Druze council (*majlis*). France's involvement was restricted to providing technical and formal "advice." The town of Suwaydā' was chosen as the Jabal capital.

Sulṯān al-Aṯrash, who wished to strengthen ties with the British, was not part of the group who had made this arrangement and did not see himself obligated to the agreement with the French. Friction intensified between him and the French, to the point that the latter bombed and destroyed his home in the town of Qrayyā. Sulṯān al-Aṯrash's attempts to recruit forces that would rebel against the French proved unsuccessful, and he was forced into exile (until May 1923) in Transjordan, which was under the British Mandate.

In July 1923, one Captain Carbier was appointed French "advisor" to the Jabal. He worked hard to develop the mountain, but his activities were too intensive for the traditional, feudal local leadership, and he became a thorn in its flesh. These leaders, most of whom were from the al-Aṯrash family, even claimed that Carbier interfered too much in their internal affairs. He was also accused of causing serious harm to their status as the traditional leadership of the sect and as the principal beneficiaries of the considerable material emoluments due to them by virtue of this status.

Armed conflict erupted on July 21, 1925, between the Druze, led by Sulṯān al-Aṯrash, and the French army, thereby sparking the great Druze revolt. This revolt reached a climax on August 2, when the French sent in planes and tanks to suppress the rebellion. The Druze, in contrast, took to guerrilla warfare, using light weapons, such as rifles and even swords. The battle earned a hero's status for al-Aṯrash in the eyes of his people.

Sulṯān al-Aṯrash's efforts to present the uprising as an all-Arab revolt, and so draw to his side all of Syria and Lebanon, gained only limited success.

After several difficult battles, the French finally put down the revolt in early 1927, and al-Aṯrash himself was again forced to seek refuge in Transjordan, with the other leaders of the uprising, this time for a much longer period of time.

In consequence of the failure of the revolt, many Druze villages were destroyed and thousands of Druze fighters were killed. From that point on, *Jabal al-Durūz* gradually began to lose its right to independent government.

Sulṯān al-Aṯrash returned to the Jabal after ten years of exile, but he no longer involved himself in political activity, not even after Syria gained the independence that he had fought so hard to attain.

In the Second World War, Britain and the Vichy government of France faced each other in the region. Many Druze in the Jabal thought the time was right to assist Britain and the Allied armies against the French forces. Syria fell to the Allies and the Free French on September 18, 1941. The process of its becoming an independent state now effectively started. Concomitantly the incorporation of the Jabal within Syria began to take place, and three years later the uniqueness of the Jabal came to an end. The Syrian parliament allotted the Druze a tiny quota of three settlements, and they had no real influence in the country.[10]

Even though the weakening of the separatism of the Jabal may be said to have been a bitter pill for the traditional Druze leadership, with the al-Aṯrash family at its center it was welcomed and supported by most of the sect who did not belong to one of the aristocratic families. Essentially, this was a natural internal process, but it was fired up by the Syrian government. Matters came to a head in the latter half of 1947, when civil war broke out between the two Druze factions.

In Lebanon, too, there was a protracted decline in the status of the Druze. The Druze population of Mount Lebanon shrank more and more until the area ceased being a kind of national homeland for this sect. The national charter of Lebanon of 1943 imparted to the Druze a relative share in the government in accordance with their size – 6 percent of the population. A tradition, though, of giving the ministry of defense portfolio to a member of this community was also created.

The Druze also had a large role in the upheavals that modern Syria has undergone: that of March 30, 1949, led by Ḫusnī al-Zaʿīm; that of August 14, 1949, headed by Col. Sāmī al-Ḫinnāwī; and then in December 1949, under the leadership of Col. Adīb al-Shīshaklī. Although al-Shīshaklī owed his advancement to the Druze, who had supported him from the beginning of his campaign, his rule as president (1953–4) was characterized by bitter and prolonged confrontation with this sect. Finally, under pressure of a broad coalition of army officers and politicians, among them Druze officers, al-Shīshaklī was forced out of office in February 1954.[11]

Druze were also involved in the abortive pro-Iraq and pro-Western coup in October 1956. On March 8, 1963, another revolt broke out with the vigorous aid of the Druze, led by Col. Salīm Ḫāṯūm.[12] As a result of this action, the position of the Baʻth Party strengthened. Still another coup took place on February 23, 1966, this one generated by Alawite and Druze officers, among whom was Ṯalāl Abū ʻAsal. Ṣāliḫ Jadīd took over, with the help of Ḫāfiẕ al-Asad. In 1971, Asad gained the presidency. The fact that he was a member of the Alawite minority influenced his relations with the other Syrian minority, the Druze. At first these relations were characterized by much suspicion, but in time they greatly improved.

With the national Zionist awakening in Palestine, the Druze in the country were faced with a dilemma as to their relations with the Jews. Generally it may be said that the national Arab movement did not succeed in mobilizing Druze to its ranks in the war against the Jewish *Yishuv* (settlement) in Palestine. Yitzhak Ben-Zvi, who was to become the second President of Israel, was one of the first to act to establish ties between the Druze and the Jews both in Palestine and in other countries in the region.[13]

Druze–Jewish cooperation in that period was manifested, too, in the ties formed by Abba Khoushy, who later became the mayor of Haifa, with the Abū Rukn family of the village of ʻIsifyā, near Haifa. This family held meetings with leading Druze public figures of the time – among them Sulṯān al-Aṯrash with whom they met in his place of exile in Transjordan, and the Druze leaders of Ḫawrān – in an attempt to persuade them to refrain from supporting anti-Zionist Islamic-Arab parties.[14]

As the Arab revolt (1936–9) went on, and even in later years, the Druze population inclined more and more to favor the Jews. There were two reasons for this: First, the Druze found that the *Yishuv* was gaining no little success in its struggle against the Arabs; secondly, many of the Druze themselves had suffered from the consequences of the revolt.[15] On November 27, 1938, for instance, Yūsuf Abū Durra, one of the leaders of the Arab revolt, descended on ʻIsifyā; along with the damage his force caused there, the insurgents also assaulted women of the village and desecrated Druze religious texts. Following this incident, Shaykh Labīb Abū Rukn traveled to Jabal al-Durūz to describe to the leadership of the mountain the serious events that had occurred.

Both Sulṯān al-Aṯrash and the spiritual leadership of the al-Bayyāḏa religious center in the town of Ḫāṣbayyā in southern Lebanon responded with fury at what had happened.

The Druze in Israel

With the UN decision on the partition of Palestine, the heads of the two camps, one favoring the Jews and the other the Arabs, each appealed to the Druze population in an attempt to recruit the community to their respective ranks. At the head of the camp supporting the Jews stood Shaykh Labīb Abū Rukn of ʻIsifyā and Shaykh Ṣāliḥ Khunayfis of Shefarʻam. At the same time, Fawzī al-Qāwuqjī, commander of the Arab forces, called for the Druze to join his army, *Jaysh al-Inqāẓ* (the rescue army). Shakīb Wahhāb, a Druze of Lebanese origin with military experience, made himself available to al-Qāwuqjī and put together a company of several hundred Druze soldiers, most of them from Jabal al-Durūz. Shefarʻam was picked to be the company headquarters, but the unit took almost no active part in the Israeli–Arab war.

The most prominent event connected with the unit took place close to the villages of Usha-Ramat Yochanan. In mid-April 1948, a battle developed between the rescue army and the Haganah. At a certain point, both sides ran out of ammunition. Haganah officers, led by Moshe Dayan and Chaim Laskov, initiated contact with the Druze officers, under Shakīb Wahhāb. These meetings laid the foundation for the neutrality of the Druze force in the war, and subsequently led to the defection of more than two hundred soldiers to the Jewish side. Officers and soldiers from this company, along with Israeli Druze, Circassians, and Bedouins, formed the base of the Israel Defense Force (IDF) minorities unit (Battalion 300).

The Six Day War (June 1967) and the Peace for Galilee Campaign (June 1982) found the Druze torn between their commitment to identify with the State of Israel and their loyalty to their brethren located beyond the borders of Israel and belonging to political frameworks that were hostile to the Jewish state. At the end of the Six Day War, the Golan Heights, with its four Druze villages, Majdal Shams, Buqʻāthā, Masʻada, and ʻAyn Qinya, passed into Israeli control. The new border separating Syria and Israel also divided Druze families, who now resided on both sides of the line. Toward the end of the 1970s, calls were heard from both Druze and others for Israel to annex the Golan formally. Both for this reason and for internal Israeli political reasons, the Knesset decided in December 1981 to apply Israeli law and regulations to the Golan Heights. The decision caused great consternation among the Golan Druze, for it forced them to identify politically with Israel, whether through receiving an Israeli residence certificate or by accepting Israeli citizenship. The Druze clergy on the Golan, with the encouragement and pressure of pro-Syrian parties on the Heights (and beyond them), imposed social–religious excommunication on anyone accepting Israeli citizenship. Most of the Golan Druze also objected – willingly or otherwise – to receiving Israeli residence certificates. The Druze objection stemmed from two important motives:

1 As already mentioned, most Druze families were split, as were their fields. The Syrians exploited this situation to force the Golan Druze not to respond favorably to the Israeli demands.
2 The Druze on the Golan Heights doubted the reliability of the Israeli authorities' declarations as to the future of the Golan. There were already two precedents for the return of Israeli-occupied lands: that of the Sinai to the Egyptians, and that of the city of Qunayṯra, not far from their villages, to the Syrians themselves. The fear that the Golan Druze would one day be returned to Syrian rule necessitated that they act with utmost caution when it came to identifying with Israel in any way.

It should be mentioned that at the same time there were respected Israeli politicians, within the government itself, who declared that it was "even possible to compromise on the Golan".

Leaders of the Druze Sect in Israel
Heads of the Druze community in Israel reviewing a military guard composed of Druze soldiers. In the background, the tomb of Jethro. Heading the marchers is Shaykh Amīn Ṭarīf, spiritual leader of the Druze community, and Shaykh Jabr Mu'addī, a member of the Israeli Knesset.

Israeli Druze, including their spiritual leader, the late Shaykh Amīn Ṯarīf, tried to close the rift that had been created between their brothers on the Golan and the Israeli authorities, but their attempts were firmly rejected by the Golan Druze, who explained that the political circumstances necessitated extreme caution.

The Peace for Galilee campaign began on June 6, 1982, and in the course of the war Israeli forces found themselves ruling the Druze population in several areas in Lebanon, such as the Shūf Mountains, Ḫās̱bayyā, and 'Aley-Beirut. Israeli policy gave preference to cooperation with the Maronite Christians, a step that engendered great acrimony among the latter's enemies, the Druze. The bitterness was especially keen among the followers of Walīd Junblāṯ, leader of the Socialist Progressive Party, who himself tended to be pro-Syrian and pro-Palestinian.

IDF officials made numerous attempts to prevent hostile acts between the Druze and the Maronites, but the traditional enmity between these two communities, which had lasted for more than a hundred years, was too bitter for the Israelis to succeed. The Druze complained that the Maronites had put up roadblocks close to their settlements, had kidnapped and even murdered their men, violated their women, and so forth. The Israeli Druze, whom their brethren in Lebanon implored to help them, were torn between their co-religionists and their loyalty to the State of Israel. It even happened that several Druze soldiers serving with the IDF deserted their units to join Junblāṯ's forces in their struggle with the Maronites.

In October 1993, Shaykh Amīn Ṯarīf passed away. He had been the spiritual leader of the Druze in Israel for more than sixty years. Owing to his personality and the reverence in which he was held, he was considered the spiritual leader of all the Druze in the Middle East. In the struggle over succession, two main parties contended: one was the Druze clergy who had been close to Shaykh Ṯarīf and wanted to carry out the will he had drawn up and to appoint his grandson, Shaykh Muwaffaq Ṯarīf, as successor. The other party wanted the new leadership decided according to modern methods and democratic elections. This latter group was comprised, among others, of public figures, academics, and retired high-ranking army officers. It also included several clergy. Thus began the process of consolidation of the Druze leadership in Israel in the modern era.

2

Fundamental Principles of Faith and the Druze Tradition

The Gates of Faith

The belief in the revelation of God (*kashf*) in the form of a human being is considered the most important fundamental principle of the Druze faith. In his book about the history of the Druze, Shakīb S̱āleẖ elaborates upon the subject of the revelation of God. He bases his account on *Rasā'il al-Ḫikma* (the Epistles of Wisdom – the common name for the Druze religious scriptures), determining that "God initiated the revelation out of an acknowledgment that it would be difficult for man to believe in his spiritual existence if he did not have some kind of manifestation in the form of a physical existence, for after all man needs his eyes in order to see and yet he is kept from seeing beyond the wall."[1] According to Druze belief, the revelation of God in human form (*al-lāhūt bi-ṣūrat al-nāsūt*) was the initiative of God, and this revelation in the form of al-Ḫākim is the final revelation.

Ḫamza ibn 'Alī is granted senior status as the connecting link between divinity and humanity. He enjoys many important titles indicative of his status: the Wonder of the Revelation (*ẖujjat al-kashf*), the Messiah of Time (*masīẖ al-zamān*), who canceled the religions, who battled Satan, and more.

The preaching to propagate the new faith did not last long. Upon the conclusion of the activities of Bahā' al-Dīn in 1043, the "gates were locked" (*ugliqat al-abwāb*) to new believers. Until that time, there were many new members from throughout the land; but from that year, the religious preaching ceased and no new believers were to be recruited. Aside from very rare and exceptional cases, the Druze since that time have been careful not to consider anyone a member of the sect who was not born to a Druze father and mother. Accordingly, there is no missionary activity or religious fanaticism, and intermarriage is considered a very grave transgression.[2]

The Epistles (*Rasā'il*)

The fundamentals of faith and the system of Druze laws (to the extent that it can be seen as a system) were inscribed in numerous Epistles (*rasā'il*) written by Ḫamza and Bahā' al-Dīn, and were consolidated during the first centuries in which the religion appeared. The Epistles are held secret from all who are not Druze as well as from those Druze not deemed worthy of being privy to their contents. The permission (and the privilege) allowing access to these Epistles as well as membership of the intimate body of the faithful wise men (*'uqqāl*) involve meeting specific religious and ethical requirements (to be discussed below). According to S̱āleḫ,[3] the Epistles, which are the Druze sacred books of wisdom (*kutub al-ḫikma*), also address the following subjects: "The foundations of Druze faith; responses to questions asked by Druze or others regarding the new faith; defense of the foundations of the faith against external criticism; appointment of Druze in different regions to propagate the faith; condemnation of believers who for some reason chose to leave the fold; information on the status of the Druze in one region or another in order to forewarn, encourage, or otherwise advise the believers."

Likewise, the books of wisdom deal with the following additional subjects: creation of the world,[4] cosmic fundamental principles (*al-ḫudūd*),[5] the prophets, responsibilities placed upon the individual, the world to come (*al-ma'ād* or *al-nashr*), reward and punishment (*al-ḫisāb wal-'iqāb*), revival of the dead (*yawm al-ḫashr*), the status of women, attitudes toward non-Druze (Jews, Christians, Nus̱ayris, Muslims, Arabs), and other issues. Some of the Epistles, and especially those written in the last years of propagating the faith, were written in the language of implication, and it is difficult to understand their content without the help of a special lexicon (*mu'jam*).

The Commentary (*Sharḫ*)

There are 111 Epistles in the *kutub al-ḫikma*. They are divided into six books, also called *rasā'il al-ḫikma* (The Epistles of Wisdom); and the religion is therefore called *maslak al-ḫikma wal-tawḫīd* (The Way of Wisdom and Uniqueness). Several hundred years were to pass before al-Amīr al-Sayyid, Jamāl al-Dīn 'Abd Allāh al-Tanūkhī (1417–79), compiled the Epistles into one codex and provided an accompanying commentary (*sharḫ*). The books and the commentary are both considered secret in the eyes of the Druze believer. Accordingly they are not to be printed, but rather are copied in handwritten volumes by special calligraphers (*khaṯṯāṯūn*). The writing is occasionally done in colored ink – apparently to lend special significance to sections of the text.

The Testimony of Benjamin of Tudela

One of the first testimonies we have regarding the Druze is that of Rabbi Benjamin of Tudela (Spain), who set forth on a journey in the region approximately in the year 1167. The part of the record of his journey regarding the encounter with the Druze includes some particularly interesting accounts. He describes them in the following words:[6] "a People called *Darazyan* . . . they have no religion, and live in the big mountains and the crevices of the rocks; no king or minister is a judge over them, for of their own will they live between the mountains and the rocks, and up to Mount Hermon is their border – a three day walk. . . . And they say that the soul, after its departure from the body of a good man, will enter the body of a child born at the same time that the soul departs its body.[7] . . . And they are loving of the Jews, and they are light of foot on the mountains and hills, and no one can battle with them."

The Prophets

The Druze faith is not a ritual-ceremonial faith in essence, but rather a neo-platonic philosophy. The Druze faith can be said to acknowledge the existence of seven prophets of different periods: Adam, Noah, Abraham, Moses, Jesus, Muḫammad, and Muḫammad ibn Ismāʿīl, who founded the Ismāʿīliyya sect.[8] Each one of these seven prophets only brought a partial religion to the world, complementing the Law brought by his predecessor.

It should be emphasized that in each generation there were several chosen individuals who were privileged to secretly study the true religion, even prior to the appearance of the sect upon the stage of history. Thus, for example, the prophet Shuʿayb, identified by the commentators with Jethro, the father-in-law of Moses,[9] was awarded the most highly regarded status – being the one to propagate the true Law in his own period.

The Druze and the Fundamentals of Islam (*Arkān al-Islām*)

The Druze do not see themselves as Muslims, despite the fact that most of the Druze believers are apparently of Muslim origin and despite the fact that they focus their activity primarily in proximity to Muslims. Thus, there are those who suggest that they be considered as Muslims, though it is clear that this is a view cultivated by people of certain political inclinations, but for which there is no genuine religious substance. Proof of this point warrants consideration of the degree to which the fundamentals of Islam (*arkān al-islām*) are implanted among the Druze:

(A) The most important fundamental of faith in Islam is the *shahāda* (the testimony). Nonetheless, the Druze do not accept a very significant component of this fundamental principle – they do not recognize the prophet of Islam, Muḫammad, as the last prophet. Instead of the second part of the *shahāda*, which testifies to Muḫammad's being the messenger of God (*"wa-Muḫammad rasūl Allāh"*) – and, in fact, his last messenger, the Druze maintain: *"Dā'im bāqī wajh Allāh,"* meaning "God exists, eternally" (or *"waḫdahu lā sharīka lah,"* meaning "He is alone, with no partner").
(B) As opposed to the five prayers (*ṣalā*) of the Muslims, the ordinary Druze is not obligated to any prayer; even the *'uqqāl* are only required to participate in minimal religious congregational meetings in their house of prayer (*khalwa*).
(C) The Druze do not fast in the month of *ramaḏān.*
(D) The Druze do not observe the commandment requiring a pilgrimage to Mecca (*ḫajj*).
(E) The Druze do not observe the commandment of giving charity (*ẕakā*) in the manner prescribed in Islam.

Ta'ālīm (Religious Teachings)

Particular significance is attributed by the Druze to the observance of seven religious teachings (*ta'ālīm*), as indicated below:[10]

1 *Ṣidq al-Lisān* (holding one's tongue).
2 *Ḫifẕ al-Ikhwān* (watching over one's brothers).
3 *Tark . . . 'Ibādat al-'Adam wal-Buhtān* (abandoning worship of the occult and vanity . . .).
4 *Al-Barā'a min al-Abālisa wal-Ṯughyān* (shirking the devil and acts of evil).
5 *Tawḫīd al-Mawla jalla dhikruhu fī kull 'Aṣr wa-Zamān* (the uniqueness of the great God in every generation and at all times).
6 *Al-Riḏā bi-fi'lihi kayfa mā kān* (willing acceptance of His deeds, whatever they may be).

7 *Al-Taslīm li-Amrihi fī al-Sirr wal-Ḥadthān* (coming to terms with both the concealed and the apparent decrees of God).

(1) *Ṣidq al-Lisān – holding one's tongue*

As a rule, the Druze is expected to be careful of what he utters. He is expected to be sincere in his remarks, be faithful to his promise, admit to his mistakes, keep his secrets, bear his pain with restraint, refrain from gossip, and be pleasant in conversation

This fundamental principle is defined as *ra's al-'īmān* (the basic principle of the faith). There are those who connect this directive with the forbidding of stealing, killing, prostitution, false testimony, and the like, as it is necessarily an obligation to speak the truth. According to Druze belief, "He who lies to his brothers . . . [it is as if] he lies to our Master."

A special matter is use of the fundamental principle of *taqiyya*, in which, outwardly, the faith is presented in a misleading way (this will be elaborated upon below).

(2) *Ḥifẓ al-Ikhwān – watching over one's brothers*

According to this directive, the Druze is to exhibit solidarity with a member of his sect (Epistle 41) in times of distress, when confronted with a struggle over a just matter. Frequently, the members of the Druze sect recall the image of the Druze as a kind of copper serving platter – if you hit any part of it, the resonating sound will be emitted from all of it (*al-durūẓ min ṭāsat nuḥās: min ayna mā ḍarabtahā – tarinn*).

Thus the Druze must watch over their brothers, refrain from patronizing them, aspire to rectifying their shortcomings, protect their property, speak their praise, and protect their honor. This is also an important fundamental principle for the reinforcement of Druze unity. Likewise, it was deigned that the transgression of this directive warrants punishment and lashing.

(3) *Tark mā kuntum ʿalayhi wa-taʿtaqidūnahu fī ʿibādat alʿadam wal-buhtān – abandoning the worship of the occult, and conceit*

The Druze has to avoid worship of gods and bowing down to idols, graven images, "sanctified" stones, and the like.

Similarly, the Druze is to shirk the paths of faith of other religions, for these worship a concealed god (*ʿadam*), whereas the Druze have been privileged to witness the revelation of God, who revealed himself to them before their very eyes (*kashf*).[11]

(4) *Al-Barā'a min al-Abālisa wal-Tughyān – shirking the devil and acts of evil*

The devil is the antithesis to every positive act – with regard both to faith and to ethics. By acts of virtue, such as receiving guests, doing justice, and avoiding acts of evil, the devil is pushed away and one distances oneself from him.

(5) *Tawḫīd al-Mawla jalla dhikruhu fī kull 'Aṣr wa-Zamān wa-Dahr wa-Awān – the uniqueness of God, of whom we should be reminded in every generation and at all times*

Despite the fact that this directive is the fifth in the order of the *ta'ālīm*, it is undoubtedly the most important of all: demanding belief in *al-Ḫākim*, which is one of the many revelations of the divine spirit that have occurred until now; and the faith that this divine revelation in the image of *al-Ḫākim* is the last of the revelations. According to this teaching, the Druze and only the Druze are worthy of the name *Muwaḫḫidūn* ("unifiers"), since they alone (*waḫdahum*) were privileged to confront God in his revelation.

(6) *Al-Riḏā bi-Fi'lihi kayfa mā kān – willing acceptance of His (Allāh's) deeds, whatever they may be*

According to this directive, everything from God has to be accepted, and one must also bless the ills that come upon one just as one does the good. The acts of God transcend the comprehension of human beings, and one should not question any harm or tragedy. The meaning of this fundamental principle is exemplified in Epistle 9: "Should God request of one of you to kill his child, he must do so without hesitation or feeling of acting against one's will; for if not, he will not be entitled to reward."

(7) *Al-Taslīm li-Amrihi fī al-Sirr wal-Ḫadthān – coming to terms (totally) with both the concealed and the apparent decrees of God*

This concept is based on blind faith in fate and predetermination (fatalism): the fate of man is predetermined by God's decree, and there is no way in which it can be changed. He determines all, and is omniscient. There are those who attribute the courage of the Druze to this fundamental principle of faith.

'Uqqāl and *Juhhāl*

The Druze are divided into two groups from a religious perspective: the *'uqqāl*, the wise, knowing the esoteric (masculine singular – *'āqil*; *'āqila* for a woman) as opposed to the *juhhāl*, the simple people, the lowest (singular –

Jāhil).[12] Since Druze society is conservative, attributing extreme importance to religion, it is understandable that *'uqqāl* enjoy the right to determine all matters of daily life for the entire sect, despite their relatively limited number.

Druze society expressed the distinction between the *'uqqāl* and the *juhhāl* in the past by the appointment of two shaykhs as leaders: one for religious purposes (*Shaykh al-Dīn*), and the other for secular matters (*Shaykh al-Balad* or *Shaykh al-Dunya*). They generally were awarded the position because of their personalities, their social status, and their belonging to particular families – granting them a "hold" over these positions.

Khalwa and Religious Gatherings

The religious Druze visits the *khalwa*[13] every evening, but *must* do so at least on Sunday evening and, especially, on Thursday evening.[14] The length of time spent by the *'āqil* in the *khalwa* is related to one's religious status, and the longer, the more praiseworthy. An *'āqil* who has violated any of the commandments of religion, tradition, or society is punished by exclusion from these religious gatherings for a period of time determined by the severity of the transgression. Such a person is called *mab'ūd* (excluded). If they want to return and join the *'uqqāl* circle, they must attend every gathering and ask the religious members to forgive them and pardon their deeds.

There are two particularly grave transgressions according to the Druze religion – adultery and murder – and anyone committing these acts is excluded from the religious gatherings for life. Such a person is called *maḥrūm* (excommunicated).[15]

The house of prayer itself is a hall empty of any furniture, decoration, or photographs, and its appearance is in no way designed to please. Only the vital accessories for seating are found inside, and care is taken to avoid any item that might distract the believer from communion with God and from the depth of the contemplation of Him. The only objects found in the hall are cupboards and stools on which the religious scriptures are placed while being studied. In addition, there are carpets, mats, or mattresses, on which the worshippers sit. Part of the *khalwa* hall is for the use of women who belong to the *'uqqāl* circle,[16] and this section is separated with a solid partition. In the women's section, scarves and blankets are spread around to be used to cover the lower half of their bodies while they are sitting cross-legged on the mattresses. At these gatherings (*sahra*), beginning approximately half an hour after sunset, indoctrination and religious guidance are heard under the direction of an important religious man, referred to as *Sā'is*[17] and permanently appointed for the house of prayer.

During the first part of the gathering, members of the sect who are not *'uqqāl*, but consider themselves candidates, may also take part; however, in the latter part, they must leave. At that point, the *'uqqāl* remain to address various community needs, to read the holy scriptures and the commentaries, and to attend to other matters. Among other things, during these meetings, the participants read *mawā'iẕ*, poems of indoctrination and ethics, singing them together to an appropriate tune. The contents of these songs have an ascetic orientation (*ṣūfī*),[18] and most of them were composed by one of the most important religious leaders to rise up among the people of this faith, Muḫammad abū Hilāl, referred to as *al-Shaykh al-Fāḏil* (the Shaykh of Great Compassion), who died in 1640.

The *khalwa* is generally located at a site remote from the center of the village for reasons of caution and maintaining the secrecy of the ritual.[19]

Ethical Demands of the *'Āqil*

The *'āqil* Druze are subject to a list of commands according to which they are expected to behave in their daily routine. Among other things, they must refrain from misusing the tongue and from speaking rudely, and must restrict themselves to the purity of ethics. Likewise, they must undertake to refrain from swearing in the name of God, even on a matter of truth; to forgo the pleasures of this world; and to aspire to a life of asceticism and modesty (*taqashshuf*) in behavior and outward appearance.

The ideal to which they should aspire is to subsist with little food, which is to be obtained by working the land or by the labor of one's hands, and to be cautious of receiving emoluments from anyone with respect to whom there is any suspicion that he acquired his belongings in unjust ways, or any doubt regarding his ethical honesty. This refers to emoluments from private individuals as well as from any institution, including state and public institutions. Card games, gambling, and the like are absolutely forbidden. Generally the Druze do not deal in commerce, since the Druze faith considers the legitimacy of this vocation questionable (*khabā'ith*).

Greed is to be avoided (*sharāha*), as is a showy appearance, while food and dress of the most modest degree must suffice. Therefore, it is not permissible to wear silk or to decorate oneself or to wear gold jewelry – for men and women alike.

The religious Druze is expected to stay away from festive gatherings other than those religiously condoned. Similarly, the joint company of men and women is to be avoided. Accordingly, they do not frequent coffee houses or movie theaters, and the stricter observers avoid watching television.

Commandments and Outward Appearance

The *'āqil* Druze man must abide by certain rules regarding his outward appearance: he should have a shaven head, covered usually by a white turban. He must grow a mustache, and it is preferable not to shave the beard, especially as one grows older. Likewise, he must wear a particular traditional dress, especially when he is in the village. He must avoid eating pork, and refrain from smoking[20] and from drinking alcoholic beverages (*muskirāt*). By the same token, he is warned against eating the *mulūkhiyya* plant and a vegetable called *jarjīr*. Before putting any food or drink in his mouth, he must call on the name of God in some way or another, as appears appropriate to him.[21]

Transition from the Status of *Jāhil* to *'Āqil*

The transition from the status of *jāhil* to *'āqil* is definitely possible, but requires certain tests by which the *jāhil* must prove himself. The essence of these tests is the requirement to observe the supreme ethical commandments and to abide by the rules of a modest lifestyle, as designated above. Age is not a relevant factor in this matter, and this status is not transmitted by inheritance. One who seeks to join the *'uqqāl* group must visit the *khalwa* at all times of religious gatherings there. At the conclusion of the first part of the gathering, in which the candidate is permitted to participate, he asks the *'uqqāl* present to allow him to join their circle.[22] Once this is granted, in the course of the stages of acceptance, which generally last from six to twelve months, he is required, like them, to fulfill all of the religious requirements, and they are permitted to include him in the study of the books of *al-Ḥikma*.

Among the religious persons, also often referred to as *Ajāwīd* (*Jawwīd* in the singular), a synonym for *'uqqāl*, there is a hierarchy. Ascending the religious hierarchy within the *'uqqāl* circle is related, among other things, to how far one abides by a lifestyle of asceticism and rules of ethics and behavior, as well as to the quantity of Epistles from the *Kutub al-Ḥikma* one knows by heart, the comprehension of these Epistles, and other criteria. The extremists among the *'uqqāl* seclude themselves from public life, and devote themselves entirely to asceticism and maintaining the religious ritual. The dress of these extremists usually includes a striped upper robe (*'abā'a mudalla'a* or *muqallama*), a covering similar to the Jewish prayer shawl, the *tallit* (see the picture on the title page). The shape of the turban changes according to the religious status of the *'uqqāl*; the highest level is distinguished by the wearing of a pyriform hat fluffed with white material (*laffa mukalwasa*), such as that worn by Shaykh Amīn Ṭarīf, the late spiritual leader of the Druze sect in Israel. Presently, only isolated Druze religious leaders in Lebanon wear such a turban on their heads.

The Religious Status of Women

Contrary to the traditions of the main monotheistic religions, the Druze woman is able to serve in a position of religious significance. There are even women who have been privileged to reach senior religious levels. Their rights in the realm of personal status are almost identical to those of men, and in certain religious matters their status is even higher than that of a man. Thus, for example, the Druze woman receives preference in the process of acceptance to the *'uqqāl* group. The number of women among all the *'uqqāl* is greater than the number of men. This may be due to the fact that men can join only after successfully proving themselves by certain "tests," whereas a woman who asks to join is immediately granted admittance to the group without "tests" (unless there are reasons for not accepting her request). In the religious gatherings in the *khalwa*, as noted, the religious women take part, but they are seated behind a partition separating them from the men. Like the men, their heads must be covered. Their head covering is a white scarf, called a *naqāb*. The more pious among them cover their hair with an additional head covering, called *'irāqiyya*, tightly wrapped around the head from underneath the white scarf.

Relations between Men and Women

It is recommended that an *'āqila* woman marry an *'āqil* man; if one of the couple does not belong to the group of religious members of the sect, it is clearly preferable that the person make a commitment, in advance, stating his/her intentions to join this group within a reasonable period of time. In the realm of marital relations, it is recommended that the *'uqqāl* not submit to their sexual drives and that they have marital relations only for the purpose of reproduction.

In the presence of a stranger, a woman is required to cover her face with a scarf, exposing only the eyes, the mouth, and the nose. The Druze man is not permitted by religious law to marry more than one woman, even if he is *jāhil.* Likewise, he is forbidden to return to his divorced wife or even to be under the same roof with her for the rest of his life.

Druze House of Prayer (*khalwa*)

The Druze prayer house is empty of any furniture, decoration, or photograph. Seating is on carpets. At the time of assembly (*sahra*), rows are not formed and the seating is not turned to any particular direction. Women are seated separately from the men, and the Sāis, the person who conducts the ritual, is nearby.

The *'āqil* is not permitted to be alone with a woman who is not a direct family relative (wife, daughter, sister, mother), and may not even respond to her greeting "unless there be a threesome." S̲āleh̲ reports that several chapters in the religious books are especially for the woman: She is commanded not "to look at a man, a believer or otherwise, except as she looks upon her son or her father"; she is to understand "that the Creator sees her everywhere and in every situation . . . Be cautious, be a member of the believers, refrain from being led astray by drives and desires, [know that] one who avoids one's own desires will be preferred beyond the closest angels."[23]

3

Holidays, Festivals, and Holy Places

'Īd al-Adḫa (Festival of the Sacrifice)

In fact, there is only one real Druze holiday, called the Festival of the Sacrifice (*'īd al-Adḫa*), referred to as "The Big Holiday" (*al-'īd al-Kabīr*).[1]

Layālī al-'Ashr (The Ten Days of Repentance)

The ten days prior to the holiday are called *Layālī al-'Ashr* (similar to the ten days of repentance in Judaism). Members of the sect, and especially the *'uqqāl* among them, often gather in the *khalwa*, the Druze house of prayer, in this period.

These ten days are considered days of mercy, and there are religious personalities who fast every day during these ten days. The eighth day is called *al-waqfa al-ṣaghīra*, and the ninth day is *al-waqfa al-kabīra*. Religious significance is attributed to the ninth day to a degree comparable with that of the days of the holiday itself, which lasts four days – beginning from the tenth day, *al-yawm al-'aẓīm*.

During the festival, the *'uqqāl* who gather in the *khalwa* sing the story of the creation and the chronicles of history – *al-Majrawiyya* – to a special tune. At its conclusion, the custom is to authorize the membership of the *'uqqāl* new believers after they have completed the stages of candidacy and have been found worthy of joining. Since the eve of the holiday is also set aside in view of its particular religious importance, there are those members of the sect who have made a practice of doing no work that day, and there are even those who exercise this practice from two days prior to the holiday.

The *juhhāl*, who do not have access to the secrets of the religion and are not permitted to be present at the regular religious gatherings, are allowed to participate in these religious gatherings during the ten days prior to the holiday; these in essence were intended to be meetings characterized by preaching and ethics, influencing the hearts of the believers to repent and correct their ways.

Holiday customs

On the holiday itself, each family has a feast, except where a family has been bereaved by the loss of one of its sons in that same year. The village leaders visit the bereaved family on the holiday and extend an invitation to take part in their feasts. Likewise, it is customary for holiday visits to be made among rivals – this being a pleasant opportunity for *ṣulḫa* (reconciliation). The distinguished members of the sect receive their guests on the first day of the holiday, primarily during the morning hours, and they reciprocate by paying their guests a visit on the following day. On extremely rare occasions, greeting cards are sent instead of making a personal visit. These holidays are a good time for acts of charity and goodwill; the Druze are then particularly inclined to donate to the poor, to holy sites, to the various ritual facilities, and the like. This is also an opportunity for acquiring new clothes and furniture and for a thorough cleaning of one's home. It is customary to buy many sweets and baked goods, and it is particularly common to bake *ka'k* – special cake rings in honor of the holiday.

Nabī Shuʿayb (Jethro)

The most important religious event after the Festival of the Sacrifice is that of the festivities in the grounds of the tomb of Nabī Shuʿayb, who is a central figure in the faith of the Druze. From the *Qur'ān* and from the different Druze traditions, we learn that Allāh sent the prophet Shuʿayb to the tribes of Madyan in order to interfere with the idol worship in which they were engrossed. Moses, who had fled from Pharaoh, king of Egypt, came to Madyan at the same time. There, he encountered two young girls, the daughters of Shuʿayb, as they waited endlessly by the well, unable to give the sheep water because the shepherds were rudely quarreling among themselves in their attempts to reach the spring. Moses assisted the girls in giving their sheep water, and subsequently he was invited in by their father, who asked to meet him and thank him. This meeting between the two resulted in the marriage of Moses to Zippora, Shuʿayb's younger daughter. After several years, during which Moses tended his father-in-law's sheep, Allāh called him to return to Egypt in order to save his people from the hands of Pharaoh.

It is also told of the idol-worshipping people of Madyan that they would cheat in their business dealings. After the attempts of Shuʿayb to correct their ways proved fruitless, Allāh instructed him to leave the place, and in an earthquake (or according to another version, in a hurricane), Allāh consumed them, their idols, and their property. It is further told that just as this event took place, Shu'ayb looked back, and was therefore blinded. He found refuge in a nearby cave in the village of Ḫiṯṯīn, where he lived until he died of old age.[2] His followers buried him at that spot and placed a tombstone on his grave.

Maqām Nabī Shu'ayb: General View

According to Druze tradition, the Maqām indicates the burial site of Nabī Shu'ayb, who is identified with Jethro, father-in-law of Moses. The site is located near the village of Ḫiṯṯīn, adjacent to Tiberias. The Druze gather there en masse on April 25 every year.

Despite the fact that the identification of Shu'ayb with Jethro is not alien to Druze tradition, it does constitute a difficulty, since his being a prophet would not have allowed him to marry, and therefore he could certainly not have had daughters. On this matter, another version warrants consideration: despite Shu'ayb being identified as Jethro, and the account of the marriage of Moses with Zippora, she was not Jethro's daughter, but a relative.

Maqām (site) Nabī Shu'ayb

The first testimonies we have about the site located near the village of Ḫiṯṯīn (near Tiberias) are from the twelfth century. Historians and various travelers, some Jews among them, mention the site in recounting their travels, and there are those who note that next to it is the grave of Zippora.[3] There are testimonies from hundreds of years ago about the Druze holidays at the

Maqām. According to Druze tradition, an imprint resembling a foot (*da'sa*), found by the grave to this day, is identified with the left foot of the prophet. Members of the sect pour oil into the *da'sa* and then rub this oil over their bodies in order to be blessed with good fortune and success.

Druze Religious Figure Kissing the Da'sa in the Maqām Nabī Shu'ayb
According to Druze tradition, the da'sa, an imprint resembling a foot, was created when Nabī Shu'ayb stamped his foot to kill a snake, the signs of which are evident across the imprint.

The appearance of the *Maqām* today reflects many years of ongoing, expansive construction and renovation of the site. Since the second half of the last century, the *Maqām* has been expanded – primarily through the input of Shaykh Muhanna Ṯarīf, who served at the time as the spiritual leader of the sect. For this purpose, he also successfully raised funds from the Druze in Syria and Lebanon. During the British Mandate in Palestine, a dispute broke out between the Druze sect and the High Muslim Council (*al-Majlis al-Islāmī al-A'la*) regarding the registration of ownership of the *Maqām*.[4] Upon the establishment of the State of Israel, the ownership rights of the Druze to this site were recognized, and approximately 100 dunams of the surrounding land were granted to them. Through the efforts of Shaykh Amīn Ṯarīf, the place was renovated and numerous rooms were added for hosting pilgrims to the site. Likewise, many improvements were added with the help of government institutions: a road leading to the *Maqām* was paved, electricity and water were installed, etc.

The Nabī Shuʻayb festivities

Today, it is customary to conduct the festival every year on April 25.[5] The State has even acknowledged the four days (April 25–28) as an official Druze holiday. During these days, mass celebrations are held in the grounds of the tomb, while religious figures gather there for ritual purposes and to deliberate on current religious questions. Until the establishment of the State of Israel, Druze from Syria and Lebanon also participated in these festivities.[6]

Ziyārāt – Visits to Religious Sites

Another kind of pilgrimage common among the Druze is the *ziyārāt* – visits to religious sites, including public visits held on set dates, and private visits made as circumstances permit.

Only religious figures participate in the public visits, which are held in the *Maqām* Nabī Sabalān near the village of Ḫurfaysh, at the *Maqām* al-Khaḏr in the village of Yāsīf, at the *Maqām* al-Ya'Fūrī on the northern Golan Heights, and at the *Maqām* Abū ʻAbd Allāh in the village of ʻIsifyā.

Sites at which private visits are conducted are intended for the entire community, and are found in almost every village (as will be noted in detail below). The sites at which public visits are held also serve as sites for private visits, but not on the fixed annual dates on which the *ʻuqqāl* congregate.

Public visits at religious sites

The most important annual pilgrimage after the Nabī Shuʻayb festivities takes place every year on September 10, at the *Maqām* Nabī Sabalān in Upper Galilee. Few details are known about Nabī Sabalān, even to the Druze. There are those who identify him with Zebulun, son of Jacob.[7]

This site is also considered among the Druze as a place at which an adversary may be sworn to tell the truth when it is necessary to confirm his account. The grave is located at the top of a hill looking out over the whole of Upper Galilee as far as the Israel–Lebanon border. In the main wing of the *Maqām*, there is a cave, and above that is a wide hall serving as a place of congregation for the religious figures. Several rooms are built around the cave and the hall, which are available for the use of visitors.

The sites connected with Elijah the Prophet, known in Arabic as al-Khaḏr (the green), also serve as a focal point for pilgrimages made by many members of the sect. These sites are referred to as *Maqām* al-Khaḏr. Such sites are found in Haifa;[8] for example near the village of Dīr al-Asad on the Acre-Safed highway, in the village of Buqʻāthā on the Golan Heights, in the

Bānyās, and in the village of Yāsīf. The latter is said to be the most important, and is the place where religious persons gather every year on January 25. This structure is composed of a large convention hall adjacent to the *Maqām*, along with rooms and courtyards that serve the visitors.

Salmān Falāẖ relates that during the nineteenth century, and at the beginning of the twentieth, the Druze on the Carmel made pilgrimages to Maẖriqa (crematorium), where they would conduct a special religious ceremony and even make a sacrifice. According to tradition, it was here that Elijah the Prophet slaughtered the prophets of Bā'al,[9] and it is from this event that its sanctity is derived.

From 1967, the Druze in Israel began participating together with the Druze on the Golan in the celebrations held in the *Maqām* al-Ya'Fūrī near Birkat Rām on the northern Golan Heights. These festivities, held every year on August 25, attract many members of the sect to the adjacent tomb, which is surrounded by fresh-water springs and rich fruit fields. The *Maqām* underwent thorough renovations in recent years, and a large hall was built there as a place for religious gatherings.

Several years ago, two more sites were added to those that are visited by the religious members of the sect on particular dates. One is the *Maqām* Abū 'Abd Allāh in the village of 'Isifyā, for which the date set for the annual visit is November 15. The site is in a delightful green spot by a spring of fresh water. The second site, *Maqām* Bahā' al-Dīn, is in the village of Bayt Jann, and the date for the annual gathering there is July 25.

Occasional visits to religious sites

Aside from the places mentioned, there are many other sites that serve as visitation sites for members of the sect, especially for invoking their vows. The time for visiting them, primarily determined by family considerations, is not a designated date, but derives from a family matter regarding which vow is to be taken or a prayer offered. An appropriate site is visited depending on the occasion, such as a request for the recovery of an ill person, or a barren woman hoping for fertility, a husband or a wife asking for reconciliation of differences, or a soldier safely returned from battle wishing to express thanks, and other similar prayers. On such occasions, it is customary to light up the *Maqām* with candles or oil lamps, and to contribute a scarf (*sitār*), usually made of silk or other costly fabric, in accord with one's means. Sometimes the family members even sleep at the site or make a sacrifice (*dhabīẖa*) there and eat the meat in the guest rooms generally located near the *Maqām.*

It is also customary to visit sacred sites in order to obtain spiritual inspiration, or to hold discussions of clarification (*tadhākur*) between a husband

and wife, or in hope that such a visit will help individuals locked in conflict or persons faced with a difficult decision make a wise choice. Such sites are found in almost every Druze village, but usually their importance is only of a local nature.

On the Carmel, the *Maqām* al-Shaykh Abū Ibrāhīm, located in Dāliyat al-Karmil, is a rectangular underground cave whose 20-square-meter area is carved into the rock where there is a lengthwise crack. Many tales have developed around the cave and the crack in the rock. At the edge of the cave, there are steps connecting it with the large hall built above it that serves visitors in the *Maqām* for purposes of religious gatherings, for offering special prayers, and for making personal requests.

The tomb of Shaykh 'Alī Fāris (who died in 1753), sacred in the eyes of the members of the sect, is in the village of Jūlis. This *Maqām* consists of a medium-sized room with a domed ceiling. At its entrance there is a large courtyard, adjacent to which the Ṯarīf family makes a practice of burying its deceased. The most important of these tombs are those of Shaykh Muhanna Ṯarīf (died 1889), who served as the spiritual leader of the sect and labored on behalf of the renovation of *Maqām* Nabī Shu'ayb, and of Shaykh Ṯarīf Muẖammad (died 1918), who built the *Maqām* al-Khaḏr in the village of Yāsīf.

There is also a small edifice in the village in the form of a dome, known as the *Kharrūbat al-Nabī Shu'ayb* (Carob Nabī Shu'ayb) or *Qubbat al-Kharrūba* (Carob Dome). There is a belief that this structure, which is as tall as a human being, marks the spot where a holy carob tree once stood.

Shaykh Amīn Ṯarīf passed away in October 1993. He had been the leader of the sect for almost 70 years. The Shaykh was buried in one of the rooms of his home, and his tomb has already become a pilgrimage destination (*maẕār*).

Close to the village of Abū Sinān is the tomb believed to be of the prophet Zechariah (*Nabī Zakariyyā*). It is a magnificent and well-maintained building, built to receive pilgrims, and located in the heart of an area filled with ancient olive trees.

The tomb of al-Nabī al-S̱iddīq is located in the village of Yarkā. According to Druze tradition, this is the grave of an Israelite, and is commonly thought to be that of Hushai ha-Arkī, an advisor to King David,[10] hence the name of the village – Yarkā. To the east of this village is a house of prayer referred to as *Khalwat* Shaykh Muẖammad or al-Rughab. It was built by Shaykh Muẖammad Mu'addī (who died in 1931) for the purpose of religious studies. Externally, the structure of this building is completely identical to *Khalwāt al-Bayyāḏa* (to be discussed in the next section below).

In the village of Sumay', there is a *Maqām* attributed to al-Shaykh al-Fāḏil. He is considered one of the greatest Druze religious figures of all time. According to the tradition of the local community, the Shaykh spent some time near the carob in their village. In memory of that visit, an edifice was built there with two components: a small hall, and beside it a niche below a cone-shaped roof. The old carob that served the Shaykh, according to this tradition, stands there to this day. Near this *Maqām* is the tomb of Shaykh Khalīl Ṯāfish (died 1911). The daughter of this religious figure, Fāṯima (Umm Nasīb), was responsible for managing all of the religious trusts (*awqāf*, singular *waqf*) in the village and was considered a senior religious authority in her village.

The tomb of Shaykh Ṣāliḫ Abū Milḫ (died 1906) is located in Peqi'in (Buqay'a). He is considered a holy religious figure by the members of the sect. At the front of the grave is an indentation intended for lighted candles.

In the village of Bayt Jann there is a grave attributed to "al-Nabī Ḫaydar." No details at all are known about him, and his sanctity is limited to the residents of this village alone.

In the town of Shefar'am can be found the tomb of Rabbi Yehuda Ben Baba, known in Arabic as *Mughārat Banāt Ya'qūb* (the cave of the daughters of Jacob). It is a holy site to Jews and non-Jews alike.

In the village of Rāma is *Qurnat Nabī Shuḫayb* (a hidden corner of the prophet Shu'ayb), and in the nearby village of Sājūr is the *Maqām* Yūsuf al-Ṣiddīq (Joseph the righteous), referred to as al-Gharīb (the wonderful). In the village of Yānūḫ is the *Maqām* Shamsa, or Nabī Shams; and in the adjacent village of Jathth is the *Maqām* Abū 'Arūs. Almost no details are known about the history of the sites in these villages or about the personalities associated with them.

Aside from *Maqām* al-Ya'Fūrī and *Maqām* al-Khaḏr, which have already been mentioned, there are other sites that are holy to the Druze on the Golan Heights and in the vicinity. Among others, there are two sites in this region named *Maqām* al-Sulṯān Ibrāhīm – referring to Ibrāhīm ibn Adham, who lived in the Byzantine period and was known for his righteousness and self-denial. One *Maqām* is near the Bānyās, and the other in the village of Ḫarfā.

Near the village of Turunjeh is the *Maqām* Abū Dhirr al-Gaffār, who according to one of the traditions is the al-Ya'Fūrī with whose name the *Maqām* near Birkat Rām is associated.

Above the *Maqām* al-Khaḏr at the Bānyās, a cone-shaped dome protrudes, referred to as the *Maqām Sitt Sāra*; it is also sacred to the Druze.

At the highest point in the village of Ḫaḏar at the foot of Mount Hermon is the *Maqām* al-Shaykh 'Alī, attributed to Shaykh 'Alī ibn Aḫmad al-Samūqī, who died at the beginning of the eleventh century.[11] According to the tradition of local residents, this shaykh spent time under a tree that stood at that spot. Now an impressive structure stands there, overlooking the village.

The story of the Maqām Sitt Sha'wāna

In the village of 'Ayn Qinya on the Golan Heights is the *Maqām* Sitt Sha'wāna. According to local tradition, the association is with a Jewish girl (from Banī Isrā'īl); however, I have found no comparable figure in Jewish literature, based on the history of her life as told to me by the local residents. Likewise, I know of no others than the Druze who attribute sanctity to this location. Nevertheless, the story warrants acknowledgment, since it is abundant with motifs taken from the fundamental aspects of both Judaism and the Druze tradition. The story is told about seven (some say ten) men from the "Sons of Israel" who were distinguished in their time for their righteousness and their self-deprivation (*'ubbād*).[12] They split up into two groups, which rotated their roles: when one was engrossed in the worship of God, lamenting day and night, the other group was occupied with weaving mats, which were later sold in the nearby town of Bānyās. In exchange, they purchased barley and oil to bake bread for the sustenance of the members of the group. These righteous men lived in huts and wore clothing made of straw, "until their skin peeled." News of these seven wonderful, righteous persons reached the king of Israel, who had only one small daughter. The heart of the king was attracted to these goodly persons, and in his heart he came to the decision to abandon his kingdom "and the vanities of this transient world." The king's daughter pleaded that he take her with him, and so he sewed her a hairy garment that lent to her the appearance of a boy, so that these good men would not object to her presence, as "it is not comely for women to be in the company of men."

The seven righteous men were pleased that the father and his "son" had joined them. From that time they saved themselves the trouble of walking to Bānyās, a chore that was assumed by the "boy." Things continued in this manner even after the father-king passed away.

And then there came a day when the "boy" went to town, as was his habit, to sell mats. The local king's daughter saw him, was charmed by his beauty and sent for him, to invite him in on the pretext that there was a dying child in her palace, and "who but you, fearful of the word of God, is worthy to teach the dying child words of God on his deathbed?" When the "boy" came to the palace, the king's daughter locked the doors and tried to entice him, but the "boy" did not succumb to her advances. The king's daughter then promised herself that she would yet take her revenge. The "boy" returned to his friends, and told them nothing of what had happened.

The vengeful king's daughter tempted one of the courtiers to lie with her, and blamed the "boy" for this. The king, who was overcome with rage, commanded that the "boy" be brought before him in handcuffs, and he accused him of hypocrisy. "Outwardly you are a righteous person, but licentious on the inside," he said to him and sentenced him to a lengthy exile. Nonetheless, the "boy" remained silent and did not divulge his secret. When a baby was born to the king's daughter several months later, the king sent him to the "boy," considering him the father. Since the baby's crying and the concern for his welfare interfered with the "righteous one's" dedicating "his" time to worshipping God, the "boy" said a prayer to "the God of Abraham, the God of Isaac, and the God of Jacob(!)," and God answered his prayer and instructed the angel Gabriel to send a doe to take care of the baby. "I swore to myself," said God, according to this story, "even if this girl should ask me to move the mountains to another location, I would do so in acknowledgment of my esteem for her."

The doe raised the baby until he grew into a youngster, when his games disturbed the "righteous man," who was again forced to pray to God to save him from this "trouble." Indeed, God responded, and took the soul of the youth. When the king heard of God's responsiveness to the prayers of the "righteous man," he decided to pardon him immediately and allow him to return to his righteous group of compatriots.

A short time thereafter, the "righteous man" became ill and was about to die. He called his seven friends to him and said to them: "Always hold God before you! I hereby command you to bury me in the clothes that are on me!" The seven righteous men were appalled by this request, as it was customary to be very strict regarding the laws of purification of the dead, and they begged him to change his mind – "and especially since you are a righteous person." The "righteous man" responded to their request, but with a condition: "First of all, the biggest of you should cut my upper garment with a knife – beginning at the upper edge of the garment and continuing toward the chest."

Indeed, when the "righteous man" died, the biggest of the group approached him to fulfill the duty, and alas, he discovered to his amazement that the "righteous man" was . . . a girl. His friends found this difficult to believe, and asked that he return and look again at the body; yet he refused, saying: "Don't you know that God forgives for the first look, but the second is considered a great sin?" Immediately, the wife of the king was summoned to check the body, and she confirmed that the "righteous man" was a girl. The shocked king, who asked to be forgiven for his treatment of the girl, suggested that she be wrapped in shrouds, that he would provide; but when the moment came "that they completed washing the body, and they came to dress it in the king's shrouds, the girl was already dressed in shrouds from the Garden of Eden, which blinded the eyes with their light and whose fragrance was like that of musk." The priest who came to conduct the prayers prior to the burial recoiled in fright and reported that he had seen "a rider on a red knight's horse casting forth his hand holding a sword glaring with a blazing fire." When the people approached in order to attend to the girl's burial, "they saw that she had been buried by herself, and they understood that the angels had attended to her burial."

The fearful king could do nothing but pray that God pardon him, and even had his daughter executed for what she had brought upon so holy a girl. The Druze identify the girl's tomb with *Maqām* Sitt Sha'wāna in the village of 'Ayn Qinya on the Golan Heights.

Religious Sites Associated with Outstanding Personalities

The Druze sect acknowledges several outstanding personalities, who owing to the special status bestowed upon them, primarily because of their religious activity, are awarded sacred recognition and admiration. Their burial sites serve as places of pilgrimage for many members of the sect.[13] The sections that follow offer selected examples.

Religious sites in Israel

In the short time in which it was still possible to act to spread the Druze faith (at the beginning of its establishment) – the period of the *da'wa* – some messengers (*du'ā, mashāyikh al-kashf*) were operating in Israel, then referred to as *Bilād Ṣafad* (the land of Safed).

The tombs of these shaykhs are concentrated in the vicinity of the villages of Yarkā-Abū-Sinān-Jathth. This seems to confirm the idea that the Druze population already existed in the area during the period of the founding of the religion. These places include *Maqām* Shaykh Abū al-Sarāya in the village of Yarkā, considered the most important of these *mashāyikh*. According to tradition, Shaykh Abū al-Sarāya is buried beneath its floor.[14]

Nearby is the tomb of Shaykh Abū Jum'a. The tomb, covered with hewn rocks, is located at the crossroads at the entrance to Bet Ha'emek. At a distance of several hundred meters are the tombs of another two "messengers" with the same name – Shaykh Abū Muḫammad. Adjacent to them are the tombs of Shaykh Abū 'Abd Allāh (in Mīmās, west of the village of Abū-Sinān) and Shaykh Abū al-Shibl. Slightly to the north, in the nearby village of Jathth, is the tomb of the seventh of this group, Shaykh Abū 'Arūs, thought to be among the first to spread the religion during the first century in which it was founded.

Religious sites in Lebanon

Maqām Nabī Ayyūb In Lebanon, there are several places known to be sacred to the Druze. One, in particular, is the *Maqām* al-Nabī Ayyūb (the prophet Job), above the town of Nīḫā in al-Shūf region. The Druze greatly admire the personality of Job, who is considered the absolute symbol of restraint (*ṣabr*) and forbearance (*iḫtimāl*). There are approximately twenty rooms at this site to accommodate the many visitors.

Maqām Nabī Ayyūb, Nīḫa, Lebanon

The Druze consider Job a prophet, his image constituting the symbol of a suffering person who endures his pain quietly and patiently.

Maqām al-Amīr al-Sayyid Another holy *Maqām* in Lebanon is the *Maqām* al-Amīr al-Sayyid Jamāl al-Dīn 'Abd Allāh al-Tanūkhī, situated to the south of the town of 'Abeh. Shaykh al-Tanūkhī (1417–79) is most sacred to the Druze because of his interpretation of the *Kutub al-Ḫikma*. His appointment immediately after Bahā' al-Dīn Muqtana, an important propagator of the religion after the disappearance of Ḫamza ibn ‘Alī, is evidence of his stature.

Khalwāt al-Bayyāḏa *Khalwāt al-Bayyāḏa* (the white houses of communion), located in southern Lebanon, are known for their special importance to Druze religious learning. They are study halls in which the religion's priests specialize in the *Kutub al-Ḫikma*, reciting them by heart and copying them. There are religious persons who stay there permanently, isolating themselves from the outside world. They live an ascetic and monastic lifestyle and are therefore held in high esteem. Over time, several structures have been built to accommodate religious figures visiting *al-Bayyāḏa*. Some of the buildings were designated from the outset for populations coming from certain regions. Large groups also come from Israel to enhance their studies of the secrets of the religion. Some of the buildings were constructed using funds raised by Druze donors in Israel. Since the land of Israel is referred to in ancient Druze religious literature by the name *Bilād Ṣafad*, one of the buildings constructed to serve the young Druze clergy coming from Israel is called *Ṣafaḏiyya*.

Khalwāt al-Bayyāḏa

The hall in the southern Lebanese town of Ḫāṣbayyā where the secret Druze religion is studied.

4

The Druze Faith in Relation to Non-Druze

Anyone seeking to learn about the relationship between the Druze and non-Druze is faced with a difficult problem and soon realizes that there are attitudes that absolutely contradict one another on this matter: Druze requesting to join the group of religious figures – the *'uqqāl* – must shirk the prophets of other peoples and commit to taking the "covenant of Ḫamza"[1] upon themselves, thereby declaring acceptance of belief in *al-Ḫākim*; wherein, among other things, it is stated: "I hereby put my faith in our Lord, *al-Ḫākim*, the one, the only, and the special . . . and, my being in my fullest capabilities of intellect (*'aql*) and body (*badan*), I repudiate, by my own free will, all other schools of thought (*madhāhib*), fundamentals of faith (*maqālāt*), religions (*adyān*), and opinions (*i'tiqādāt*), without professing anything except for submission to our Lord, *al-Ḫākim*, his memory should transcend . . . and without participating in the worship of Him, who He was, is, or will be, I hereby surrender (*sallama*) my soul, my body, my possessions, my offspring, and all that I have to our Lord, *al-Ḫākim*, and accept all of his decrees . . . for better or for worse . . . and should I stray from the religion of our Lord . . . or violate any of his teachings . . . I shall be deserving of punishment from God, the exalted . . . "

On the other hand, upon examining the lifestyle of the Druze, one cannot help but discern the great similarity between them and the Muslims in language, culture, food, and popular beliefs. In the religious sphere, too, the matter is particularly noticeable – the Festival of the Sacrifice (*'īd al-Aḏḫa*), for example, is considered the most important holiday for Muslim as well as Druze believers. The traditions characterizing ceremonies such as engagements, marriage, birth, circumcision, divorce proceedings, funerals, and even burial prayers are identical.[2]

Indeed, Muslim religious figures (*'Ulamā'*) from the Egyptian al-Azhar religious university, after following the behavior of the Druze in *Jabal al-Durūz* in Syria, decreed that the Druze are Muslims, since, like the Muslims, they recite the two testimonies[3] and believe in the *Qur'ān*.[4]

The Muslim Muḫammad al-Zuʿbī, who has researched the subject, is among those who maintain this belief. He bases this perspective on the following:

> "If there is a man whose name is Elijah and his father's name is Cohen and his mother's name is Dina, and his wife's name is Esther, and they are all speakers of Hebrew and celebrate the holiday of the Feast of Ingathering (*al-Mazall*), Passover (*al-Fiṭr*), and Hanukka (*al-Ḫanukka*) – what would you say about this family?"
>
> "We would say: They are Jews!"
>
> "And if there is a man whose name is Muḫammad, and his son's name is ʿAlī, and his daughter's name is Fāṭima, and his wife's name is Khadīja, and they speak fluent Arabic – what would you say about this family?"
>
> "We would say: They are Arab Muslims, Arab Muslims!"[5]

There is, however, no consensus of opinion that the Druze are in fact Muslims. Among the Druze, it is very rare for a religious figure to voice any opinion on this issue. In addition, among the Muslims, there are those who are vehemently opposed to associating the Druze with Islam. For example, Jalāl al-Dīn al-Suyyūṭī,[6] one of the greatest sages of Islam of all time, adamantly claimed that the Druze should be seen as agnostics, in a religious ruling (*fatwa*)[7] relying on the opinions of several *ʿUlamā'* who preceded him, and on which al-Suyyūṭī elaborates in his opening remarks. He discusses the question of whether the Druze can be granted the status of "People of the Book" (*Ahl al-Kitāb*). The Jews and the Christians are included in this category; accordingly, they are permitted to reside in *Dār al-Islām,*[8] with all of the laws derived from this status,[9] in exchange for a head tax (*jizya*).

From studying the Druze religious texts, it becomes apparent, in his view, that the Druze believe in the "divinity of al-Ḫākim bi-Amr Allāh, in reincarnation (*Tanāsukh*), and in abrogating the prophecy of Muḫammad. At the same time, in concealing themselves among Muslims, they outwardly exhibit adherence to Islam in their prayer, in fasting, and in the other religious commandments of the *Sharīʿa.*" For this reason, al-Suyyūṭī rules that the willingness of the Druze to repent (*tawba*) need not be considered seriously. Rather, they should be seen as agnostics, from whom "it is permissible to extract property, for they are heretics (*zanādiqa*), apostates (*murtaddūn*), whose repentance should not be accepted, as they should be killed . . . cursed . . . their scholars should be killed . . . their homes should not be slept in, nor should one keep their company, or take part in their funerals."

In this chapter, as far as possible, the relationship of the Druze faith to the different monotheistic religions – Islam (*Sunnī* and *Shīʿī*), Christianity, and Judaism – will be examined.[10]

Relationship of the *Khalīfa* al-Ḫākim bi-Amr Allāh to the Monotheistic Religions

Before we examine the attitude reflected in the Druze faith with regard to the monotheistic religions, to which we will relate below, it is important first to gain an understanding of the attitude of al-Ḫākim himself, as a *khalīfa*, with respect to members of these religions during the twenty-five years of his rule in Egypt.

The attitude of the *khalīfa* can be divided into three periods with reasonably distinct characteristics.[11] During what were approximately the first ten years of his rule (996–1006), for most of which the executive tasks of the khalifate were administered by his advisors, he behaved like the Muslim *Shī'ite* khalifs, whom he succeeded, exhibiting a hostile attitude with respect to *Sunnī* Muslims, whereas the attitude toward "People of the Book" – Jews and Christians – was one of relative tolerance, in exchange for the payment of the *jizya* tax.

During the second period, which lasted five or six years (1007–12), there was a notably tolerant attitude toward the *Sunnīs* and less zeal for S*hī'īte* Islam, while the attitude with regard to the "People of the Book" was hostile. During the third period (1012–21), he became more tolerant toward the Jews and the Christians and hostile toward the *Sunnīs.* Ironically he developed a particularly hostile attitude with regard to the Muslim *Shī'ites.* It was during this period, in the year 1017, that the unique religion of the Druze began to develop as an independent religion based on the revelation (*Kashf*) of al-Ḫākim as God.

The first period

During the first period of his rule (996–1006), which concluded at the age of 20, al-Ḫākim, a *Shī'ite* Muslim, took a hostile attitude toward the *Sunnīs.* In 1005, he ordered the public posting of curses against the first three khalīfs: Abū Bakr al-S̱iddīq (632–4), 'Umar ibn al-Khaṯṯāb (634–44), and 'Uthmān ibn 'Affān (644–56). 'Ā'isha, the beloved wife of Muḫammad, who was included among the leading fighters of the time against the fourth *khalīfa* 'Alī, the cousin and son-in-law of the prophet of Islam, who demanded the position of the khalifate for himself and his descendants, was also publicly cursed, and curses were registered against the warrior Mu'āwiya, founder of the Umayyad khalifate, and against others in the inner circle of Muḫammad from the *S̱aḫāba* – the compatriots of Muḫammad in the way of Islam.[12] This decree, however, was canceled after two years.

In the realm of religious ritual, al-Ḫākim ordered the cancellation of the addition introduced by the *Sunnīs* that followed the call to morning prayer (*ādhān*) with "*al-Ṣalā Khayr min al-Nawm*" (Prayer is preferable to sleep). He decreed that in its place, the following summons should be proclaimed: "*Ḥayyī 'Ala Khayr al-'Amal*" (Come to the best of deeds). Likewise, he forbade the reciting of two prayers – *Ṣalāt al-Tarāwīḥ*[13] and *Ṣalāt al-Ḍuḥa*[14] – apparently because they were established by the *Sunnī* sages.

In accord with the khalifate tradition, in 1005 al-Ḥākim ordered the enforcement of the ordinance requiring Jews and Christians under his rule to wear "distinguishing signs" (*ghiyār*) – belts (*zanānīr*) and black scarves (*'amā'im*).

It seems that his attitude toward the Christians was particularly hostile. A recently built church was destroyed and replaced by a mosque in 1003, and he transformed two other churches into mosques. The use of wine (*nabīdh*) or even intoxicating drinks not made from grapes (*fuqā'*) was forbidden not only for Muslims but for non-Muslims, as well.[15]

He issued more rigid restrictive ordinances (*sijillāt*; singular – *sijill*) regarding matters of ethics, probably owing to the fact that the *Shī'a* was more rigid than the *Sunna* in this area. Thus, for example, entrance to a public bath was forbidden without covering the loins (*mi'zar*), women were forbidden to appear in public with their faces uncovered, and clubs and places of entertainment were closed.

The second period

The attitude of al-Ḥākim with regard to the *Sunnīs* became considerably more moderate in the second period (1007–12) and he exhibited tolerance toward them. In the year 1008, a *sijill* was published in which this trend was evident with respect to several matters.[16]

Sunnīs were permitted to begin and conclude the times of fasting in accordance with their own calculations. The *al-Khamīs*,[17] *al-Tarāwīḥ*, and *al-Ḍuḥa* prayers, which had formerly been forbidden,[18] were now permitted. Likewise, the use of the *ādhān* was permitted – in the manner acceptable to each individual. The order to register all statements against the greatness of *Sunnī* Islam was canceled along with other ordinances.

The *sijill* concludes with the words, "No Muslim is above another in his faith, and no man has the right to oppose his neighbor."

The attitude toward Jews, and all the more so toward Christians, continued to be hostile during this period. Many therefore converted to Islam or fled from Egypt. Alongside the restrictions against wine and intoxicating beverages, which were renewed,[19] many churches and monasteries were confiscated and others were destroyed or looted.[20] Christian religious parades were forbidden – especially those in which crosses were carried or in which there were distinct Christian symbols.[21] The persecution of the

Christians reached a climax in 1009 with the destruction of the Church of the Holy Sepulcher in Jerusalem.[22] During that year the use of *Nawāqīs*[23] was also forbidden; and there was a renewed issue of the edict to adhere to the sign distinguishing Jews and Christians. This order has been revised again and again. Among other things, the edict stated that Jews and Christians were required to wear pendants[24] while in public bathhouses – a cross for Christians and a small bell (*juljul*) for Jews. These medallions were hung on Jewish bathhouses built for the use of "the People of the Book." In addition, in 1012, they were forbidden to ride horses, being permitted to ride only donkeys or mules, led by leather reins with no decorations and using only wooden saddles. Likewise, they were forbidden to purchase a Muslim slave or maid or to hire the services of a Muslim for purposes of riding or sailing.

The third period

The attitude of al-Ḫākim toward Muslims, *Sunna* and *Shī'a* alike, became more and more acrid in the third period (1012–21), from the time he reached the age of 27 and until his disappearance at the age of 36.

It is known, for example, that in the year 1017, at the latest, al-Ḫākim severed the long-standing tradition whereby Egypt would contribute *kiswa* (covers) to the *Ka'ba*.[25] He ceased to pray the five daily prayers and claimed that the prayer of the heart was more important.[26] During this period, the great gap was created between Islam and the believers in the new religion (*al-'ārifūn*), who believed that the Deity was expressed in human form (*ārifū al-lāhūt mutajassid fī al-nāsūt*) while all the members of the other religions refer to the One who is "unseen" (*tawḫīd al-'adam*).[27] The hostile attitude exhibited by al-Ḫākim toward the Jews and the Christians became more moderate during this period, tending toward an attitude of tolerance. Those who had previously converted to Islam as a result of religious, economic, or other pressures were allowed to return to their original religion. The property of these communities was returned to them, and believers were permitted to carry out their commandments and rituals.

Attitude of the Druze Faith toward Monotheistic Religions

The prophets of all the nations who preceded Ḫamza ibn 'Alī are charged with grave offenses: each operated to deny the religions of the others, such that what one permitted, the other forbade.[28] This is the reason for the hostility between the different religions, as each ordered its people to sanctify a holy war (*Jihād*) against the people of another nation.[29] They are described as being negligent in their duties (*muqtaṣirūn*), their faith tainted by "connivance" (*mushrikūn*). Similarly, they are described as apostates (*kāfirūn*, *mulḥidūn*), all sharing one message though they are different in their external appearance.[30] Their prophets are accused of betraying their mission, which was the propagation of the idea of monotheism: all of them, from Noah to Muḥammad ibn Ismā'īl,[31] are as one soul, which is the accursed soul of Satan (*Iblīs al-la'īn*).[32] The role of Ḥamza was to condemn the behavior of these prophets,[33] who only introduced confusion among the different nations.[34]

Since the appearance of Ḥamza, it seems that there is no longer any value to religions, which are as "a shell without a pearl as being without a soul."[35] The seven pillars (*arkān*) upon which the religion of Islam stands (according to the *Shī'a* perception): testimony (*al-shahāda*), charity, fasting, pilgrimage to Mecca, prayer, holy war (*jihād*), and loyalty to the House of 'Alī (*Wilāya*), are rejected in favor of seven principles of faith unique to the Druze.[36]

There are times when the Druze are forced to outwardly demonstrate their belief in Muḥammad, and even to praise him and to profess the *shahāda*.[37] But this occurs because they are involved with the Muslims and hidden among them as a minority; "however, in fact, we praise Muḥammad ibn Bahā' al-Dīn al-Muqtana."[38] The prophet of Islam is charged with permitting forbidden matters and presuming to speak in the name of Allāh. The following are two examples:

(1) Conflicting instructions that he issued to his believers – according to an edict from Allāh, he claimed – to turn toward Jerusalem in prayer on one occasion and toward Mecca on another,[39] are said to create a misleading impression of internal contradiction as though it were the word of God.

(2) His claim that he made a night-time journey (*isrā'*) from Mecca to the mosque in Jerusalem, at the conclusion of which he also went up to the seventh heaven (*mi'rāj*), where he met the angels and heard the voice of the sovereign of the worlds,[40] is rejected.

Mecca, the *Ka'ba*, and the black stone are described in a negative light: they are doomed to be destroyed, since they are the source of evil. The sanctity that Islam ascribes to the black stone is compared to the sanctity that the Christians ascribe to the cross, and wonder is expressed that anyone should run through the desert to that lifeless black stone.

The criticism of the *Ḥajj*[41] ritual is even greater than the criticism of the sanctification of the cross. The reason for this ridicule is that in order to reach the black stone, one must make an exhausting journey, while doing things such as uncovering one's head, removing one's shoes, and throwing pebbles.

The main claim of the Druze against Christianity concerns the means of determining the identity of the Messiah. The qualities of Jesus as the evangelist (*injīl*) are attributed not to him, but rather to the "real Messiah" – Ḥamza ibn 'Alī.[42] The Christians themselves are described as idol (*awthān wa-Asnām*) worshippers, and in their rejection of the Messiah, Ḥamza, they behave like "the Jews who killed the prophets."[43] The blindness and hermetically closed nature of the Christians preclude their ability to distinguish the true Messiah.[44]

و مذ موت بقوله قاتلوا
ايمة الكفر انهم لا ايمان
لهم لعلهم ينتهون وهم
روسا الشريعة الناموسية
وقد اعتقد المسلمون في
كتابن من الامامة مثل الشا
فعي وابي حنيفة ومالك وسفيان
الثوري وغيرهم مما يطول
به الشرح وانما قالوا انهم
ائمة حيث يحرمون الحرام
ويحللون الحلال واقتدوا بهم
نوقع

نوقع عليهم اسم الامامة
فهولاء الخمسة الذين ذ
كرناهم كل واحد منهم
امام لمن يطيعه ويتبعه
ويقبل منه وقد جعلنا السلف
كبيرهم وامامهم الاعظم
لانه بمنزلة الناطق محمد ابن
عبد الله فقاتلوهم بقلوبكم
وتبروا مما يعتقدونه في مولانا
البار العلام العلي الاعلى حاكم
الحكام سبحانه وتعالى عما

The Druze Attitude toward Islam

The Druze religious texts (*Kutub al-Ḥikma*) contain expressions of the Druze attitude toward people of various faiths. In the section shown here, in reference to Islam, it says, in part: "Fight apostate leaders, for you should not believe them . . . the greatest of them, who has the status of a prophet, is Muḥammad ibn 'Abdallah. Fight them in your hearts, and shake yourselves of their outlook toward our Lord, who is pure, wise, supreme, the master of all, may he be praised and exalted. . . ."

Likewise, criticism is made of the Jews, though more moderate than that of the Christians and certainly more moderate than the criticism of the Muslims. This criticism was made primarily by Bahā' al-Dīn, during the later period of the founding of the Druze faith.[45] It is directed against the claim of the Jews that there can be no Torah or prophecy after Moses. This claim is countered by the claim that there have been many significant prophets after him, and there is a place for them precisely as there was a place for the prophecy of Moses. Not only was Moses preceded by Noah and Abraham, but he himself emphasized that there would be many prophets after him. The critics hold that the denial by the Jews of the authenticity of Ḫamza is equivalent to their rejection of the words of the prophets who preached to them, and their scorned status is a direct result of their obstinate nature.[46]

Shortly, the Messiah, Ḫamza, will arrive in order to punish those who do not acknowledge his role, including the Jews, the Christians, and all of the Muslims.[47]

"The Reflection" of the Druze Faith in Monotheistic Religious Literature

The *Qur'ān* in its own right, is considered a sacred book in the Druze faith. The Druze, however, attribute a special significance to it entirely different from that which is acceptable to Islam. Essentially, the Druze also consider the Bible and the Evangelical texts in this manner. Several examples follow.

In the *Qur'ān*, it is stated: "And remember – As Jesus, son of Mary said, 'Woe to the Children of Israel! Here I am the messenger of Allāh to you to uphold that which came before me from the Torah, and to proclaim that another messenger will follow after me.' . . ."[48] In the opinion of the Druze, that messenger is none other than Ḫamza.

They interpret other verses in the *Qur'ān* in a similar way. Thus, the verse, "You shall worship the God of this house,"[49] is understood to express the need to believe in the unity of al-Ḫākim, and not in Allāh, who is the "Master of the *Ka'ba.*"[50]

The verse, "Fear Allāh and be the People that speaks the truth,"[51] is explained as an expression of the need to fear al-Ḫākim and to be counted among those who seek unity with him.[52]

In the opinion of the Druze, the four books of the Christian Gospel, Matthew, Mark, Luke, and John, deal with the "true Messiah," who is none other than Ḫamza. In fact, this is alluded to in the texts, but the Christians have been deprived of the proper comprehension of them.[53] Thus, for example, when the Gospel According to John speaks of "the night,"[54] they interpret this reference to be to the teachings of the prophets, as opposed to the light of the mission of the true Messiah, which is the "Gospel of Ḫamza."[55]

Another testimony to the identity of the true Messiah is found in the Gospel According to Matthew, where it is stated: "From Egypt, I called to my son."[56] The Druze see this as a clear reference to Ḫamza, who operated in Egypt. In the Gospel According to Matthew there are apparently even allusions to the period of Bahā' al-Dīn. For example, in the following excerpt, they see a reference to the denial of the chosen people and the apocalyptic punishment that will be brought upon the Christians: "Therefore I hereby send to you prophets, sages, and scribes, and from among them you will kill and crucify, and from among them you will lash with whips in their churches, and you will pursue them from city to city, in order that all the clean blood spilt in the Land will come upon you . . . Amen, I say unto you: all of them will surely come."[57]

It was the true Messiah, Ḫamza, who directed the deeds of the messiah Jesus, but when Jesus strayed from the path of the true Messiah, Ḫamza filled the hearts of the Jews with hatred for him – and for that reason, they crucified him. After Jesus was placed in the grave, they took the true Messiah and concealed him in a garden, announcing to the people that the Messiah was also among the dead, and that "He who enters among the disciples while the doors are locked is Ḫamza, the true Messiah."[58]

There is, then, a clear distinction between the Christians and the Evangeline. The heart of the Christians was sealed against understanding who was the true Messiah, and therefore the Druze faith actually "foresaw" that the time had come to eradicate the "Christian Kingdom."[59] Unlike the Christians, the Druze act in admiration of the Evangeline because he exalts Ḫamza, and he has divine wisdom, "whose inner meaning demonstrates faith in one God."[60]

The Jews, too, like the Muslims and the Christians, are criticized for not believing in the coming of the designated Messiah (*al-Masīḫ, al-Muntaẕar*) despite the fact that there are verses from the Bible[61] that "allude" to al-Ḫākim and Ḫamza, his Messiah. The following are several examples.

The verse, "The Lord came from Sinai, and shone forth from Seir unto them; He shined forth from Mount Paran, and came from Ribeboth kodesh . . . "[62] deals, in Druze religious opinion, with the three religions that preceded the Druze faith: Moses appeared from Mount Sinai; Jesus appeared from Seir; and Muḫammad appeared from Paran, which is the Mount of Mecca; while the light and sanctity appear from Ribeboth-kodesh in a manner that exceeds all that preceded it.

Isaiah is much quoted as the one who foresaw the coming of a new age, which in fact alludes to the period of the revelation of Ḫamza:

> Behold the former things are come to pass,
> And new things do I declare . . . [63]
>
> Don't remember the former things,
> Neither consider the things of old,
> I will do a new thing . . . [64]

A voice rings out:
Clear in the desert
A road for the Lord
Level in the wilderness . . .
Let every valley be raised,
Every hill and mount made low.
Let the rugged ground become level
And the ridges become a plain
And the presence of the Lord shall appear.[65]

And even David is mentioned as one who prophesied the renewed coming of al-Ḫākim and of Ḫamza:

Sing to the Lord a new song,
His praise in the congregation of saints.
Let Israel rejoice in its Maker . . .
For God has chosen His people
He adorns the humble with salvation.
Let the faithful exult in glory
And praise him upon their couches
Exalting God;
Let the high praises of God be in their mouth
And a two-edged sword in their hand;
To execute vengeance upon the nations
That do not worship Him, nor profess His unity.[66]

Likewise, Malachi promoted the belief in al-Ḫākim when he was commanded to go to the People of Israel with a clay vessel, saying to them:

Thus said the Lord of Hosts
So, I shall break this nation and this city
As the potter's vessel is broken and cannot be repaired.
Sacrificing the lamb like immolating a dog,
Slaughtering the ox as though sacrificing the swine,
I have hated you and I will take no more of your burned offering.[67]

From different sources, it is apparent that disagreements occurred between the leaders of the new religion, particularly al-Ḫākim and Ḫamza, and the leaders of the Jewish community in Egypt. One of these disputes[68] broke out when al-Ḫākim was still at the outset of his appearance as a divine image. A select group of Jews (and Christians?) turned to him and complained that he was violating the tradition that had been forming from the beginning of the period in regard to the Muslim rulers' treatment of their subjects, the "People of the Book" (*ahl al-kitāb*).[69] According to this tradition, which relied upon the *Qur'ān*,[70] the Jews enjoyed protection and respect for their religious principles in exchange for the payment of a head tax (*jizya*). The Jews claimed that al-Ḫākim and his followers were not honoring this tradition. In reaction to al-Ḫākim's grievances with regard to the Jews' reservations in recognizing him as the Savior, they replied that their opinion relied on the following three claims:

1 The timing of his appearance was not compatible with their view on this matter.
2 He for whom they were waiting would call for the perfected worship of the Creator and not for the abandonment of their religion.[71]
3 It was inconceivable that the revelation of God should be in the form of a human being.

Al-Ḫākim promised them that he would continue to honor their religion in exchange for the payment of the *jizya* until "that time which, according to them, is the time of the coming of the Messiah," then he would force them to join his religion. In response to a renewed Jewish claim that it was inconceivable that God would reveal himself in the form of a human being, Ḫamza countered[72] that this idea was more conceivable than the story told of the revelation of God to Moses in the bush[73] or from the mount.[74] Revelations in which Moses is called the one "with whom God spoke" (*Kalīm Allāh*) – and where it is the tree ("the bush") in which God was revealed, and the tree was destined to burn – are a far less honorable means for the revelation of God than a human being.

The Monotheistic Religions at the Time of the Apocalypse and on the Day of Judgment

The attitude of the Druze faith to the other religions is unique from an eschatological perspective. At the time of the apocalypse (*ākhir al-zamān: al-yawm al-akhīr*), the Messiah, Ḫamza, would return in order to obliterate the different religions and to take revenge upon the enemies of the Druze. He would do this primarily by "the selected persons of the tribes of Naphtali, Benjamin, and the descendants of the tribes of Menashe and Gad."[75] Similarly, the "imminent" appearance of al-Ḫākim is described, as being with sword in hand, in order that he should "destroy the apostates and fight the heretics." Those who escaped his vengeance would have to pay a tax (*al-Jāliya*)[76] and wear a distinguishing sign (*ghiyār*), a mark of their contemptible nature.

On the Day of Judgment (*yawm al-dīn*), al-Ḫākim would be revealed in a human image (*nāsūt*), and would judge the world by means of the sword (*sayf*) and in a brutal manner (*'unf*).[77]

Al-Ḫākim would be worshipped by all people, each in his own language. Throughout the world would be heard the question: "For whom is the Kingdom today and every day?" And the answer would be given – "For our Lord, al-Ḫākim the victorious, the powerful, who shall be praised and exalted."[78]

Come the Day of Judgment, there would be an end to the false beliefs of the members of the other religions, according to which God will reveal himself to his creations in order to settle accounts with those who are not of the faith. The emphasis, according to the Druze belief, would be placed upon "the cancellation of the other religions."[79] The time of the Day of Judgment was not known; however, there were signs (*'alāmāt*) of it: kings will fall and rise, and the Christians will rise above the Muslims.[80] It was said that al-Ḫākim would destroy all religions and kings, "and he will control the reincarnation of their souls."

Aside from all of this, an allocation of curses was made for members of other religions: for the *Mutawālīs* (*Shī'ītes*) – 50 curses; for the *Sunnīs* – 40 curses; for the Christians – 30 curses; while for the Jews – 20 curses.[81]

In addition to the curses, suffering was also designated for members of other religions: the Muslims, for example, were to be the victims of "hard torture – everything they eat or drink will be bitter . . . They will walk around with an *amah*-long cone-shaped hat (*ṯarṯūr*) from the skin of swine," apparently in an attempt to embarrass them. Likewise, on each of their ears there would be a black glass earring – "In summer, scorch it like fire, and in winter, chill it like ice."[82] The men's chests would be infected by color, they would be humiliated, and they would have to pay a 20-dinar tax each year.[83] Particularly difficult would be the status of the *Shī'ītes*, who were to serve the "legions (*katā'ib*) of our Lord, al-Ḫākim."[84]

For the apostates–proselytes (*murtaddūn*, *munāfiqūn*), "who have reconsidered their faith in the unity of our Lord," it was determined that they should also have black glass on both of their ears, each weighing 40 dirham. It was also said of them: "in the summer scorch it like fire, and in winter chill it like ice. On their heads they shall don a long cone-shaped hat from the skin of a fox. The front of their clothing would be dyed a grayish color, and each will pay a 5 dinar tax. All that they drink and eat will be bitter."

For the Christians, it was determined that a 30-dirham earring of iron would be on each ear; that the edge of their right sleeves would be dyed black, and the tax upon them would be in the amount of 3.5 dinars. They would be barefoot, naked, and on their backs they were to carry wood "to the ovens and the baths of our Lord." At the time of the apocalypse, Ḫamza would come and would strike a victorious blow upon the Christians for the suffering and humiliation that they had caused the Druze.[85]

The Jews were to be in a less grave situation. They would have 20-dirham earrings of lead on each ear. The left edge of their sleeves would be dyed a yellowish color.[86] The tax imposed upon them would be in the amount of 2.5 dinars.[87] The relatively favorable status of the Jews is connected to the attitude of the Druze faith toward Moses. He is defined as a man of sharp intellect (*dhū 'aql thāqib*) and focused vision, who directed his people with wisdom because he would ascend the mountain and transcribe the words of our Lord and obey them. Moreover, it was determined that Moses formed a people that listened to him "even though he doesn't belong to us," and even Muḥammad and Jesus recognized that he was a wise man of sharp intellect. "It is permitted to curse his people, but less than the others . . . Furthermore, he [Moses] was not a prophet, and prophecy was not his occupation . . . On the day of the appearance of our Lord, he will appoint them as managers of his accounts, as messengers in his service . . . Their food will be only berries . . . The Lord will allow us to associate with them . . . Since they have been privileged to see (God), difficulties have not been imposed upon them as has been done to their rivals."[88]

A Faith that Excludes All Outsiders

Based on all that is written above, it can be stated with certainty that the Druze religion is an independent religion, absolutely different from other religions. It regards Islam with hostility. Ordinarily, this is not evident from the outward religious behavior of the Druze as is indeed clear from the examples presented at the beginning of the chapter.[89] In this regard, it is important to mention the command to the members of this faith not to openly expose the fundamental principles of their faith. This injunction includes, among other things:

> Keep the *Ḥikma* from those who are not worthy of it, and do not withhold it from those who are worthy . . . Don't expose yourselves to those whose desires and ignorance overtake them, and you are (thereby) observing them without their having the capability of seeing you – the words of their Law are familiar to you, while their knowledge is diverted from that which is in your hands, and the light of wisdom is withheld from them that is kindled in you:
>
> They are dumb — While you are speaking;
> They are deaf — While you are hearing;

They are blind	While you are open-eyed;
They are ignorant	While you are knowing.[90]

The Druze feeling of being chosen because of their singular privilege of wisdom was to provide them with compensation at the time of the apocalypse. Other nations would be punished – some more and some less, all depending on their religious affiliation. Of the three monotheistic religions, the status of the Muslims would be the worst, and especially that of the *Shī'ites*; followed by the Christians; while the Jews would suffer the least punishment of all the nations. The members of the Druze faith were to be considered as the chosen among the nations and as the best of those "whose feet have trodden the earth. The monotheistic believers will be so privileged that the simplest amongst them will be masters over the rulers of other nations, to the extent that the greatest of them [i.e., the nations] will listen and bow down to each and every one of you."[91]

Since the Druze were a minority subject to the rule of Islam and there are principles in their religious belief considered as complete heresy in the religion of Islam, they were thus compelled to develop two systems of behavior: outward behavior (*ẕāhir*) suited to the beliefs of the Muslim rulers;[92] and on the other hand, genuine, internal behavior (*bāṯin*), concealed from the eyes of the surrounding society. This situation was compared to the human body, wrapped in clothing – the garment may be white, black, red, or green; but it neither raises, lowers, nor changes the body: "wear, then, what is suitable to be worn, and outwardly appear in the same religion in a manner that is comfortable to you." It was even permissible to pray with members of the other religions in public prayer and to hold religious ceremonies with them of the type noted at the beginning of the chapter. At the same time, they were commanded to: "Preserve me in your hearts."[93]

This provides an explanation for the outward resemblance that exists in several areas of religion between the Druze and the Muslims: "Since we are obligated to hide behind Islam, we have to acknowledge the book of Muḫammad . . . and to conduct the burial prayer."[94] The Druze give a

Fatwa (Religious Ruling) of al-Suyyūṯī Concerning the Druze

(on facing page)

Jalāl al-Dīn al-Suyyūṯī (1445–1505), one of the greatest Islamic sages of all generations, ruled that Muslims had to view Druze as apostates, "whose property it was permissible to expropriate . . . and whose requests to repent should not be answered, but one is to kill them . . . to curse them . . . and to kill their wise men. . . ."

السيف المسلول على اهل التناسخ والحلول
من الدروز والنيامنه الطايفتين الضالتين
الفراعنه رحم الله مقيله وجامعه
وتاليه وسامعه من المسلمين
آمين

سيل في طايفة الدروز القايلين بالهية الحاكم بامر الله العبيدي وبالتناسخ وبعدم نبوة محمد نبينا صلى الله عليه وسلم وغير ذلك وهم مع ذلك يستترون بين المسلمين بالصلاة والصوم وغير ذلك من شرايع الدين هل يقبل اسلامهم ويترتب عليه احكام الاسلام ام لا لما اشتهر عنهم من اخفاء الكفر واظهار الاسلام واذا اغار المسلمون وسبوهم فاشترى مسلم من تلك السبايا فما حكمها اجاب ...

ليس لهم ضرر على احد من ادعايا فمن باب اولى من يقطع الطرق ويهجم على القرايا ويتجرى على الدما والاموال فكيف لا يجب دفعه ومنعه وردعه ... القادرين بالحال والقال والله الهادي وهو حسبي وعليه اعتمادي كتبه عبد القادر بن مصطفى الصفوري الشافعي حامدا ومصليا ومسلما انتهى من خطه نقلت رحمه الله تعالى
ورايت جواب شيخ الاسلام ابن تيمية على نظير هذا السوال ونص عبارته مارايته عليه هذا واجاب العلامة الشيخ تقي الدين شيخ الاسلام ابن تيمية من السادة الحنبلية تحت نظير هذا السوال رفع اليه في زمن تولية ملك الامراء خرم بن عبد الغفار في اوايل شهر المحرم سنة اربع وثلاثين وتسعمايه بقوله كفر هولاء مما لا يختلف فيه المسلمون بل من شك في كفرهم فهو كافر مثلهم وليس هم بمنزلة اهل الكتاب ولا المشركين بل الكفرة والضالين فيباح اكل طعامهم وسبي نسايهم واخذ اموالهم فانهم زنادقة مرتدون لا تقبل توبتهم بل يقتلون اينما ثقفوا ويلعنون كما وصفوا ولا يجوز استخدامهم فيما هو مباح للمسلمين ولا استخدامهم للحراسة والبوابة والحفاظة ويجب قتل علمايهم وصلحايهم لئلا يضلوا غيرهم ويحرم النوم معهم في بيوتهم ورفقتهم والمشي معهم وتشييع جنايزهم اذا علم موتها ويحرم على ولاة امور المسلمين اضاعة ما ... من اقامة الحدود عليهم باي شي يراه المقيم لا المقام عليه والله المستعان وعليه التكلان انتهى ما رايته ووقفت عليه من فتاوي الايمة الاربعة رضي الله عنهم اجمعين ووفق الله ولاة امورنا للعمل بذلك امين
ذكر الناسخ الاول ولا ادري هل هو الجامع او لا قوله وكان الفراغ منها نهار اثنين ... من شهر ذي القعدة المبارك على يد افقر العباد الى الله تعالى الامير محمد بن الامير احمد الغزاوي نسبا الحنفي مذهبا غفر الله له ولوالديه ولمن دعا لهم بالمغفرة امين وتم الصلاة والتسليم على اشرف خلقه محمد وعلى آله واصحابه اجمعين في شهر ذي القعدة من شهور سنة مايه وستة بعد الالف هـ

نقلت منها هذه النسخة في اوايل شهر ربيع الثاني سنة ١٣٠٦

prominent place to the discussion of this issue of Druze–Muslim relations and emphasize the basic difference between the two religions. As opposed to the Muslims, who were never privileged to witness the divine revelation and who worship the "missing" (*'Adam*), the Druze saw the revelation of al-Ḫākim when he revealed himself to human beings as a human being.[95]

The "fact" that the religion of Muḫammad spent some 410 years "without . . . overcoming all of the other religions . . . but rather the Jews and the Christians are greater in number than they" constitutes "proof" that the true messenger of God (al-Ḫākim) is Ḫamza. Nonetheless, precautions have to be taken with respect to the Muslims, as can be inferred from the following excerpts:

> Stay far from the ways of coercion and going astray
> And go in the ways of the honest and the perfect
> And know that every man that leads a crowd and stands at the head of it
> He is their *Imām*
> Because he directs them, in speech and in deeds . . . [96]

> Muḫammad ibn 'Abd Allāh is the Master of the Muslims,
> Their great and revered *Imām*,
> Who maintains the status of *Nātiq* . . .
> Fight them [the Muslims] in your hearts
> And shirk from their thoughts about our wise,
> Pure Lord, the supreme, exalted, ruler of rulers,
> He shall be praised and raised above all that describes him
> And all that resembles him in human perception.[97]

What is the ruling for a non-Druze seeking to adopt the religion professing unity?

It is not possible, since "the propagation of the religion has been completed, and the gate has been locked. He who denied – denied; and he who believes – believes."[98] If, despite this, such a man should "recognize the religion, believe in it, and observe it," it will not help him, since "the gate is locked, and the matter is closed, and the pen is dry, and upon his death, his soul will return to his previous religion."[99]

Is there not unfair discrimination in this against one who does not "profess the unity?"

In the Druze religion an opinion is given on this query, but "the deeds of al-Ḫākim should not be questioned, in accordance with the verse in the *Qur'ān*: 'He will not be asked of his actions.'"[100]

5

The Life-Cycle of the Druze Individual

The life-cycle of the average Druze revolves around a very small number of events – birth and circumcision, engagement and marriage, death and burial – and is devoid of special Druze-religious ritual. In addition to these subjects, this chapter will survey other characteristics of Druze life as individuals and as a society: the woman's place in this society, popular beliefs, the generation gap.

Birth and Circumcision

The birth of a baby is seen as the realization of a higher destiny for the sake of which the Druze family is established. Indeed, the most important aim of the Druze is establishing a new generation, and the young couple will gain the greatest happiness if their first born is a boy. Immediately after the birth, it is the custom to rub antimony (*kuḫl*) on the baby's eyelids as a sign that the infant should be given added grace and beauty and also, some believe, health. This blue tincture is spread on male children for just a few days, but it continues – with no particular time limit – for girls.

The birth of a child necessitates safeguarding the baby from the evil eye (*'ayn al-ḫasūd* or *al-'ayn*). The best way to ward off such a threat is through a blue bead or beads (*khirz* or *funduqliyya*) plaited in the baby's hair, put on his hat, or placed on his shoulder. These beads are generally threaded. Another popular custom employed to protect the baby from the evil eye is to hang up a good-luck charm, a pendant made of a piece of leather (*taḫwīṯa*) stored inside a case on which are written words of encouragement and a prayer against the evil eye and its adverse effects.[1]

Druze society has no custom of celebrating the birth of babies, though the parents may mark the birth of a male child with a big celebration if at the outset they have pledged to do so. The birth of a baby is, first and foremost, an assurance of a succeeding generation that will proudly bear the father's name. This is manifested in the blessing customarily given to the parents in such circumstances: "May he live and bear his name" (*ya'īsh wa-yaḥmil ismuhu*). Special attention is given to a woman who gives birth (*nifās*), on account of both the effort involved in pregnancy and childbirth and the fact that she will nurse her baby for a very long time: a year and a half for a male and two years for a female child. For some forty days after giving birth, the mother enjoys a special drink – *maghlī*, which is a tonic containing nuts, pinenuts, cinnamon, sugar, cloves, and other spices. This drink is said to have a double purpose: strengthening the woman who gives birth and enriching her milk.

A short time after the birth of a male child, the practice is to circumcise (*ṭuhūr*) him, but unlike Judaism there is no special date for this act in the Druze religion: some have it done when the baby is but a few days old, others wait until he has reached the age of ten or even older. The circumcision is performed by a professional circumciser (*muṭahhir*), no matter his religion, or by a physician if the child is still hospitalized. No special religious event or significance is attached to the act, but it is customary upon such an occasion to hold a festive family meal. The traditional blessing is "*ṭuhūr mubārak*" ("a blessed circumcision").

Engagement, Marriage, and Divorce

Druze family life is not rich in religious experiences, but marriage is considered a central event. The most striking phenomenon in the marriage procedure is the absence of social ties between the couple prior to their wedding. So long as no *'aqd* – the religious–legal act that binds the couple and that constitutes the second of three stages leading to a marriage – has been conducted, they are not allowed to meet alone. Another especially prominent phenomenon is the care that is taken to obtain the consent of the bride to the marriage. It should be mentioned that marriage between cousins is still acceptable among the Druze; however, the number of such marriages is rapidly decreasing.

The groom's contact with his bride-to-be is made through his parents. The parents, and with them respected figures (*jāha*) of the locality, approach the girl's parents with the request that they consent to the marriage. If her parents agree, there is an engagement, with the two families and their close friends meeting in the home of the bride's parents. This meeting, called *khuṭba* (engagement), constitutes the first stage leading to the marriage. At this point, the conditions that the groom must fulfill to merit his bride are agreed, such as the bridal price (*mahr*) that must be paid to her family, the couple's place of residence and its condition, several particulars relating to religion and society, and one more important item – setting a date to conduct the *'aqd*.

The *'aqd* itself, which has been mentioned as the second stage, is arranged by the *Imām*, who records on a special form the details about the couple and the agreed terms. He also has the witnesses sign the document and obtains the renewed agreement of the bride to the marriage. This part is generally sealed with the phrase, *Sūrat al-fātiḥa*, which is the opening chapter of the *Qur'ān*. When this phrase is uttered, it is the custom among the Druze for the father of the bride to press his thumb against the groom's thumb, their hands covered with a cloth, to symbolize the transfer of the bride to the groom's domain following the *'aqd*. There is another custom in which the groom waves a stick above the bride's head or slightly lifts the veil (*naqāb* or *mindīl*) covering her face – also a symbolic expression of this transfer.

The length of time between the *'aqd* and the third and last stage of the marriage procedure, which is a party (*zawāj*), is not fixed. It can last several weeks or a number of years, depending on the ability of the groom to live up to the terms that he took upon himself to fulfill at the engagement. During this period, the groom must visit his bride at her parents' home, especially during holidays. At each such visit, he gives her some sort of gift (such as a sum of money, jewelry, or clothing). On his first visit after the *'aqd* (*shōfat khāṯir*) he showers her with expensive gifts, in particular with items agreed upon as part of the bridal price (*mahr*): household appliances, jewelry (*ṣīgha*), clothing, etc.

The amount of the bridal price varies with the circumstances. It may vary according to the bride's age, her education, her appearance, and her intelligence. Owing to the development of Druze society, as well as to prolonged efforts by the Druze spiritual leadership, the demand for an exaggerated bridal price has been halted almost completely as has the phenomenon of the bride's father pocketing the money for himself. This money is really meant to be an important contribution to cover the expenses of the new couple. Similarly there exists the custom of dividing the *mahr* in two: the part that the groom pays immediately (*muqaddam* or *mu'ajjal* – advance *mahr*) and a supplementary amount that he (or someone on his behalf) pays off only in the event of divorce or death (*mu'akhkhar* or *mu'ajjal* – later *mahr*).

The wedding ceremony (*zawāj*), the third step concluding the marriage, is usually a three-day affair: a festive meal takes place at the groom's parents' home on the evening of the first day, but the bride dines with her friends at her parents' house at the same time; the couple are then escorted by a large crowd from these respective houses to their own home. It is customary for the bride to stick some dough (*khamīra*, *'ajīna*) to the entrance of her new home before she enters it and for the groom to put some dough on her piece, a sign of their life together. The third day is called *yawm al-kubba* because the young couple's friends who have come to greet them are given a food delicacy (*kubba*), made of wheat groats and spicy meat.

One of the customary blessings at a wedding is the following: *Ij'alhu tawfīq wa-lā taj'alhu ta'wīq bi-barakat sayyidinā wa-nabiyyinā yūsuf al-ṣiddīq* (Let us have success, my God, and not ruin, on the merit of the blessing of our Lord and Prophet, Joseph the Righteous).

Druze society acknowledges the great financial expense of a wedding celebration to which many guests are invited; and because of that, some of the invited guests give the couple gifts of food. From time to time, the religious figures warn against exaggerated celebration and expenditure, which they consider improper, for "this world is a kind of prison for righteous men and a heaven for the wicked; and therefore, it is not proper for a prisoner to rejoice and have a good time" (*Inna al-dunya sijn al-abrār wa-jannat al-ashrār fa-lā yaḥiqq lil-sajīn an yafraḥ wa-an yaṭrib*).

Loyalty to the family is a supreme value among the Druze. This is not to say that there are no deviations from this general rule; but these are exceptional cases. For instance, when the bride or a woman is "kidnapped," this usually involves a young unmarried woman who has agreed to be "kidnapped" by her partner, whom she finds more acceptable than the intended spouse chosen by her parents. There is also the case of a married woman who goes astray and wants a partner who is not her legal spouse. The "kidnapped"[2] woman will stay for a period of time in the home of one of the community notables until her legal–religious status and that of her "kidnapper" are legally settled, or at times, until the anger at this action has subsided. This is a rare phenomenon in the community, and such an event is impossible to find among the *'uqqāl.*

Divorce is not unknown among the Druze, but is relatively infrequent. There have been cases in which the break-up of the marriage was initiated by the wife, usually because of the husband's immoral behavior, such as leaving her for another woman.[3] Unlike religions that permit the return of a divorced woman to her former husband, Druze religious law forbids this and even imposes severe sanctions on anyone who does this. Still, there are couples who have divorced but who continue to live together – to the bitter distaste of the elders.

Status of Women and Education of Children

A female *'āqil* (*'āqila*) will generally prefer an *'āqil* for a husband, and vice versa, for belonging to this social group obliges *takāfu'*, or equality between spouses. Nevertheless, there are frequent exceptions to this rule. A complaint by an *'āqil* that his spouse is not an equal – in other words, that she is not religious – is an accepted grounds for a divorce.

The Druze Religious Court on the Golan has adjudicated a typical case of this sort. The court approved the divorce, but exempted the husband from having to give his former wife special rights. Their joint home was divided in two, in accordance with the relevant religious instruction, and the divorced couple had to see to the permanent blocking off of all passages between the two parts of the apartment "in order to preclude the possibility that one of them might see the other."[4]

More interesting still is a case in which an *'āqila* complained about the secular way of life of her *jāhil* husband. In the arguments that were heard in the Druze Religious Court on the Golan, the woman contended that her husband "is not religious . . . lacks initiative, is illiterate, smokes, drinks liquor, and so forth." The court gave great weight to her claims and obligated the husband to obtain guidance from his brother-in-law, who, in his wisdom, would try to save the marriage, "but if not the court would rehear the case and issue a final verdict."[5]

The social status of the Druze woman is incomparably preferable to that of her Muslim counterpart, and this emanates from the attitude of the Druze religion to women.[6] This is true for every Druze woman, but all the more so for the *'āqila*. There are a number of cases of women who found themselves at the center of religious–social action aimed at fulfilling all demands of modesty in relations between men and women.

Since the objective of setting up a family is to bring offspring into the world, there are Druze religious figures who take care not to have marital relations from the time the woman becomes pregnant until forty days after she gives birth. There are some who completely refrain from relations with their wives during their monthly period and for seven days thereafter; at the end of this period, the woman gives herself a thorough hygienic bath.

The commandment that a woman must marry her deceased husband's brother if she has no children is unknown among the Druze. Mention, however, should be made of a practice that is accepted for social motives: if a young married man dies, it may happen that his unmarried brother will agree to marry his brother's widow in order to preserve the unity, and property, of the family. This custom exists whether or not the widow has children from her late husband.[7] There is no foundation to the opinion that the Druze widow is forbidden to marry, although the frequency of widows with small children marrying – particularly marrying someone outside the late husband's family circle – is very low. The main reason for this is that the widow is obligated in such a case to transfer her small children to the custodianship of her late husband's father.

As a rule, it may be said that the concern for educating and rearing the children – and this means imparting to them educational and moral values at home, religious values, and the tradition of the house of worship (*khalwa*), as well as formal education – stands among the top priorities of the average Druze family.

It is customary for Druze children to help their parents with their work, especially manual agricultural work such as picking olives, tobacco, citrus fruit that has fallen from the trees, and so forth.

Transmigration of Souls and the End of Days

The beliefs in the transmigration of souls (*tanāsukh* or *tanāsukh al-arwāḫ*) and in life after death constitute important foundations of Druze theology and considerably influence the everyday life of the Druze, including their tendency to social equality, their bravery, their religious tolerance, and more. An attempt should be made, therefore, to clarify this issue on the basis of available Druze sources.[8]

According to the belief in the transmigration of souls, a person's body is a kind of clothing (*qamīṣ, taqammuṣ*) for the soul, and with the person's demise the soul passes over to the body of a newborn child. Najjār states that the number of souls in the upper world or in the nether world never changes,[9] and that reward and punishment (*'iqāb wa-thawāb*) for the soul are given after many transmigrations – all according to the degree of knowledge that it acquires in its various migration cycles. The soul that is prepared can even attain the level of *Imām* (a kind of prophet).[10]

As to the question of the soul's limitations in connection with the body in which it resides, Najjār provides two contradictory answers: In one place,[11] he argues that the soul of a Druze (*Muwaḫḫid*) passes to the body of a Druze child, and the soul of an apostate (*Mushrik*) to another non-believer. Later, however, he contends that the soul migrates from body to body without consideration of whose it is – whether male or female, and regardless of the "new" person's race, place of birth, etc.[12] It appears that even Ṭalī' is of the latter opinion; still, he emphasizes that the soul transmigrates among human beings and does not pass to animals.[13]

Another Druze scholar, Sāmī Makārim, believes that there is no intergender migration of souls – a soul that leaves a male body will re-enter a male child and one that leaves a female will re-enter a female.[14]

Ṯalīʿ raises another point in regard to the transmigration of souls: He is of the opinion that with the passage of the soul from one body to another, the whole complex of traits, or at least the most prominent ones, passes with it. Further, he says, the souls of the prophets and messengers transmigrate amongst themselves from generation to generation, improving their traits.[15]

The concept of the "end of days" in the Druze faith requires the clarification of two issues: Judgment Day and reincarnation. According to the Druze faith, a human being is given freedom of choice, but at the same time is ruled by God (*musayyar wa-mukhayyar fī ān wāḥid*).[16] On Judgment Day, the scales of justice are brought out to weigh the cumulative deeds of the soul in its various incarnations.[17]

A Common Burial Structure

According to Druze belief, the body has no value; only the soul does, which is eternal and transmigrates from body to body. It is for that reason that Druze cemeteries are neglected, and there is a common grave, called *khushkhāsha*, in many cases.

The accepted belief is that there will be one judgment day for all souls and that they will end their transmigration and improvement on that day. The date of that day has been lost to human knowledge; however, there are several signs attesting to its approach: an intensification of wickedness and corruption and a decrease in the value put on religion and morals.[18] The Druze also believe that Judgment Day will come on a Friday on which the Festival of the Sacrifice (*'īd al-aḏha*) occurs.

The next stage following Judgment Day is the resurrection of the dead.[19] It will not be the bodies that will come to life on this day, for they have been used up and lack any value in Druze belief. Rather, on this day the superior status and governance of the Druze will be recognized: "You are the chosen among nations and the best among those who have trod the earth, for you have worshipped that which exists whereas they were keen on worshipping what has disappeared, the hidden."

In Druze belief, every person's lifetime is decreed in advance and is impossible to change. The belief in fate (*al-qadr*) is imbedded deep in the heart of the Druze, and this belief very much affects his/her life's course. One can point to many cases in which Druze took unreasonable risks, explaining their action by reference to the concept that nothing happens in this world in any case without its having been preordained. The will (*mashī'a*) of the individual is but marginal in managing one's life. This seems to explain the exceptional bravery for which the Druze are known.[20]

Since this world is only a bridge leading to the principal objective – the world to come – one should not wonder at the customary neglect of Druze cemeteries and the infrequency of headstones. The only sign indicating the existence of a grave is generally a pile of dirt surrounded by stones. In recent years, there has been a tendency for the dead to be placed in a common burial structure (*khushkhāsha* or *fustuqiyya*).

Death and Burial

There are many Druze traditions connected with death, but at their base lies the outlook that the soul does not cease to exist when the body comes to an end and that every person is allotted in advance a fixed and unchangeable period of life.

The Druze are not accustomed to mourning, and grieving women do not dress themselves in black, since they believe this contradicts the heavenly plan. Close family members, however, do stay indoors for several days in order to receive those who come to console them and memorialize the deceased. During the first few days after a person's death, the close male

Druze Women Mourning Col. Nabīh Mar'ī *(on facing page)*
The Druze custom is to dress the deceased in the same clothes that the person normally wore in his/her lifetime.

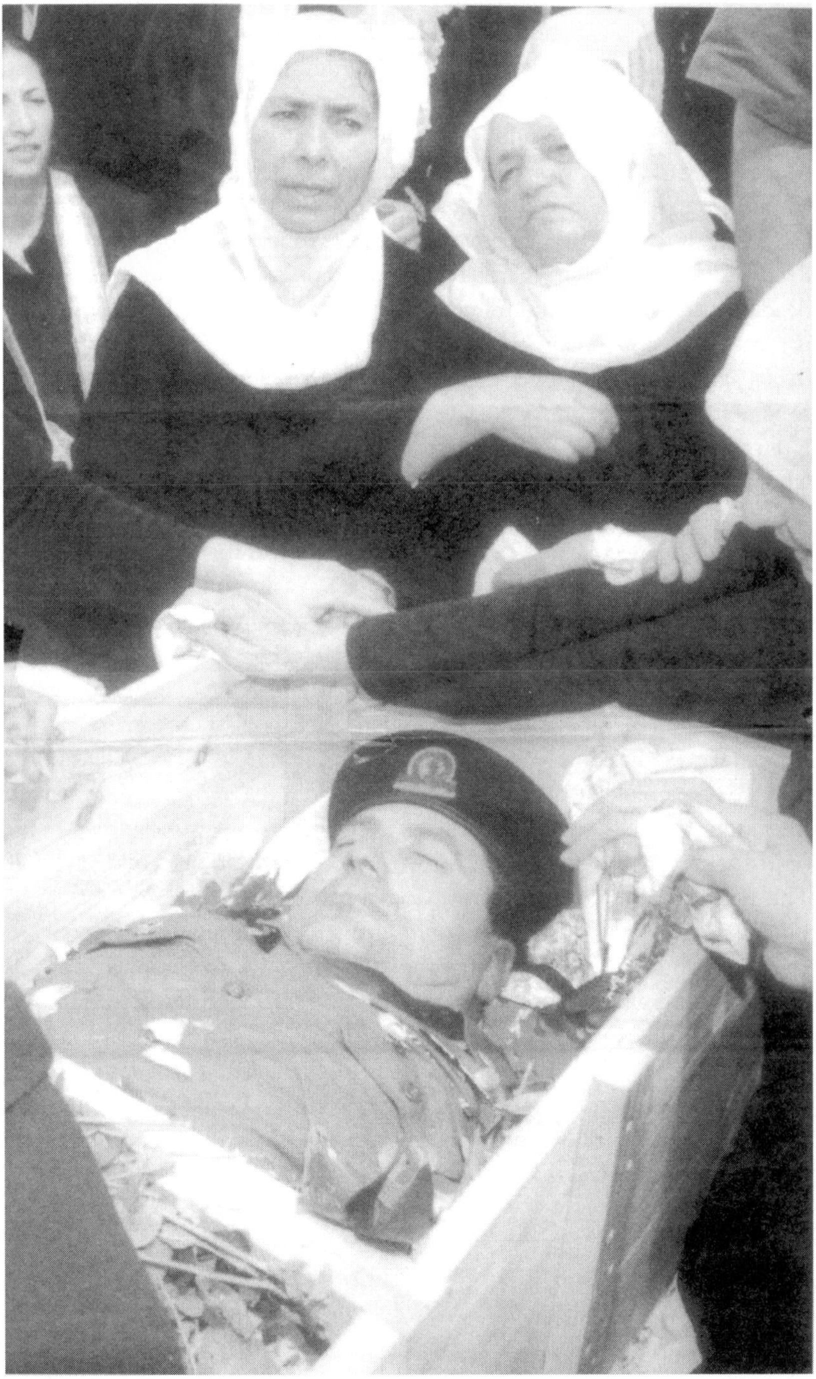

relatives refrain from shaving, having their hair cut, and eating meat; but this period of denial is not defined ahead of time. Generally the custom is that it lasts seven days for the closest family members (father, mother, brother, sister, son, daughter, husband or wife).

The Druze look upon undue delay in burial as being disrespectful to the deceased (*karāmat al-mayyit – dafnuhu*; respect for the dead – in his burial). Various preparatory measures (*tajhīz al-mayyit*) are taken prior to the funeral: the body is washed, and sometimes dressed in the clothing that the deceased used to wear when alive, then wrapped in a shroud (*kafn*). The dead person's relatives and friends ask his/her forgiveness before the body is placed in a coffin. The women congregate in a special public structure (*ma'tam*) to bewail the deceased, but they are forbidden to participate in the funeral itself.

Until the funeral procession, the men of the family wait in a large hall, where those who have come to take part have assembled. The procession goes on foot to the cemetery. Along the way, the mourners recite the Druze version of the *Shahāda* and sing words of praise and thanksgiving to Allāh. When they arrive at the cemetery, the mourners will at times place the coffin on a raised bench, with the feet of the deceased pointing south, then eulogize the dead person, and say a special prayer.[21] After the burial, the members of the family stand in a row close by the grave in order to receive those who have come to offer condolences. It is also customary to give charity at this occasion to honor the soul of the deceased, as well as donations for the upkeep of the various religious sites (*na'wāt*). The members of the family, and with them the local religious figures, assemble at the *khalwa*, or in a special room, for the purpose (*ghurfat al-waṣiyyāt*) of reading the will. The deceased person's family customarily eats the first meal after the funeral at the home of strangers or else eats food supplied by strangers.

Participants in the funeral procession or those who have come to console the family and who are not from the locality are not permitted to eat in the same village unless they have brought their own food with them or bought it, at full price, in the village. For this reason, there is no custom of offering food at such occasions, except for water, which is given to non-Druze, as well.[22] The Druze follow this custom even when taking part in the funeral of a non-Druze person.

Part II

Spiritual Leadership and Community Organization

6

The Druze Spiritual Leadership in the Middle East

Beginnings of Spiritual Leadership

In the first generation of the existence of the Druze religion – in the first half of the eleventh century – the fundamentals of the religion were open to all; there was even a campaign to propagate the faith among the public at large in order to attract new adherents. At the end of this period, the "gates were shut," and it became forbidden to reveal the secrets of the faith to outsiders. Furthermore, among those who were counted as believers in the new faith there began to crystallize a limited circle of pious men for whom the tenets of the faith were their exclusive lot. These were the *'uqqāl* – the sages. In generations to come, these men would shape the nature of the sect and its fundamental beliefs. They also became the leaders – both in matters of religion and in overall community affairs.

The activity of the spiritual leadership in this initial period concentrated on two geographical areas: Wādī al-Taym[1] and al-Shūf.[2] Those who were part of this select group bore the title of "spiritual head": *shaykh 'aql*, *ra'īs rūḥī*, *shaykh 'aṣr*, and others. The modest lifestyle of these shaykhs served as an example for the other members of the community, who behaved toward them with deep respect and even regarded them as holy. These pious men generally operated within a united religious leadership, the spiritual leadership (*mashyakhat al-'aql*), whose members were chosen for their personality, their experience in life, and their knowledge of the secrets of the faith. Heading the spiritual leadership generally was the most prominent shaykh, with alongside him four or five senior shaykhs, who assisted in the leadership of the community.[3]

No details are available on the shaykhs who served as the spiritual leadership in the first centuries after the founding of the sect. We effectively have no clear picture of this area until the end of the fifteenth century.

Spiritual Leadership up to the Eighteenth Century

One of the most striking religious figures in the second half of the fifteenth century, and perhaps among the Druze religious leadership of all generations, was al-Amīr al-Sayyid Jamāl al-Dīn 'Abd Allāh al-Tanūkhī (1417–79). His grave, found in the town of 'Abeh in Lebanon, still serves as a pilgrimage site for Druze. Al-Amīr al-Sayyid is considered the person who formulated the tenets of the religion. He wrote many exegetical works (*sharḥ*) on the Druze scriptures (*rasā'il al-ḥikma*); these commentaries are regarded as secret like the *Rasā'il* itself. All his works quote profusely from the scriptures of monotheistic religions. Al-Amīr al-Sayyid was a modest man who shied away from all material pleasures. He is said to have fathered four children, three of whom died young. The fourth was killed when he was kicked by a horse on the eve of his wedding when he was but 18 years old; al-Amīr waited until the end of the wedding feast and only then informed his guests that his only son had died, adding: "Allāh has received his deposit back."[4]

Two of al-Amīr al-Sayyid's followers particularly stood out: Shaykh Abū Yūsuf 'Alam al-Dīn Sulaymān, and Shaykh Sayf al-Dīn al-Tanūkhī, who was a relation and eventually inherited the spiritual leadership. It is said that al-Tanūkhī used to ride from village to village with two sacks. If he saw a poor person, he would say: "Take what you need." If he saw a rich person, he would tell him, "Put something into the two bags" (*ḥiṯṯ fī al-khirj*), which has become a well-known Arabic expression.[5]

In the sixteenth century, one name is worthy of mention: Shaykh Abū Zayn al-Dīn 'Abd al-Gaffār Taqī al-Dīn (1503–57), who was born in the village of Matta in Lebanon. His religious status is considered to be just below that of al-Amīr al-Sayyid. He composed several treatises, the most important of which are "The Book of Dots and Circles" (*kitāb al-nuqat wal-dawā'ir*), "Lexicon of Wisdom" (*qāmūs al-ḥikma*), and "A Short Explanation of the History of Time" (*mukhtaṣar al-bayān fī majra al-zamān*).

The one striking figure in the seventeenth century was Shaykh Abū Hilāl Muḥammad (who died in 1640), better known as al-Shaykh al-Fāḏil (the most compassionate shaykh). He is thought of as a great authority in religious matters, his standing in this area approaching that of al-Amīr al-Sayyid. He was born in the village of al-Sha'īra, west of Mount Hermon, studied in Damascus, and lived in the village of Kawkaba. Like al-Amīr, he was orphaned as a child. As a youth, he was a shepherd, and when he became an adult he devoted himself to religious studies and asceticism. He used to wear clothing made of crude cloth and was known to be very stringent when it came to food. It was said that he would plant barley in the dirt and harvest it with his own hands. As was customary among ascetics he would kneed the barley with its husk, bake it that way, and eat the resulting bread without having sifted the flour. Wherever he went, al-Shaykh al-Fāḏil took along his own food in order to avoid eating anything that might have been obtained in an improper manner.

When the Turks arrested al-Amīr Fakhr al-Dīn al-Maʿnī II and also wanted to apprehend al-Shaykh al-Fāḏil, who was the Amīr's cousin, on the assumption that the Druze would be willing to pay a good ransom for his release, al-Shaykh al-Fāḏil proclaimed a ban on anyone paying even the smallest amount toward the ransom money,[6] thereby causing the Turks to rescind their orders for his arrest. Residents of the village of Sumayʿ in Israel are known to relate how the man visited their village once, and the foot of a carob tree is identified as the spot where he stayed. He is generally regarded as the religious leader who formulated many of the practical laws of the Druze religion, such as the prohibition against eating at funerals, rules of conduct in society, and so forth. He also composed many religious poems about the work of the Creator.

Al-Shaykh al-Fāḏil put two requests into his will: one, that he be buried in a cultivated field so that no remnant would remain of his grave; the other, that no publicity be given to his death, and no eulogies delivered at the burial – so as not to bother the public unduly. Because of his elevated status, his peers refrained from carrying out his request in regard to a burial place, and his grave may still be found in the village of ʿAyn ʿAṯā in Rāshayyā (Wādī al-Taym). Druze customarily visit the site in the belief they will be blessed.

In the eighteenth century, the most prominent personality was Shaykh Abū ʿAlī Nāṣīf Abū Shaqrā (died 1750), who was very wealthy and became famous when he directed in his will that his fortune be divided among his co-religionists and that allocations be set aside for the maintenance of the holy places. Another well known personality from this same family was Shaykh Abū Zayn al-Dīn Yūsuf Abū Shaqrā, who lived at the time of Amīr Yūsuf al-Shīhābī, who ruled in Lebanon in the second half of the eighteenth century.

Spiritual Leadership in Recent Generations

In recent generations, a religious leadership developed separately in each of the three large Druze concentrations in the Middle East: Syria, Lebanon, and Palestine. The status of this leadership in these localities was anchored in separate legislation in each state. To a large extent, the hold of certain families on particular functions of the spiritual leadership crystalized in this period, and members of these families filled these positions by virtue of inheritance. Until 1948, the spiritual leaders of the three centers used to meet to discuss religious problems and to formulate policy in connection with ongoing current events. Meetings of this kind came to a halt in the wake of political events accompanying the establishment of the State of Israel, but were resumed in 1982 when the spiritual leaders of the Druze of Israel were able to meet with their counterparts in southern Lebanon, who were in charge of operating *Khalwāt al-Bayyāḏa*, the most important center in the world for studying the secrets of the Druze religion. There has also been a degree of communication between the Druze spiritual leadership of Lebanon and that of Syria.

The spiritual leadership in Lebanon

The institution of the Druze spiritual head in Lebanon began to crystalize gradually 200–250 years ago. Simultaneously, religious centers were also created in Syria and Palestine. At the end of the eighteenth century there were two striking figures among the Druze religious leaders in Lebanon: Shaykh ʻAlī Junblāṯ and Shaykh Ismāʻīl Abū Ḫamza. The two died in the same year, 1778. The next prominent leader was Shaykh Ḫusayn Māḏī (died 1801), who was known for his ascetic way of life. He used to dress in simple clothing, abstained from eating meat or ripe fruit, and fasted often.

Foremost among the figures in the nineteenth century were Shaykh Fakhr al-Dīn Ward and Shaykh Aḫmad Amīn al-Dīn. In the early part of the century, a feud broke out between the ruler of Lebanon, Amīr Bashīr al-Shīhābī II, and one of the Druze leaders at the time, Bashīr Junblāṯ. In the wake of this struggle (*al-gharaḏiyya*), a split occurred in the leadership, and from then on two Shaykhs (*ʻaql*) served the Druze of Lebanon concurrently, one from the House of Yazbak and the other from the Junblāṯ family.[7]

After Shaykh Ḫasan Taqī al-Dīn, of the Junblāṯ dynasty, Shaykh Ḫasan Ṯalīʻ served as spiritual head from 1945, and he was followed by his son Muḫammad Ṯalīʻ in 1949. Representing the Yazbakī faction as spiritual heads were Shaykh Ḫusayn ʻAbd al-Ṣamad, from 1915, and Muḫammad ʻAbd al-Ṣamad, from 1946. In 1954, quite unusually, two Shaykhs representing the Yazbakīs served together, Rashīd Ḫamāda and ʻAlī ʻAbd al-Laṯīf. They, too, both died in the same year, 1970.

In more recent times, Shaykh Muḫammad Abū Shaqrā served as spiritual leader of the Druze community in Lebanon until his death in 1991. In accordance with Shaqrā's will, Shaykh Bahjat Ghayth took over the leadership. Many Lebanese Druze expressed bitterness at the way he had been appointed as well as at the appointment itself.

The al-Bayyāḏa seminary for religious studies in southern Lebanon has a separate spiritual leadership: Shaykhs Muhanna Badr, Ghālib Qays, and Sulaymān Sujā'.

The modern period has seen legal expression given to the double *'aql* leadership in the form of a 1962 law covering the Election of the Spiritual Head of the Druze Community in Lebanon, stipulating that two pious figures (Shaykhs, or *'aql*) will serve as spiritual leaders of the Lebanese Druze.[8] These spiritual heads do not receive a state salary, but only a symbolic sum "for covering expenses" as the law defines it.[9]

The spiritual head is appointed for life. He is chosen by secret ballot of the male Druze citizens of Lebanon who have the right to vote in the Lebanese parliamentary elections. The Druze community council conducts the election. Requirements for the position of spiritual leader include being at least 40 years old, a religious person, expert in the Druze tradition, and a man possessing a good name who has not committed any religious or other transgression that would disgrace him.[10]

According to the legislation in force until 1962, the Druze Court of Appeals was composed of two spiritual leaders and another senior Druze judge from the civil court system. Then, a step was taken to remove the establishment–judicial authority from the religious leadership. The new law stated that the Religious Court of Appeals would be composed of the *Qāḏī-madhhab*, as chairman, and two advisors, appointed, like the *qāḏī-madhhab*, on the recommendation of the Justice Minister. Thus the Druze spiritual leadership would no longer be represented in Lebanon's judicial system.[11]

The spiritual leadership in Syria

The institution of the Druze spiritual head in Syria began to take form some two hundred years ago, when the Druze were based on Mount Ḫawrān (*jabal al-durūz*). The leadership body had three members with the positions passing by succession among a fixed set of families: the al-Hajarī, Jarbū', and al-Ḫinnāwī. The members were elected by the entire Druze leadership in Syria – the religious and the secular worthies alike.

Until 1959, the three spiritual leaders also served as members of the Druze Court of Appeals (*hay'a isti'nāfiyya*). That year, the court was disbanded and its members were transferred to a new department: the Department for Religious Law Decisions of the Druze Community (*dā'irat al-iftā' lil-madhhab al-durzī*), which was not intended to serve a judicial function; rather, its activity was to focus on expressing opinions in matters of religion and ethics only.

Recent spiritual leaders have been Shaykh Aẖmad al-Hajarī of Qanawāt,

Shaykh Ḫusayn Jarbū‘ of al-Suwaydā’, and Shaykh Shiblī al-Ḫinnāwī of al-Sahwā.

The spiritual leadership in Palestine

Spiritual heads The first person to serve as spiritual head in Palestine was Shaykh Muhanna Ṯarīf (1850–84). His father, Shaykh Sulaymān Ṯarīf, had died when Muhanna was 15 years old. Shaykh Muhanna was known principally for the ten years he devoted to constructing the *Maqām* Nabī Shu‘ayb near Tiberias. At one time, April 25 was the date of the annual assembly of the whole Druze community – from Palestine, Syria, and Lebanon – held at this site.[12]

A letter circulated by Shaykh Muhanna had urged his co-religionists to donate money to the building of the *Maqām* al-Khaḏr in Kafr Yāsīf, but he never lived to see it built. Shaykh Muhanna died before his 40th birthday, leaving two sons, Sulaymān and Sa‘īd. It was his brother Shaykh Muḫammad Ṯarīf, however, who was appointed *shaykh mashāyikh al-‘aql*.

Two other religious figures who had taken part with Shaykh Muhanna in collecting money for construction and renovation at the *Maqām* Nabī Shu‘ayb were Shaykh Abū Qāsim Muḫammad Farhūd of Rāma (who died in 1894) and Shaykh Abū Muḫammad Khalīl Ṯāfish of Sumay‘ (died 1911). Shaykh Qāsim is known to have taken a little dirt from the grave of Nabī Shu‘ayb when it was opened, and this is still used in giving blessings. Shaykh Ṯāfish is buried in the courtyard of the *khalwa* in his village. Carved on his gravestone are the details of his life. He left two daughters, one of whom, Fāṯima (umm Nasīb), attained important religious status.

Shaykh Muḫammad Ṯarīf, who succeeded his brother, appealed to the Turkish authorities to recognize him as *Qādī-madhhab* of the Druze community in Palestine, similar to the situation of the Druze in Syria and Lebanon. His request was granted and he served in this position until his death on September 28, 1918. He was thus in charge of both the spiritual affairs of the community and its religious–judicial matters. Shaykh Ṯarīf also played an important role in the building of the *Maqām* al-Khaḏr and added rooms to the *Maqām* Nabī Shu‘ayb. At his death, he left four sons: Salmān, Amīn, Muḫammad, and Ṣalāḫ. Two of his sons succeeded him. Shaykh Amīn was selected as spiritual head of the Druze in Palestine (he died in October 1993). Shaykh Salmān was put in charge of religious–judicial matters, including conducting marriages for the members of his community (he died in 1978).

In addition to the members of the Ṯarīf family, representatives of the Khayr and Mu‘addī families also served as Druze spiritual leaders. When Shaykh Ṯarīf Muḫammad was alive, the representative of the Khayr family was Shaykh Abū Muḫammad Yūsuf Ṣāliḫ (who died in 1965), assisted by his brother, Shaykh Abū Najīb Ṣāliḫ Khayr (died 1952). Shaykh Abū Muḫammad was an important religious figure who dedicated his life to matters of the spirit. Despite his great wealth, he lived modestly. He aided the needy and financed the renovation and development of sacred property in the village of Abū Sinān. More recently, Shaykh Aḫmad Khayr served as his family's representative to the spiritual leadership, until his death on February 1, 1993.

Alongside the Shaykhs of the Ṭarīf and Khayr families, Shaykh Abū 'Alī Muḫammad Qāsim Mu'addī (died 1931) served as family representative to the Druze spiritual leadership in Palestine. Shaykh Mu'addī was known as an important religious personality who devoted much activity to strengthening the foundations of the faith. He also did much to set up and strengthen charitable enterprises. He became especially known for cultivating moral values in his society, particularly among the women of the community. His house served as a refuge for the politically persecuted (of whom there were many, especially at the end of the first quarter of the twentieth century), among them many of the religious leaders of Lebanon at the time. Adjoining his village, Yarkā, Shaykh Abū 'Alī put up the Khalwat al-Rughab, which for a short time served as a religious studies seminary for young Druze in the region. After his death, this enterprise waned until it became completely inactive at the time of the Arab disturbances of 1936–9. During this period, Shaykh Kamāl Mu'addī served as family representative to the Druze spiritual leadership (he died in 1984).

Local religious figures Besides the Shaykhs, other religious figures, generally people who worked to strengthen the religious foundation of their villages, served as religious leaders. In only a very few cases, however, did the Druze leaders in Palestine gain prominence and recognition even among the other Druze populations in the Middle East. The most striking of these was Shaykh 'Alī Fāris (died 1753), who is considered of very high religious standing. Shaykh 'Alī Fāris came from a poor family in the village of Yarkā. As a young man, he immersed himself in religious studies and maintained an ascetic way of life. Delegations from Druze populations throughout the Middle East would call at his home. He was a superb calligrapher (*khaṯṯāṯ*), and composed many religious poems. A subject that arises again and again in his poetry is a request to Allāh for forgiveness and atonement for his sins. His *dīwān* (poetry anthology) serves religious Druze throughout the Middle East even today. For a while, Shaykh 'Alī Fāris studied at the Khalwāt al-Bayyāḏa in south Lebanon. Afterwards, he moved to the village of Jūlis, where he died in his mid-50s. Details of his life are written on a panel at the entrance to the room above his grave, to which people go on pilgrimage and to receive blessings.

The two Druze villages on Mount Carmel, Dāliyat al-Karmil and 'Isifyā, have produced several religious figures of high stature. From 'Isifyā came Shaykh 'Alī Khatīb Abū Rukn (died 1930), who was among the leaders in the fight against the move toward Islamicization being preached by one of his peers, also from 'Isifyā, Shaykh Abū Ṣāliḥ Sulaymān Abū Tamīma (died 1951). Abū Tamīma set up a movement calling for a "return to Islam" (*al-rujū' lil-Islām*), on the basis of the *taqiyya* (self-preservation) principle, without regard for the basic differences between Druze and Muslims. Members of this movement demanded outwardly Islamic behavior, including performing Muslim rites in mosques, fasting at *Ramaḍān*, and other Muslim rituals. The movement lasted seven years.

Supporting Abū Tamīma and his movement were Shaykhs of the Ḥalabī family in Dāliyat al-Karmil and the Khayr family of Abū Sinān as well as many other Druze from Palestine, Syria, and Lebanon. Opposing them was the Druze leadership in the Khalwāt al-Bayyāḍa. They issued a proclamation ostracizing anyone who followed Abū Tamīma and excluding them from the '*uqqāl* society.

The spiritual leadership (Religious Council) in Israel

The formal institution of the Druze spiritual leadership in Israel (*al-ri'āsa al-rūḥiyya*, or the Religious Council, as the law terms it) is relatively new, its initial patterns having begun to take shape only a few generations ago. The three families from whom the members of the Council are chosen live in nearby villages: Ṭarīf in Jūlis, Khayr in Abū Sinān, and Mu'addī in Yarkā. This body did not receive official recognition until April 15, 1957, when the Minister of Religions, Moshe Haim Shapiro, by virtue of the authority granted him as "Supervisor of Religious Communities (Organization), 1926," issued regulations making the Druze a recognized religious community.[13] He also appointed a Religious Council for this community, composed of Shaykh Amīn Ṭarīf, as chairman, and Shaykhs Kamāl Mu'addī and Aḥmad Khayr. The regulations said nothing about the functions of this institution. Recognition of the Religious Council came about during the establishment of the Druze Religious Courts. The first activity of its members immediately after their appointment was to "adopt" the laws in regard to the personal status of the Druze in Lebanon as the substantive law of the Druze Religious Courts in Israel, with the introduction of certain changes necessitated by the existence of Israeli legislation.

Simultaneously the members of the Religious Council were appointed – in person, and seemingly without any affinity to the position – as members of the Druze Religious Court of Appeals.[14] In this way, a connection was assured between the judicial authority and the supreme religious power in the community.

The practical work of the Druze Religious Council consisted of discussing various topics of concern that arose from time to time in the religious and social life of the community. The Council would publish regular statements containing the Council's decisions on these matters, which were then circulated among the community. Below is a selection of such resolutions and topics discussed by the Council, which give an idea of the prevailing state of mind and feelings of the Druze public in a previous generation.

Religious education The preface to this book describes religion as a distinct factor characterizing the Druze community, but points out that the Druze religion is a secret religion, which makes it difficult to propagate it even among the members of the community itself. This issue is of critical importance in the matter of education for the young generation, who wonder more and more about their identity.

Shafīq Manṣūr, a journalist from ʿIsifyā, stresses the commitment of the community to preserving its religious principles, but also "the obligation of religious figures to open up the gates of religious studies for Druze youth." In his opinion, "The religious figures have a multiple responsibility because the future and the honor of the community are placed on their shoulders."[15]

Shaykh Labīb Abū Rukn, who served as *Qāḍī* on the Druze Court of Appeals, places special emphasis on the importance of giving religious education to girls "because if the woman does not learn the religion, it will be difficult for her to instill in her home moral values and the foundations of a positive way of life."[16] Nā'if Ṣāliḥ Salīm of Peqiʿin expresses a grievance against the elders of the community for not opening a religious studies seminar for girls in Israel "in order to improve the standing of the community and to prevent it from standing still."[17]

Shaykh Salmān Māḏī, a religious figure and important poet from Jūlis, proposed appointing teachers to instruct school children in the basics of the religion in every Druze elementary school, beginning from grade 6, "in order for the youth to be educated in the basics of ethics and religion." The same proposal advocated that these teachers be paid for out of State coffers or from the yields of Druze endowments.[18]

The late spiritual head of the Druze community, Shaykh Amīn Ṭarīf, addressed this subject at the Nabī Shuʿayb celebrations in 1970. He talked of the need for religious education and called on the religious figures in every village to "intensify religious instruction and training, especially among the youth, and to strengthen the foundations of the religion and tradition among the young generation, which is sunk in materialism."[19] The Shaykh even made contact with government education officials to formulate appropriate frameworks. It was agreed that the Ministry of Religions would finance expenditure in connection with religious studies, including paying the salaries of the teachers and covering attendant organizational expenses. Indeed, for several years, courses were offered in accordance with this arrangement. Moreover, the spiritual head, with encouragement and finance from the Ministry of Religions, would tour the various Druze villages, preaching and giving religious instruction. Following the 1982 war, the way was opened for hundreds of young Druze a year to take courses in their religion at Khalwāt al-Bayyāḏa in the town of Ḫāsbayyā in southern Lebanon.

Mixed education for boys and girls One of the more sensitive issues for the community related to the question of mixed education for boys and girls. According to Druze tradition, mixed company is forbidden, from the age of 7 or 8. It should be emphasized here that the elders of the community do not object in principle to giving girls an education. They even encourage it and see in it a religious goal. Shaykh Aḫmad Khayr, who served as a member of both the spiritual leadership and the Druze Court of Appeals, even insisted that boys and girls be given an equal education.[20] Shaykh Jabr Mu'addī, a former member of Knesset and Deputy Minister of Communications, was active on several occasions in setting up a Druze high school near Yarkā and, at the same time, a high school for girls "to ensure a balance in the field of education between children of the community of each sex."[21]

This question of mixed education generated sharp debate in Shefar'am with the town's decision to open a mixed elementary school, which infuriated many in the Druze community. The issue even led to Court appeals. The Druze spiritual leaders published a statement that "mixed education is religiously forbidden . . . except for higher education – and the latter by force of reality and in the absence of any possibility of maintaining separation there."

Besides the general view in favor of girls' acquiring knowledge, there was a desire to impose limits in the hope of maintaining the modesty of the girls and the separation of the sexes. Thus, girls were forbidden to join the Scouts, to study outside the village, and so forth.[22] Several years ago, a course for Druze nurses was offered so that these women would be able, when the time came, to serve their villages. The Druze spiritual leaders, who were not favorably inclined toward this course, wrote to the Ministry of

Health and the Ministry of Religions to register their objection because "the duties of nurses do not accord with the way of life of young female Druze insofar as the tenets of our religion are concerned." They requested that the Ministries shut down the course and refrain from accepting Druze girls into such frameworks.

Avoiding exhibitionism The Druze individual should aspire to a modest, simple lifestyle, but it appears that contrary external influences have not passed the younger generation by, even though most young people are villagers. These outside influences are manifested in all walks of life, and are very common even in matters that by their very nature are protected by the tradition of generations, such as wedding customs, traditional clothing, etc.

Community leaders have devoted a lot of attention to this matter, sometimes threatening to ostracize or even excommunicate those who violate existing tradition. Cracks, however, have appeared in the rigid nature of the traditional Druze wedding, once characterized by its modest style. "Innovations" have been introduced in recent years, such as a band and lavish receptions to the point of exhibitionism. The spiritual leaders published a statement attacking these innovations and threatening a religious ban on anyone participating in weddings of this sort. They have also come out against the custom of the groom's families giving exaggerated gifts to the bride, since this extravagance is tantamount to circumventing the limitations placed on a maximum bride price (*mahr*).[23]

Innovations in Druze tradition may also be seen in the area of dress. Druze brides have begun to wear fancier wedding gowns, contrary to a generations-old custom of having a local seamstress sew such dresses, and to decorate themselves with expensive jewelry. Community leaders warned against this practice and forbade brides from using a bridal veil instead of the traditional white scarf, and from "decorating themselves with gold ornaments, expensive chains, and various jewelry on their hands and necks."[24] In another proclamation, the community's religious leaders issued a prohibition against Druze girls wearing miniskirts or trousers.[25]

The bride's price (*mahr*) One of the difficulties standing in the way of the young male Druze who wants to raise a family is the *mahr*, the money that he must first pay the potential bride's family. This difficulty, especially severe in the past, eventually brought about the intervention of the Druze religious leadership. Muḫammad Mursil of Peqi'in, for example, complained of the level of *mahr* required in his village and called on the community leadership to express its opinion on the matter. He feared that in the absence of an appropriate solution, there could be serious implications for the young generation of males, even "leading to marriages with non-Druze girls."[26]

Shaykh Kamāl Muʿaddī, who served as a member of the spiritual leadership and of the Druze Religious Court of Appeals, urged his people a number of times to stop exaggerating the bride price. He demanded that the sum be reduced to a minimum. He also asked grooms not to go overboard in buying clothes for their brides and to be satisfied with spending the minimum necessary for a wedding. Another proposal was to increase as much as possible the amount of "late *mahr*" (*mu'ajjal* or *mu'akhkhar*, the *mahr* granted to a woman in the event of divorce or the death of her husband). This, in his opinion, would have three advantages: (a) it would ease the immediate financial burden placed on the young husband; (b) it would ensure material means for the woman in the case of divorce; (c) the husband would be deterred from any hasty divorce.

A special meeting of the spiritual leadership was convened to discuss the matter. A statement issued upon its conclusion said that "since the prophets stated that it was forbidden to exaggerate the bride's price," the leadership had resolved to fix a certain maximum sum, which would include clothing expenses and other expenditures.[27] It should be mentioned that several years previously, the *Qāḍīs* Shaykh Labīb Abū Rukn and Shaykh Ḫusayn ʿAlayān had discussed the subject and offered a similar proposal.[28]

The status of the woman There is no doubt that the respected status of the Druze woman, especially in the realm of family life, was influenced by the position of honor granted to her by the religion. Her agreement has to be obtained before she is married, and in the family she must be accorded equal standing with her husband.[29] The husband must, by law,[30] guarantee her lodgings and see to it that she is not neglected in his will or in the matter of inheritance.[31] In certain cases, she is entitled to request separation from her husband, and she is given full authority to leave her property to whomever she wishes. The spiritual leadership was asked on several occasions about the woman's rights and ruled that she must have a modest appearance, is forbidden to work outside her village or go into a cinema, and among other prohibitions, cannot be photographed, even for an official document.[32] She also cannot give birth in a hospital that has no women doctors.[33]

Autopsies, especially of women, are entirely forbidden. In 1970, the Druze sent a request on this matter to the Ministries of Health and Religions that said, among other things:

> The Druze spiritual leadership has been informed by a reliable source that

> the phenomenon of operations on women after their death has increased of late . . . Because of this, the leadership of the Druze community in Israel has decided to appeal to the Ministers of Health and Religions to inform hospitals and appropriate institutions of our reservations and concern at the performance of such operations, since our religious tenets strictly forbid operations of this kind, particularly those conducted on Druze women.[34]

Wills and inheritance The *Qāḍīs* Shaykh Labīb Abū Rukn and Shaykh Ḫusayn ʻAlayān contend that according to Druze religious law, "a believing Druze may not go to sleep without having prepared a will." Following a statement published on this subject, the two called on members of their community not to deviate from the rules of justice and not to give in to passing emotions when they wrote their wills, and also not to neglect the wives' and daughters' share of the inheritance.[35]

Oaths An interesting issue discussed by spiritual leaders is the question of the book on which a Druze may swear an oath. This question, which arose with the establishment of the Druze Religious Courts, originated in the fact that Druze religious books are secret. Members of the Druze spiritual leadership decided that "it is best if the oath is taken on one of the sacred books that show the unity of the Creator." As an addition to that resolution (of March 3, 1967),[36] Shaykh Kamāl Muʻaddī stated the following:

> We, members of the Druze community, believe in the holiness of the Torah of Israel in that it teaches about the existence of the almighty God and because our first prophet is mentioned there, Shuʻayb [Jethro], the High Priest of Madian, along with the other prophets of Israel who are holy in our eyes. We also believe in the holiness of the *Qur'ān* in that it teaches about the uniqueness of the Almighty God . . . and because our prophet Shuʻayb, of blessed memory, is mentioned there – he is Jethro the Priest . . . These are the sacred books in the eyes of the members of the Druze community, and oaths may properly be taken on them.

Sacred trusts An issue that annoys the community from time to time relates to the management of assets considered sacred trusts (*waqf*) of the community. This property constitutes, in essence, public charitable trusts (*waqf khayrī*) as opposed to family sacred assets (*waqf dhurrī*). Every village has someone in charge of these trusts, who collects the income from them, and distributes it among the needy or expends it for maintaining religious facilities. These charitable trusts are not numerous, and it may safely be assumed that the income from them is not high. Nevertheless, the nature of their management is sometimes criticized. Complaints have been heard that the money from these trusts has not been put to the charitable purposes for which they were intended. Shaykh Kamāl Mu'addī has argued on several occasions that the managers of these trusts in every village, must keep precise books, which should be open to anyone for inspection, as is the case in Yarkā. In the past, the issue became acute in Rāma, where it led to a civil suit. Shaykh Nimr Abū Zaydān of Mughār in Galilee called for a public body of members of the Druze community to be set up to deal with the sacred trusts of Nabī Shu'ayb, the largest and most important of the group. He also offered several suggestions for putting sacred trust monies to public use, such as establishing and maintaining a seminary for religious studies.

Laws of mourning The Druze have no laws dealing with mourning in the sense familiar to Jews. Druze are commanded to take part in funerals, but if this takes place outside their home village they may not eat unless they brought along their own food or purchased it at the full price. Similarly it is not customary for Druze to hold memorials, and it is strictly forbidden to place flowers on graves. After much deliberation, the religious leadership withdrew the ban on wreaths and flowers when the occasion was in memory of fallen Israeli Druze soldiers buried in military cemeteries.

The Druze Religious Council in Israel

Shaykh Amīn Ṯarīf, spiritual leader of the Druze community in Israel, passed away in early October 1993. The Shaykh had fulfilled three important public functions: First, he had been spiritual head of the Druze community, a position that from 1957 involved being head of the Druze Religious Council. Secondly, he had been chairman of the Druze Religious Court of Appeals, a position he first took up in 1963. Thirdly, he had managed the assets of *Maqām* Nabī Shu'ayb (Jethro's gravesite), a task he had inherited from past generations.

Until his demise, Shaykh Amīn Ṯarīf had served as spiritual leader of his community for more than sixty years. His death led to a bitter struggle over the Druze leadership in Israel between, for the most part, two forces. One group was composed of religious men close to the Shaykh when he was alive, who wanted to carry out his last will and testament by appointing his grandson, Shaykh Muwaffaq Ṯarīf, as successor.[37] The opposing group[38] demanded that the head of the community and the person responsible for Jethro's grave be appointed in accordance with democratic rules, with careful attention paid to proper administrative arrangements.

The struggle essentially revolves around two issues that have a major influence on determining the leadership. One concern is the method of appointing the Religious Council, as well as the nature of this Council, which is the body that elects the spiritual head of the community. The second issue concerns the person who has the authority to administer *Maqām* Nabī Shu'ayb. This is very important, since the administration of this *Maqām* was always in the hands of the spiritual head. Many lawsuits were filed that revolved around the two issues, but especially the second.[39]

To understand the legal background to the struggle over the two institutions, one should first read the directives contained in Article 2 of the Religious Communities (Organization) Executive Order. According to this Article, the Minister of Religions may, at the request of a religious community in Israel, produce regulations for its activities as a religious organization and for its acknowledgment as such by the Israeli government. Furthermore, "for each and every community, special regulations will be instituted that are appropriate for the special circumstances and organization of that community." By virtue of this authority, the Minister of Religions instituted the regulations known as Religious Communities (Organization) (the Druze Community), 5717–1957, which announced that "the Druze community is a recognized religious community in Israel."

Along with the legal recognition of the Druze community, a Religious Council was established for the community, with three members, chosen according to title and name. Shaykh Amīn Ṯarīf was selected as chairman. Besides the Religious Council, a Druze Religious Courts Law, 5723–1962, was enacted. This court system has special authority in matters of marriage and divorce involving Druze and – what is particularly important – in matters pertaining to the creation and management of Druze sacred trusts.

Of the original three members of the Court of Appeals and the three members of the lower court, only one *Qāḏī-Madhhab* remained at the time of the death of Shaykh Amīn Ṯarīf (and even for many years before that). In other words, appeals were effectively frozen for many years.

Shaykh Amīn Ṯarīf had been aware of the struggle that was to be expected over the spiritual leadership and the management of the Nabī Shu'ayb assets. His will, dated March 30, 1985, nine years prior to his death, stated that he willed to his grandson, Shaykh Muwaffaq Ṯarīf, both the leadership and the authority to manage the *Maqām*. At the heart of his conception was the view that these positions were a right acquired by the Ṯarīf family by virtue of the fact that this had been the situation for untold generations. Accordingly, at Shaykh Amīn Ṯarīf's funeral, his mantle was literally placed on his grandson's shoulders to show – according to ancient tradition – that the transference of the succession from grandfather to grandson was completed.

It was this act that incensed significant sections of the community who took part in the gravesite ceremony for the elder. Thanks, however, to police reinforcements that were present, no real commotion erupted, and the essence of the struggle passed to the courts.

The rest of this chapter will be divided into two parts. First, the focus will be on the Druze Religious Court, how it was set up and how it operates; the second part deals with the rules determining who heads it, a position of great importance and prestige as we have seen.

The first lawsuit was presented close to the time of Shaykh Ṯarīf's death, and its concern was simple: it appealed to the Prime Minister (and Minister of Religions) to refrain from appointing the members and chairman of the Druze Religious Council by virtue of his authority according to the rules of the Religious Communities (Organization) Act.[40] At the same time, the suit included an appeal for urgent action to "make a secondary set of regulations concerning the manner of the election of the members and chairman of the Druze Religious Council as well as of Druze community institutions in democratic, egalitarian elections."[41]

In the end, the Minister of Religions formulated regulations for putting together the Religious Council. The essential elements were as follows:[42]

- 30 *sā'ises* (those in charge of Druze houses of worship, the *khalwas*);
- 15 candidates of local authorities where Druze live;
- 15 members appointed by the Minister, following consultation with the Druze local authorities and all serving *sā'ises.*

Opposing this view, significant parts of the community were of the opinion that a body should be created that would represent the community in a democratic manner, or at least the religious figures of the community. Therefore, it was suggested that elections be conducted in the Druze houses of prayer. Instead of the automatic appointment of *sā'ises*, it would be those elected who would represent the *khalwas.*[43]

The Supreme Court, sitting as a Court of Appeals, deliberated over this issue. The three-man bench was clearly inclined to introduce more democracy into the composition of the Religious Council. In the end, though, they decided by a two-to-one vote to adopt the suggestion of the Minister of Religions as the lesser of two evils. The majority opinion stated that

> the trap into which the Druze community has ensnared itself obliges a solution that will enable returning community institutions, which are so vital to the individual and the public, to normal activity, as rapidly as possible, after so many years of absolute paralysis. This goal would have come to nothing

> were the community now put into another maelstrom of elections, which would deepen the polarization, and it would not be difficult to assess that it would also draw other legal action in its wake . . .

There was, however, a minority opinion supporting the other group's position, which demanded more democratization in the community. The government, which held this view, as is indicated in the proposals of the Minister of Religions, was

> entitled and authorized to ask the community to make these and other changes in the structure of the community and its institutions as a condition of its being recognized by the law – and these changes, if effected, would be made by the community or on its behalf, and not by the government. The government was not authorized and was not given permission to coerce the community into particular courses of action, for autonomy and coercion are contradictory. And so, in accordance with the law, the Minister does not obtain authority except if the community petitions him. Recognition comes on the basis of this appeal, and autonomy follows recognition. Coercing the maintenance of certain institutions instantly negates the petition to the Minister and stands in contradiction to the idea of autonomy.

As to the second area of contention, management of the assets of *Maqām* Nabī Shu'ayb (and other religious property), which seemingly is not connected to this discussion, it should be noted that a short time after the death of the head of the Druze community, the Druze Court was requested to exercise its authority in accordance with Article 4 of the Druze Religious Courts Law, which states: "In its exclusive jurisdiction will be matters pertaining to the creation or internal management of sacred trusts." In other words, the Court was asked to expropriate the Nabī Shu'ayb assets from the Ṯarīf family and to deny the Shaykh's right, expressed in his will, to make his grandson heir to the assets of *Maqām* Nabī Shu'ayb and its management.

The Druze Court thus found itself engrossed by a very intriguing issue: How should it relate to the Nabī Shu'ayb assets? Should it recognize the right of the Ṯarīf family to manage these assets as had been the case for a number of generations prior to Shaykh Amīn Ṯarīf's demise? Put another way, should it allow a continuation of the existing situation, or should it respond positively to the view of these assets as public holdings of the whole community and, therefore, subject to the application of legal rules and public administration, and all that this implies?

Moreover, in the *tabu* books (land-title registers), these assets are apparently recorded as sacred trusts of the Druze community in Israel, with no exact reference to the Ṯarīf family. Because of the sensitivity of the issue, the Druze Court turned to the litigants and proposed that they set up an agreed-upon joint public committee for managing the Nabī Shu‘ayb property, its administration involving great prestige along with not a little financial involvement. In addition, Shaykh Muwaffaq Ṯarīf was requested not to take any further steps in relation to these assets without the court's agreement in writing. Various public figures were recruited to bring the two camps to negotiate. Particularly involved in this was Professor David Libai, a former Minister of Justice, who drew up an agreement for cooperation that was signed at a public convocation at *Maqām* al-Khaḏr in Kafr Yāsīf on December 11, 1997. The understandings sum up three principal points:

1 The Religious Council will be composed of 78 members:
(a) 30 *sā'ises* serving in Druze houses of worship;[44]
(b) 15 members of local authority councils where Druze reside, as detailed in the appendix;
(c) 15 members appointed by the Minister of Religions after consultation with the local authority councils and all the serving *sā'ises*.
(d) The 60 foregoing members will be joined by another 15 selected by those objecting to the Ṯarīf family, and three chosen by the Ṯarīf family.[45]

2 The tenure of the head of the Religious Council will expire at the end of five years from the day of his election or at the expiration of the validity of the regulations.[46]

3 Concerning the management of the monies of the holy sites, it was decided that a management committee would be set up composed of 11 members: six to be chosen by a representative of the Ṯarīf family, who would also serve as chairman of this committee, and five chosen by the opposite side.[47]

There is no doubt that this agreement constitutes an important foundation for the building of understanding between the different factions of the community and for advancing proper, balanced administration, despite the fact that the implementation of the agreement has in the meantime encountered certain difficulties.[48]

7

The Status of the Druze and Their Community Organization

The Druze do not enjoy identical legal standing in their three large concentrations in the Middle East: Syria, Lebanon, and Israel.

The first attempts at an official definition of the community status of the Druze in the region were made in the second half of the nineteenth century. Until then, their standing was not at all clear although there was known to be an arrangement, which relied mainly on long tradition, according to which a man of the Druze faith would be in charge of several matters in the area of personal status, especially matters having to do with marriage.

The Ottoman Period

One of the first documents known to us about the status of the Druze deals with their standing in the Ḫāsbayyā and Rashayyā districts in Lebanon. It is an epistle that the *Wālī* (governor) of Damascus sent in 1890 to the district officers (*qā'im maqām*) of the two districts, instructing them "not to alter in any way the existing arrangements and practices of long standing." The spiritual head of the Druze community was the official authorized to handle matters of marriage, divorce, and wills for the members of his community.[1] This epistle was sent in response to a complaint made by the heads of the Druze community in Ḫāsbayyā against the local *Qāḏī Shar'ī*, who had tried to violate this tradition. The *Qāḏī*'s action was not an isolated event, and the Druze leaders were forced to lodge further complaints when he did not abide by the *Wālī*'s instructions. In the end, there was need to involve the *Mashyakhat al-Islām*, or Islamic religious leadership, in Constantinople. That year, the Islamic leader, Shaykh Aḫmad Luṯfī, in answer to a query, reiter-

* This chapter was written with the participation of Salmān Falāḫ.

ated that matters of Druze marriages and wills "have always been adjudicated by their religious leader." Accordingly the *Qāḏī Shar'ī* of Ḫāṣbayyā was ordered not to handle these matters unless all parties to the dispute agreed to his involvement. The Shaykh's letter also mentioned that this arrangement "had at the time received the imprimatur of the High Porte [the name given to the Ottoman government in Constantinople]."[2]

In 1908, a directive was issued by the *Mashyakhat al-Islām* to the *Wālī* of Syria in reference to the *Qāḏī Shar'ī* of Ḫāṣbayyā, and copies were sent to every *Shar'ī* court in Syria, Lebanon, and Palestine. The directive mentioned the Druze's repeated complaints that *Shar'ī* courts were adjudicating matters of Druze marital status, and repeated the order to refrain from doing so. The document also stated that because of the special status of the Druze, their leaders, and their character, and because of the desire to maintain the status quo, the Muslim *Qāḏīs* were not to intervene in matters of the personal status of Druze.

In contrast to the Druze in Lebanon under the Turks, who were recognized as an independent community on the basis of an order from the High Porte, the Druze in Palestine did not gain this right. In 1909, however, the ruling council of the *Wālī* of Beirut decided that the Druze in Palestine were within its jurisdiction and began to apply the High Porte's order to the Druze of Palestine. In a letter of clarification, the *Wālī* of Beirut, Adham ibn Mas'ūd, wrote to the District (*mutaṣarrifiyya*) of Acre stating that the order sent by the *Shaykh al-Islām* to the *Qāḏī* of Ḫāṣbayyā in 1890 applied also for the Druze of Palestine. He added that it was necessary to apply the order of the High Porte to all Druze and to prevent *Shar'ī* courts from handling Druze affairs in matters of marriage, divorce, wills, and inheritance. It may be said, therefore, that from 1909 the Druze of Palestine gained recognition – though of doubtful legal value – as a separate, independent community group and were not subject to adjudication before *Shar'ī* courts.

Two months later, on April 20, 1909, the *Wālī* of Beirut informed the Acre authorities that, relying on petitions sent by Druze notables and their *mukhtars* in Palestine to the Ministry of the Interior (*Naẓārat al-Dākhiliyya*) in Constantinople and subsequently transferred to him, and following the decision reached by the *Wilāya* council, he recommended appointing Shaykh Muḥammad Ṭarīf as *Qāḏī* for the Druze. The Acre district officer (*mutaṣarrif*) therefore appointed Shaykh Ṭarīf as judge of the Druze in Palestine. Thus, by the end of the Ottoman period, the local Turkish authorities had recognized the Druze as a separate independent community and appointed a Druze judge to adjudicate matters of Druze personal status. This recognition, though, ensured the establishment of neither community institutions nor Druze religious courts. The Druze were not obliged to go to Shaykh Ṯarīf with their disputes. In fact, the *Shar'ī* courts could still try Druze affairs if the parties concerned so requested. Moreover, this recognition did not come from an order of the Sulṯān (*firmān*) or the legal regulation of a certified authority. It was only a local decision taken by the ruling council of the *Wālī* of Beirut.[3]

The British Mandate Period

The British Mandate did not view the Druze as an independent community and was unwilling to allow them to establish a community court. At first, they restricted the authority of the Druze judge, limiting it to narrow personal affairs; the judge's right to adjudicate matters of inheritance and wills was recognized only on condition that both parties agreed to this. In 1922, the community courts of the various communities living in Palestine were given legal standing in accordance with a King's Order-in-Council. Since the Druze had no recognized court, they were not given the right to set one.

The powers of the Druze religious *Qāḏī* were constricted further in 1932. His authority to adjudicate matters of inheritance and wills was abrogated entirely, and he was left only to rule on matters of divorce and marriage.

The steps to greatly reduce the area of judicial authority for the Druze and to negate any recognition of their community independence were undertaken gradually. In the first two years of British rule in Palestine, the Druze turned to the military administration with a request for recognition of their communal independence and for a renewal of the appointment of the Druze *Qāḏī*, Shaykh Ṯarīf, whom the Ottomans had recognized. The British military governor of Haifa at the time replied to Shaykh Ṯarīf on July 7, 1919, that the authorities had approved his right to adjudicate matters of marital status involving Druze. As to matters of wills, this authority required the agreement of the two parties to the dispute, otherwise the matter would be turned over to the *Shar'ī* court. Following this response, Shaykh Ṯarīf appealed to the presidency of the Haifa Municipal Court to order the court's judges (*ḫakam al-ṣulḫ*) in Acre and Haifa to transfer to him all Druze-related suits in regard to estates, wills, marriages, and divorces.

The president of the Haifa Municipal Court informed the Shaykh on October 11, 1919, that the authorities had instructed the Municipal Court judges and the *Shar'ī Qāḏīs* in Haifa and Acre to take into consideration the permission given to the Druze to handle matters of marital status that arose on the basis of their own laws. As to suits on matters of inheritance, it had been decided that "if the two parties to the case do not agree to be judged by you, then the file will be transferred to the *Shar'ī* court for a ruling." The reply did not at all satisfy the Druze, who demanded full recognition of their community and the establishment of community institutions. They sent a petition signed by all Druze notables, demanding full recognition, but they were met with refusal. The northern district officer, in a letter dated May 2, 1924, informed Shaykh Ṯarīf that the Mandatory government could not fulfill the Druze's request to establish community courts that would handle matters of personal status, because the 1922 legislation, on the basis of which the other community courts operated, recognized only those courts that had existed at that time and whose authority stemmed from Ottoman law in the form of a *firmān* or some other order issued by the Sulṯān. Apparently the British feared the ire of the supreme Muslim council on this matter.

As for the directive sent by the *Wālī* of Beirut, the district officer said that it did not fulfill the conditions set down in Article 7 of the Palestine laws and that it did not grant the required authority for setting up courts because Shaykh Ṯarīf's authority was limited to ruling on matters of marital status, whereas issues of inheritance had first to gain the consent of all parties. Relying on military regulations, the district officer confirmed Shaykh Ṯarīf's authority to adjudicate matters of marital status (marriages and divorces) without setting up a Druze court, whereas all other matters were to be decided in civil courts. This order, then, effectively transferred authority over the personal status of Druze – except for issues of inheritance – from the Muslim *Shar'ī* courts to the civil court system. But it also effectively put an end to any chance that the British Mandatory authorities would recognize the Druze in Palestine as a separate and independent community.

There were other appeals on the issue, but the British stance did not change. In a letter that the Haifa district governor sent on January 16, 1929, to confirm the appointment of Shaykh Salmān Ṯarīf after the death of Shaykh Muḥammad Ṯarīf, the new *Qāḏī*'s authority was not spelled out. The letter only said that he had the same authority as his predecessor. The appointment did not clarify anything with regard to recognition of the community and the setting up of its own community institutions.

In 1932, the Druze once again appealed to the British to award them the right to organize as a community and to establish recognized community institutions. The district governor, however, contended that the British could not recognize the Druze as an independent community, since the Druze were not included in the detailed list in Article 51 of the King's Order-in-Council of 1922, for at the time of the drawing up of the law, there was no Druze court with legal sanction. Early in 1932, Shaykh Salmān Ṯarīf again requested that he be appointed as *Qāḏī*, the same standing held by his father during the Ottoman period. The Acre district officer's letter of April 18, 1932, replied in the negative. His argument was that the British authorities did not possess the Ottoman order on which Shaykh Ṯarīf relied for his claim.

That was the last of the Druze appeals to the British Mandatory government on the subject. Meanwhile, internal conflicts broke out in the community itself over who was to hold leadership positions. These conflicts adversely affected Druze unity as well as the validity of their claims for full recognition by the government.[4] Bloody events in the 1940s and the onset of the Second World War removed the issue from the agenda, and neither the Mandatory authorities nor the Druze themselves returned to it again.

The French Mandate of Lebanon

The status of the Druze community did undergo changes for the good in Lebanon under the French Mandate. The changes began with an agreement by the French to preserve the situation that had prevailed during the Ottoman period, and ended with their *de jure* recognition of the Druze as an independent community. In a document dated March 13, 1936, the French governor discussed the special status of the Druze and cited the fact that the Druze constituted one of the communities whose uniqueness was recognized, and that "it has the right to legislate its own laws, which will be valid after their proper approval."[5] The same document stated that the Druze community had the right to manage its assets and to establish educational and charitable institutions and that the head of the community would represent it in all these matters.

In regulations published in October 1938, official recognition was given to Druze courts. Druze *Qāḏīs* were awarded equal standing to the other *Qāḏīs* in Lebanon, and, a Court of Appeals was established, on which, according to these regulations, three members served: the two community heads (*shaykh ʻaql*) and a senior Druze judge from the civil court system.[6]

Lebanon in the Modern Era

Between 1960 and 1962, three laws were published in Lebanon that related to the Druze community. Together with the personal status laws that had been enacted there in 1948, these constitute the set of basic laws by which the Druze religious judicial system operates in Lebanon to this day. The three laws are the Organization of the Druze *Madhhabi* Judicial System, 1960; Establishment of the *Madhhabi* Council of the Druze Community, 1962; and Election of the Spiritual Head of the Druze Community, 1962.

Madhhabi courts

The *Madhhabi* courts in Lebanon consist of courts of first resort and the Supreme Court of Appeals. Both are part of the country's judicial system. Beirut was fixed as the location of the Supreme Court of Appeals, while the lower-level courts were placed in each of five areas where there was a large Druze concentration: Beirut, 'Aleh, B'aqlīn, Rāshayyā, and Ḫās̱bayyā. The court of first resort is composed of one *Qāḏī-Madhhab*; and the Court of Appeals, of three members: one *Qāḏī-Madhhab*, who serves as chairman; and two advisors. All are appointed on the recommendation of the Justice Minister.[7] Those who occupy these positions must be citizens of Lebanon and at least 25 years old, and they should not have transgressed any law that would bring shame upon the family. Another requirement is that they have a legal education or, at least, an academic degree.

The authority of these courts focuses on "matters relating to the performance of religious law and Druze tradition and the laws of the personal status of the Druze community." To supervise the Druze courts, a Druze judge was chosen who served on the civil Supreme Court. His appointment, too, was made by the Minister of Justice, but with the consent of the members of the Druze religious leadership.

The Druze community council (al-majlis al-madhhabī lil-ṯā'ifa al-durziyya)

Besides the religious judicial system, the Druze community in Lebanon also has a council that handles secular matters and the community's money, management of the sacred trusts,[8] supervision of the community's institutions and associations and determining their functions, appointing teachers for the educational institutions run by the community, and so forth.

Two groups comprise the council's membership:

1 Permanent members: the religious leadership and those who serve or have served as government ministers or members of Lebanon's parliament;
2 Elected members: 10 who represent various professional/academic organizations (lawyers, engineers, physicians, etc.) and 18 representatives of the different regions of the country. These members are

elected every four years by Druze who serve as *mukhtars* and heads of local authorities.

The two spiritual heads, who are chosen by the president of the country and alternate in this function annually, head the council. Members of the council operate through committees: treasury, administration, education, sacred trusts, and others. The council is located in Druze House in Beirut.

Syria in the Modern Era

Until the mid-1950s, the community status of the Druze in Syria was almost identical to that of the Druze in Lebanon. In the annotations to the law governing the personal status of Muslims that was enacted in 1953, it was stated that certain laws included in this legislation would not apply to the Druze. According to laws passed between 1945 and 1946, the Ministry of Justice appointed the Druze *Qāḏī-Madhhab* on the advice of the spiritual leadership.[9]

The Druze courts were granted "the right to preserve their character and their special community independence in matters of inheritance, wills, alimony, marriages, divorces and their outcomes, and also in their special community affairs." Once officially confirmed, their verdicts would be valid and could be executed through the government's operations department. Three members of the spiritual leadership served as an appeals body (*hay'a isti'nāfiyya*), located in Jabal al-Durūz.

In 1959, meaningful changes began to take place in the religious–judicial system: the number of *Qāḏī-Madhhab* positions was reduced to one,[10] and from then on the government decided on appointments – in accordance with the suggestions of the Minister of Justice, but without having to obtain the consent of the spiritual leadership. The court's verdicts were subject to appeal only before a civil appeal court, which sat in Damascus and whose members generally were not Druze. As mentioned in the previous chapter, the Druze Court of Appeals was disbanded, and its members moved to a new department known as the Department for Religious Rulings of the Druze Community (*dā'irat al-iftā' lil-madhhab al-durzī*).

This tendency to pull the carpet from under the religious figures in the Druze community's judicial institutions was manifested, too, in the new requirement that *Qāḏīs* had to be jurists.[11]

Israel in the Modern Era

With the establishment of the State of Israel, the Druze renewed their claims to be recognized as a separate religious community. In the first meeting between this group's leaders and the first Minister of Religions Rabbi Y. L. Maimon (Fishman), the Druze raised their demand for official recognition and the establishment of community institutions in the framework of an overall community organization. Despite the understanding and good will shown by those in charge, the Druze's request was not fulfilled so quickly. In fact, several years were to pass before official recognition was given to the independence of this community.

Soon after this meeting, the Druze Department in the Ministry of Religions appointed certified registrars to record marriages and divorces,[12] relying on the 1927 "Law for Recording Marriages and Divorces" for its action. In accordance with that law, certified registrars had been appointed to record marriages and divorces among the Bedouins, who did not have day-to-day contact with *Shar'ī* courts.[13]

After the marriage registrars were appointed, a supervisory body was needed since there was no Druze religious court dealing with the matter. Accordingly, on April 9, 1954, the Ministry of Religions set up a committee to supervise the registration of marriages and divorces, with Shaykh Salmān Ṯarīf of Jūlis as chairman, and Shaykh 'Abd Allāh Khayr of Abū Sinān and Shaykh Ḫusayn 'Alayān of Shefar'am. Representatives of the Ministry of Religions were also on the committee, which convened regularly once every three months. All the Druze registrars took part. The function of the committee was to check all registries used by Druze registrars, especially to see whether the marriage or divorce had been performed and recorded in accordance with the religious law of the Druze community,[14] as well as in accordance with Israel's Marriageable-Age Law of 1950 and its Woman's Equal Rights Law of 1951. The committee was also to investigate whether the fees were being collected according to religious court instructions and transferred to the State Treasury.

Recognition of the community

The previous chapter dealt with the issue of the recognition of the independence of the Druze community and the establishment of its own religious council.[15] The Minister of Religions, in consultation with the Druze Religious Council, was permitted to appoint a temporary cultural council that would serve until the establishment of community institutions not detailed in the regulations. As to how long such institutions would serve, their authority, their functions, and the arrangements for their management, it was stated that the Minister would decide on all these matters, again after consulting with the Religious Council. All such institutions were permitted, with the approval of the Minister of Religions, to impose fees for services rendered.[16]

On April 23, 1957, an official ceremony was held in the office of the Minister of Religions to mark the important event of the recognition of the Druze community as an independent community.[17] Two days later, on April 25, the annual celebrations took place alongside the grave of Nabī Shu'ayb at Ḫiṯṯīn. Druze speakers expressed their appreciation and thanks, and accented the importance of this historic event.[18]

Since the Druze's recognition as a religious community, the *Shar'ī* courts have not been authorized to adjudicate matters of Druze personal status or Druze sacred trusts. In the absence of Druze religious courts, judicial authority for these matters was transferred to the civil courts. In effect, though, no Druze has turned to these courts to decide on matters of personal status. On *Waqf* (sacred trusts) matters, one such suit was brought to the civil courts. This occurred in December 1961, and the plaintiff, Shaykh Salmān Farhūd, was the person in charge of *Waqf* income in Rāma.

In May 1959, the Druze Department in the Ministry of Religions appointed another committee that, on the surface, had to deal with matters of sacred trusts. In actuality, it handled matters of personal status. The members of the committee were Shaykh Salmān Ṯarīf (chairman), Shaykh Kamāl Mu'addī, and Shaykh Ḫusayn 'Alayān. The establishment of this committee was related to an arrangement in regard to land in the Galilee. The committee's function was to approve sacred trusts belonging to the Druze community, and the courts and lands officials had to honor such acts. From the time this committee was appointed until the end of February 1960, when the Minister of Religions disbanded it, the body held some thirty meetings but issued only one approval on a trust matter. Instead, it dealt with marriages, divorces, wills, and alimony – subjects under the authority of the civil judicial system – which the marriage registrars were unable to straighten out themselves.

Lacking statutory recognition, these two committees could not operate as judicial authorities but provided arbitration and settled disputes among the parties involved. The registrars and the committees could not fulfill all the directives laid down in the personal status law, in particular matters connected with legal proceedings, such as divorces, which had to be conducted in a religious court.[19]

Druze Religious Courts Law, 5723–1962

In 1962, the Druze Religious Courts Law was enacted. This law, however, had been preceded by two other proposed laws, the first in 1959[20] and the second in 1960.[21] A third proposal[22] was presented in April 1962, and formed the basis of the currently existing law. The main parts of this law, which was accepted unanimously, deal with the following (listed after the tables):

Table 7.1 Marriages and divorces among Israeli Druze, 1975–97

Year	Marriages	Divorces	Divorce %
1975	600	44	6.7
1980	622	59	9.5
1985	632	59	9.3
1990	642	74	11.5
1995	830	84	10.1
2000	952	92	9.7

Table 7.2 Druze religious courts' activity, selected years

File	1965	1970	1975	1980	1985	1990	1995	2000
Divorce	22	21	44	59	59	74	78	95
Proof of Marriage	—	11	50	35	25	17	37	52
Bride's Price, Dowry	—	8	8	3	—	—	—	—
Alimony	—	19	12	20	15	11	17	5
Household Peace	8	7	12	17	10	9	8	9
Children's Maintenance	5	2	2	2	7	4	8	9
Wills, Inheritance	16	61	73	90	122	131	146	144
Guardianships	7	14	44	13	13	22	50	26
Sacred Trusts	4	1	—	4	1	—	1	—
Misc.	9	8	11	17	18	14	24	20
Total	71	152	256	260	270	282	369	360
Appeals	—	—	2	12	6	4	—	—

Judicial authority: Druze courts are given special jurisdiction in matters of marriage and divorce and also, to a great extent, in matters of sacred trusts. As for other areas of personal status, they are given parallel authority. In other words, they have authority only after the two sides have agreed to turn the matter over to them.

Composition of the courts: The law lays down two levels of adjudication – first, the lower court, composed of three *Qāḏīs-Madhhab*,[23] and then a court of appeal, with a similar number of members.[24]

Appointments committee: Nine members constitute the appointments committee: the Minister of Religions (chairman), the Minister of Justice; the chairman of the Religious Council; the president of the Appeals Court (but if he serves as chairman of the council in addition, a *Qāḏī-Madhhab* will take his place, to be chosen for a three-year term as a representative of the *Qāḏīs-Madhhab*); two other *Qāḏīs-Madhhab*, to be chosen on behalf of this group and to serve three years; a Druze member of the Knesset, to be elected by the Knesset in a secret ballot and to serve on the committee so long as he is an MK, and when his term ends, until the new Knesset chooses someone in his place (if there is no Druze Knesset member, the Knesset will hold a secret ballot to choose a Druze to serve until such time as the Knesset selects another Druze to replace him); another Druze Knesset member (or a Druze who is not a member of Knesset, to be chosen as above); a lawyer, to be chosen by the National Bar Association and to serve three years.

Oath of allegiance: After the President of the State appoints him, the *Qāḏī-Madhhab* must declare that he "obligates himself to remain faithful to the State of Israel, to give fair judgment to the people, not to subvert justice, and not to be biased." He is also forbidden to serve in any other public position, unless with the approval of the Minister of Religions and so long as the position does not harm the standing of the *Qāḏī-Madhhab*.

Retirement age: This is set at 70,[25] but an interim directive states that anyone appointed as *Qāḏī-Madhhab* within a year of the enactment of the law will not retire before the end of three years from the enactment of the law.[26]

Qualifications: The candidate for the position of *Qāḏī-Madhhab* must have appropriate training in Druze law,[27] a lifestyle and nature that are appropriate to the status of *Qāḏī-Madhhab* in Israel, and must be aged 30 or over, and married or formerly married.

Toward the end of 1963, the following were sworn in as *Qāḏīs-Madhhab* in the lower court: Shaykh Salmān Ṯarīf, Shaykh Labīb Abū Rukn, and Shaykh Ḫusayn 'Alayān.[28] Sworn in to serve on the Court of Appeals were Shaykh Amīn Ṯarīf as chairman, and Shayks Aḫmad Khayr and Kamāl Mu'addī as members.

The substantive law, and court activity: The Religious Court Law does not stipulate any substantive law according to which the Druze religious courts must adjudicate matters. This is done in accordance with the recommendation of the Ministry of Religions, which considers this to be an internal Druze matter. The Druze Religious Council, being the supreme religious institution of the Druze in Israel, decided on November 2, 1961, to adopt the personal status law of the Druze community of Lebanon of February 24, 1948, as the substantive law of Druze religious courts in Israel.

Druze religious courts have heard thousands of cases on matters within their authority. The vast majority of these cases have dealt with wills, inheritance, and divorces. In recent years, some 800 marriages have been conducted yearly, and divorces have reached 13 percent of this number, double the 1975 rate, as may be seen from tables 7.1 and 7.2 on page 94.

Part III

Population, Society, and Identity in Israel

8

The Druze in Israel – Demography, Settlement, Residence

The world population of Druze currently numbers fewer than one million.[1] They are concentrated principally in three countries: Syria, Lebanon, and Israel. In Syria, there are some 500,000 Druze, constituting 3 percent of the Syrian population. Lebanon has 350,000 Druze, or 7 percent of its population. Israel has about 100,000 Druze, who make up 1.7 percent of its citizenry.[2] Druze are also found in South America (in Brazil, Venezuela, and Mexico), in the United States, Canada, Australia, the Philippines, Jordan, Saudi Arabia, and a few other countries. Their total number outside the Middle East is estimated at 100,000.[3]

In general, it may be said that the Druze population in Israel is rural in character (more than 90% are non-urban) and lives almost entirely in the northern (70%) and Haifa (25%) districts of the country. The Acre (Akko) district alone contains two-thirds of the Druze in Israel.

The most striking feature characterizing Druze settlement throughout the Middle East is that it is hill-based. This fact is motivated by security, since hostile relations have always seemed to prevail between this minority and its environment. Basing themselves in hilly regions, however, the Druze have preserved both their physical existence and the mysteries of their faith.

The Druze Population of Israel

Of the twenty settlements in Israel that have significant Druze populations, the Druze constitute the vast majority in thirteen villages: Dāliyat al-Karmil, Jūlis, Yarkā, Sājūr, ʻAyn al-Asad, Bayt Jann, Jathth-Yānūẖ, Kisra-Sumayʻ, Ḫurfaysh, Majdal Shams, Buqʻāthā, Masʻada, and ʻAyn Qinya. Druze also constitute more than 50 percent of the population of three other villages:

Mughār, Peqi'in, and 'Isifyā. They are a minority in four locations: Shefar'am, Kafr Yāsīf, Abū Sinān, and Rāma; but in all four of these locations, they and the Christian population together form a majority. In the mixed settlements, the Druze live in their own neighborhoods.

The Israeli Druze population is, relatively, very young. A comparison of the median age of the country's various communities is shown in table 8.1.

Table 8.1 Average age of religious communities in Israel

	1985	1993	1997
Muslims	15.9	18.1	18.6
Druzes	16.9	19.7	20.9
Christians	24.2	27.0	27.6
Jews	27.2	28.9	29.6

Demographic Statistics

In 1949, the Druze population of Israel numbered 14,500. It grew more than six-fold over the next half-century (see table 8.2).

Table 8.2 Growth of Druze population in Israel

Year	Population
1950	15,000
1955	19,000
1960	23,300
1965	29,800
1970	35,900
1975	42,200
1980	50,700
1985	72,000
	(including Golan Druze)
1990	82,600
1994	90,000
1995	92,200
1996	94,500
1997	96,700

Table 8.3 Estimated Druze population of Israel, by settlement, in 1998[4] (in thousands; percentages rounded)

Settlement	Total Population	Muslims	Christians	Druze in 1998 Total	%
The Carmel					
Dāliyat al-Karmil	13.0	0.5	0.0	12.5	96
'Isifyā	8.8	0.8	1.4	6.6	75
Lower Gaililee					
Shefar'am (Shafā'amr)	27.5	15.4	7.7	4.4	16
Western Galilee					
Jūlis	4.6	0.0	0.0	4.6	100
Yarkā	10.3	0.0	0.1	10.2	99
Abū Sinān	9.9	5.1	1.8	3.0	30
Kafr Yāsīf	8.0	3.8	3.9	0.3	3
The Galilee (al-Shāghūr)					
Sājūr	3.0	0.0	0.0	3.0	100
Rāma	7.3	1.9	3.0	2.4	33
'Ayn al-Asad	0.7	0.0	0.0	0.7	100
Mughār	15.9	3.5	3.1	9.3	58.5
Upper Galilee (al-Jabal)					
Bayt Jann	8.6	0.0	0.0	8.6	100
Yānūḫ-Jathth	4.5	0.0	0.0	4.5	100
Peqi'in (Buqay'a)	4.8	0.2	1.2	3.4	70.8
Kisra-Sumay'	5.5	0.5	0.3	4.7	85.5
Ḫurfaysh	5.3	0.5	0.5	4.3	97
Golan Heights (Haḏabat al-Jūlān)					
Majdal Shams	8.0	0.0	0.0	8.0	100
Mas'ada	3.7	0.0	0.0	3.7	100
Buq'āthā	4.8	0.0	0.0	4.8	100
'Ayn Qinya	1.6	0.0	0.0	1.5	100
Total				100.5	

Data supplied by the Israel Central Bureau of Statistics.

History of Druze Settlement

Reference to *Bilād Ṣafad* (the land of Safed) is found in ancient Druze literature, dating back to the era of the founding of the religion. There are also references to other Druze villages, some of which exist to this day: Yarkā, Jathth, and Peqi'in. Some of these villages were destroyed in the course of time and some saw the Druze population give way to peoples of other faiths. Most of the existing Druze settlements, however, were established several hundred years ago. Belonging to this category, for example, are the villages of Dāliyat al-Karmil and 'Isifyā, which were founded at the time of the important Ma'nī Emīr, Fakhr al-Dīn II (1586–1635). The Druze researcher Salmān Falāḥ has produced evidence that the Druze population of Palestine at the end of the nineteenth century numbered 7,860. According to statistics from 1931, during the British Mandate, 9,148 Druze were living in Palestine, and the figure jumped to 13,000 in 1945/46.

Professor Arnon Sofer has pointed to the fact that Druze settlements in Israel were positioned so that people could see from one to the next: from Dāliyat al-Karmil to 'Isifyā, from 'Isifyā to all the Druze villages in the Galilee, including Shefar'am; from Yarkā to Jūlis, to Abū Sinān and Kafr Yāsīf, to Jathth and Yānūḥ; from Yānūḥ and Jathth to Kisra, and from Kisra to Sumay', to Peqi'in and Bayt Jann; from the latter pair to Ḥurfaysh and 'Ayn al-Asad, and from there to Rāma, Sājūr, and Mughār.[5]

He also remarks that living in the mountains, where it is quite cold in the winter, necessitated heating, which had a cumulative economic cost in contrast to that demanded of residents of the coastal plain and the low-lying areas:

> And if that were not enough, because of their location in the most beautiful areas of Israel and in proximity to the very few green belts found in Israel, many Druze settlements have for years been mired in constant confrontation with the planning authorities, nature reserves officials, and the National Parks Authority, for these settlements border reserves and parks and were the first to pay the price – an expensive price – for land, which in any case is poor in these regions, for the benefit of the nature reserves and parks.

The Druze Settlements in Israel

The following are some details about Israeli Druze settlements, or localities where there is a large Druze concentration. (Demographic statistics are estimates from 1998.)

Abū Sinān

A village in the Acre (Akko) District. The Druze constitute 30 percent of the population of this village of close to 9,900 residents. *Maqām* Nabī Zakariyyā (named for the Hebrew prophet Zecharya, who is sacred to this community) is found on the outskirts of the village, which also has some antiquities, a Druze house of worship (*khalwa*), and a museum rich in Eastern folklore, in the possession of the Khayr family.

'Ayn al-Asad

A small Druze village of 700 residents, in the vicinity of Rāma. It was established a hundred years ago by a group of people who came mostly from Bayt Jann. The village has a Druze house of worship.

'Ayn Qinya

A small Druze village of 1,600 people, located on the Mas'ada–Bānyās road on the Golan Heights. It once had a Christian population, but these people left the village during the 1967 Six Day War. There is a Druze house of worship, and in the center of the village is *Maqām* Sitt Sha'wāna.

Bayt Jann

This village is 10 kilometers west of Safed in the vicinity of the Jarmaq (Mount Meron). Its population of 8,600 is all Druze. The village is situated on one of the highest points in the Galilee. On one of the hilltops adjoining the village is a grave that is sacred to the Druze – *Maqām* Nabī Ḫaydar (*maqām Bahā' al-Dīn*). The village contains three Druze houses of worship.

Buq'āthā

Located on the Golan Heights, 8 kilometers north of Quneitra, Buq'āthā it has a population, all Druze, of 4,800. It has two Druze houses of worship.

Dāliyat al-Karmil

This village of 12,000, of whom 96 percent are Druze, lies 10 kilometers east of Haifa on the Haifa–Elyakim Junction road. It was founded some 300 years ago by, among others, Druze who had emigrated from Ḫalab, or Aleppo, in Syria. Hence the family name Ḫalabī of many residents. The village has five Druze houses of worship and a sacred site – *Maqām* Abū Ibrāhīm. The village has a community center dedicated to Druze soldiers who fell in battle.

Ḫurfaysh

In the Acre district, Ḫurfaysh has 4,400 residents, 97 percent of them

Druze. The village has a Druze house of worship. Close to the village is *Maqām* Nabī Sabalān, one of the holiest sites for the Druze. There is also a Greek Catholic church.

'Isifyā

Located seven kilometers south-east of Haifa, this village has 6,600 Druze residents out of a population of 8,800, or 75 percent of the total. In the Byzantine period, there was a Jewish settlement here called Husifa. The location has various archeological sites, including a mosaic floor and an ancient synagogue. The village has a Greek Catholic church and three Druze houses of worship. There is also *Maqām* Abū 'Abd Allāh, a sacred site where Druze religious figures assemble every year on November 15.

Jathth–Yānūḫ

Jathth is found at the site of the Jewish Second Temple-era settlement of Gath. The village has a Druze house of worship and the grave of Shaykh Abū 'Arūs, one of the first propagators of the Druze faith in the first generation of its founding. Yānūḫ, mentioned in the Bible and in the Talmud, has a Druze house of worship and a holy place called *Maqām* Sitt Shamsa or Nabī Shams. The Jathth–Yānūḫ population numbers 4,500, all Druze.

Jūlis

Located 10 kilometers east of Acre, this entirely Druze village has 4,600 residents. Testimony to the existence of a Druze population in this village goes back more than 600 years. At the time of the Talmud there was a Jewish settlement here, which lasted until the Ottoman period. The village has a Druze house of worship and a number of sites sacred to the Druze, one of which is *Maqām* Shaykh 'Alī Fāris ('Alī Fāris died in 1753). Close to this site is the traditional burial ground of the Ṭarīf family. Another sacred spot in the village is the Nabī Shu'ayb carob tree, where residents light candles to receive a blessing. In October 1993, Shaykh Amīn Ṭarīf, who had served as spiritual head of the Druze population of Israel for over sixty years, died. He was buried within the village itself, in one of the rooms of his former house.

Kafr Yāsīf

In the Acre district, 10 kilometers north-east of Acre, this village of 8,000 has only 300 Druze. Tradition has it that this village was named for Yoseph ben-Matityahu, or Josephus Flavius. Until 100 years ago, it was the location of a Jewish settlement. For a long time afterwards, the Jews of Acre continued to bury their dead in the cemetery still preserved in this village, which also has the remains of a synagogue, a mosaic floor, and other remains from the Talmudic period. The village contains *Maqām* al-Khaḏr (site of Elijah the Prophet, who is also holy to the Druze).

Majdal Shams

This is the northernmost and highest village on the Golan, located in the foothills of Mount Hermon. It has an all-Druze population of 8,000. The village has a Druze house of worship.

Mas'ada

This village is located four kilometers south of Majdal Shams and has 3,700 residents, all of them Druze. There is a Druze house of worship, and also a Religious Court that handles matters to do with the personal status of Druze residents of the Golan Heights. Close to the village is *Maqām* Nabī Ya'fūrī, considered holy by the Druze.

Mughār

The village of Mughār is located 10 kilometers south-east of Karmiel and has 15,900 residents, of whom 9,300 (58%) are Druze. The name of the village is related to the many caves (*mughār*) found in the area. There are two churches, a mosque, and two Druze houses of worship.

Peqi'in (Buqay'a)

This is a mixed village: 3,400 of its 4,800 residents are Druze. There is a synagogue here, built on the remains of an ancient synagogue. There is also a cave in which, according to tradition, Rabbi Shimon Bar Yochai found refuge from the Romans. The village has a Jewish cemetery, alongside which are the graves of three Talmudic-era rabbis: Rabbi Yossi of Peqi'in, Rabbi Yehoshua ben-Hanania, and Rabbi Oshaya. Evidence shows that Jews have never abandoned this village. The locality has two Druze houses of worship and two churches.

Kisra-Sumay'

Sumay' is thought to have been the location of the Second Temple period settlement of Sama, mentioned in the Talmud. There is a Greek Orthodox church here as well as two Druze houses of worship. In the past, a woman, Umm Nasīb, fulfilled a senior religious function in the village. Kisra has antiquities and a Druze house of worship. The two villages have a joint municipal framework, and their Druze population numbers 4,700, or 86 percent of the total population.

Rāma

This village has 2,400 Druze residents, or 33 percent of the 7,300 inhabitants. It has a Druze house of worship, a mosque, and a number of churches.

Sājūr

Located in the Acre district between Rāma and Karmiel, Sājūr is an all-Druze village of 3,000 people. The place is identified with the town of Sājūr mentioned in the Mishnah, and it contains the remains of an ancient settlement. It has one Druze house of worship.

Shefar'am (Shafā'amr)

A city of 27,500, it has 4,400 Druze residents who live in two neighborhoods: Ḫārat al-Qal'a and another, relatively new, area of this city. The city is mentioned in the Talmud and has almost always had a Jewish presence. There are still the remains of Talmudic-era antiquities. Located here is the grave of Rabbi Yehuda ben-Baba, known in Arabic as Mughārat Banāt (or Bunāt) Ya'qūb, whom Druze also consider holy. The locality was the interim site of the Sanhedrin, the Jewish court and law-making body in the Second Temple Period, which had been transferred from Usha. The city has a mosque, churches, and a Druze house of worship.

Yarkā

This village is located in the Acre district and has an all-Druze population of 10,300. *Maqām* al-Nabī al-Ṣiddīq is found here as is *Maqām* Abū al-Sarāyā, commemorating one of the most ancient propagators of the Druze faith; thus a Druze population has lived in Yarkā since the dawn of the religion. East of the village is the *Khalwat* Shaykh Muḫammad, built by Shaykh Muḫammad Mu'addī at the end of the 1930s. The village has antiquities, a comprehensive high school, and an ancient metalworks plant.

9

Social and Economic Changes among the Druze in Israel

Two features shape the character of the Druze sect: kinship (*ḫamūla*) and, especially, religion. The Druze have no consciousness of nationality according to the accepted criteria of the concept. Even the element of religion suffers from a severe disadvantage, that of the strict instruction to preserve scrupulously the secrets of the Druze faith. Thus, the religion cannot provide an experience for the whole community, but only to the *'uqqāl*, the restricted group of sages.

During the thousand years of the existence of this religion, the social–traditional framework and the topographic conditions of their places of residence concealed this limitation[1] as well as the absence of other elements characterizing a national collective. The affinity of the individual to his/her community in this religious group was manifested mainly in the individual's belonging to its social–traditional framework.

The Druze Social Structure

From the day of its founding, the nature of the Druze community, an essentially feudal–patriarchal regime – just like all of Arab society in the countries of the Middle East – was supplemented by elements stemming from the essence of the faith and Druze tradition. In general, it may be said that this regime was characterized by the absolute authority of the father in his extended family (*ḫamūla* or *dār*): his wife, unmarried daughters, sons, daughters-in-law, and their children. His broad authority often included management of the family coffers, to which the current income of all family members was added and from which their expenses were financed. Such a family head had an important role in choosing his daughters-in-law and sons-in-law, and even to a large extent in deciding the political framework to which the members of his family would belong. In this society, the individual had no great weight, and all his loyality was given over to the *ḫamūla*. The father's status was largely a function of the economic dependence on him of the members of the family.

Threshing, Village Style, Majdal Shams, Golan Heights

The National Singularity of the Druze

The Druze have no national affinity beyond the realm of religion, whose value cannot be imparted to all members of this community. Similarly they have almost no special culture of their own, since there is no great difference between them and the Arab society insofar as language, dress, food, or even literature, popular art, or any other cultural areas are concerned.[2] Nonetheless, it would be too simplistic to attach them to the Arab nation, because the principal foundation on which Arab nationality is built, except for matters of culture, is not at all found in the Druze *Weltanschauung.* On the contrary, at times it even contradicts their outlook: the Druze do not accept the concept of Arab nationalism in the sense of an affinity to a specific territory that they view as a homeland. It is true that there are various regions in the Middle East in which there are large concentrations of Druze: the Shūf Mountains, Mount Lebanon, and Wādī al-Taym in Lebanon; Jabal al-A'la, Jabal Ḫawrān, and the Ghūta district in Syria; as well as the Galilee, Carmel, and Golan areas in Israel. Nevertheless, no Druze concentration was ever established on a nationalist ideological basis; it merely formed owing to chance circumstances.

Druze history is composed of a string of confrontations between Druze believers and those of the Muslim faith, who constitute the overwhelming proportion of the Arab nation. The same is true of the religious conception of the Druze; they completely reject the five bases of Islam: they deny the belief that Muḥammad was the last of the prophets; they do not fast during the month of Ramaḏān; they do not observe the pilgrimage to Mecca (*ḥajj*); they do not pray five times a day; and they do not practice charity according to Islamic *Sharī'a* rules.

Social Identity and Crisis in Modern Times

In more recent years, the traditional social framework that characterized the Druze in the past has been growing weaker. This process has greatly accelerated in Israel both because of the reduced weight of agriculture as a principal source of livelihood in Arab society and because of the new means of earning a living that have taken its place, such as construction, the security services, industry, transportation, and other vocations found outside the Druze villages. Members of the young generation can now free themselves of economic dependence on the father, a development that leads to a weakening of their attachment to to his way of life.

There are other important factors assisting in this weakening of the social framework. The young son is generally more educated than his father, and his frequent visits to the nearby city, whether for work, social, or other reasons, expose him to "Western culture." They also result in an expanded circle of friends, as he establishes contacts in a different milieu, whether the association is on a social, political, ideological, academic, economic, military, or other basis – people whom he would not come to know "locked" away in his village. More and more, the individual's recognition of his own power has been taking the place of the *ḥamūla* as a basic social framework. In Israel, there is another aspect to this loosening of ties, connected with military service. In contrast to Christians and Muslims, the young Druze male serves in the Israeli army. In the early years of the State, this service was voluntary, but in 1957/8 it became compulsory for Druze. During the relatively long term of duty (three years, as it is for Jews), the young Druze comes to know a way of life that is completely different from what he had been used to in the village. Many of his outlooks, particularly in regard to the *ḥamūla*, begin to lose much of their significance.

Young Druze today, who differ from the previous generation in way of life, outlook, and of course education, have nothing to shield them from external influences. The community elders cannot – or, owing to religious restrictions, do not see themselves as entitled to – assist him in forming guidelines for expressing his special Druze identity or in responding to his perplexities in this area. The development of means of mass communication and the loosening of the traditional social framework have increasingly weakened the force of religion among the young generation. All this has implications for the spiritual future and distinctive identity of the community.

The first sparks of a crisis can already be seen. The number of Druze youth who seek, openly or covertly, to loosen their attachment to the community has been growing. There is a tendency today for them to marry girls who are not from the community, though this phenomenon is still limited. There are those who seek to alter the "Nationality" designation in their identity cards from Druze to Arab, and some have demanded an exemption from army service altogether. New Druze neighborhoods in non-Druze settlements are another example of this trend. In some cases this has led to dissociation from the community and a clear aspiration to become submerged in new social frameworks.

Society and Family

Druze society distinguishes between the special status of the religious figure known as *'āqil* and that of the rest of the community. The former are considered as leaders, and their opinion is given due consideration even on matters not dealing with religion. Nevertheless, it should be emphasized that this does not affect the basis of equal standing between *'āqil* and *jāhil*, between rich and poor, between men and women, for in Druze belief the souls of all revolve from person to person. The soul of somebody poor today may transmigrate and be born in a rich person tomorrow, and so forth. The belief in the transmigration of souls has implications for many areas of Druze society: the attitude of the mourner to the deceased, the care of cemeteries, external appearance, solidarity, hospitality, tolerance, religious fanaticism, and more; though the question of family origin can produce exceptions to the accepted conception of equality.

One of the striking features distinguishing Druze society is the respected status of women afforded by the religion. Forced marriage is forbidden, as is polygamy. Injury to a woman's honor gives her the right to demand the dissolution of her marriage. In the religious sphere, too, the woman is given equal standing to the man, if not one step above him. Her acceptance into the *'uqqāl* grouping is not only possible, in contrast to other Middle Eastern religions, but the conditions of her acceptance are minimal compared with the demands placed before a man who seeks acceptance. The woman is also given decisive weight in managing the household, in educating offspring, and in other matters. At the same time she is expected to be very strict in her outward appearance and way of life.

In relations between men and women, several points should be emphasized. A man is forbidden to surrender to sexual passion. The divorce rate in the community is the lowest of all religious communities in Israel. Bridal price (*mahr*) constitutes an important basis for building a joint household; though it is becoming more common for it to be a symbolic *mahr*, while payment of the balance is put off until divorce or the death of the husband. Providing a daughter with an education is considered more important than educating a son, since she is responsible for teaching the next generation. On the other hand, there are firm conditions required of a girl's school or college, such as segregation of the sexes, the need for the school to be located in or near a Druze area, and the demand that the girl return home every evening.

Conscription into the Israel Defense Force

Since 1957, Druze have been subject to compulsory military service, and they do so with exemplary loyalty. Here are some statistics about their service in the Israel Defense Forces:

(1) One of every three Druze soldiers inducted makes the army a career.
(2) One of every six Druze soldiers conscripted becomes an officer in the regular army.
(3) Sixteen percent are not conscripted: 10% for medical reasons, 5% for religious reasons, and 1% for ideological motives. (In this respect, the situation is similar to the Jewish population.)
(4) Forty percent of those inducted are integrated into organic Druze units.
(5) Eighty-six percent of all conscripts volunteer for combat units (the figure is 80% among Jewish males).
(6) As of 2000, more than 280 Druze soldiers had been killed while serving in the army or one of the security forces. There are villages in which the percentage of fallen soldiers relative to the population exceeds that in Jewish settlements. The following Druze villages "stand out" in this regard: Bayt Jann – 37 fallen; Ḫorfaysh – 26; Yarkā – 31; Mughār – 24;

> ʻIsifyā – 25. There were complaints that not every IDF unit was open to young Druze soldiers: intelligence and the Air Force being notable examples. Security officials, however, argue that the considerations in regard to this issue are solely those of a candidate's suitability.

In 1982, after the army had decided to enable youngsters from the community to integrate into all units of the armed forces, an IDF cadet scheme began to operate. The pre-army activity is meant for high school students in grades 9–12, and has two principal aims: (a) taking care of disaffected youth by helping them find learning or work appropriate to their skills; (b) preparing youth for army service from the point of view both of motivation and of physical fitness and community values, so that they are better prepared to cope with the problems they will face as soldiers, and as Druze soldiers in particular. This activity is conducted in the schools and in youth centers and involves both those in school and those who are working. A preparatory week takes place at IDF bases, one of its objectives being to expose young people to Druze soldiers and officers serving in the IDF. The need for such an activity as early as the ninth grade was recognized because there are very few Druze educational personnel employed in the local authorities who have the ability to deal with the problems these youths face.

In general, there are no complaints of discrimination against Druze during their army service, which is not the case in regard to the attitude toward them after completing their service. Discharged officers are not given proper treatment, or suitable compensation. At times, looking for work, the discharged Druze soldier finds himself being handled by an Arab clerk who managed to acquire a vocational or academic education while the Druze was doing his three years of service.

Government Handling of the Druze Population

The involvement of the Israeli establishment has many important implications for what goes on in the Druze population. This is certainly true of education, but it also holds for other fields, such as employment, housing, and industry. Following is a short survey of these areas.

In recent years, the government has been requested several times to give attention to its treatment of the Druze community. On June 1, 1975, the government decided (Resolution 792) to set up an inter-ministerial committee to take care of Druze affairs. On October 26, 1975, an additional decision was made (Resolution 128) in regard to a Ministries' Directors-

General Committee to ensure the purposeful and effective realization of the previous resolution. On April 21, 1987, a five-year plan was decided on for the Druze (and Circassian) sector (Resolution 373): Druze settlements would be classified as development areas or put in the same category as nearby equivalent Jewish settlements.

There is no doubt that these and other government decisions have gone a long way towards offering Druze the same level of service as the Jewish population. The basic infrastructure for caring for the Druze community, however, lags far behind that of the Jewish population, and the gaps between the two societies are still significant. On May 1, 1991, the Druze local authorities called a strike of the municipal services in their settlements, demanding that they receive full equality in practice. After two weeks, their demand to make the Druze local authorities comparable to the Jewish local authorities within a specified time was accepted.

In the area of developing the Druze settlements, it should be noted that crowded, difficult living conditions are the lot of this community, whose economic situation is not a comfortable one. In general, Druze are forced to pay high building costs because of the nature of the land on which their settlements lie. Still, anyone who visits a Druze village today sees construction going on of modern, spacious apartments. Also striking is the fact that almost every Druze village contains special neighborhoods for discharged soldiers, constructed with government aid.

On July 16, 1995, the government unanimously adopted Resolution 5880 summarizing the negotiations between the Minister of Finance and the heads of the Druze (and Circassian) local authorities, according to which a development budget in the amount of NIS 1.19 billion (in 1995 budget-year prices) would be made available to these settlements from 1995 to 1999. Most of this sum was to come from the State budget. The aim of this special budgetary allotment was to raise significantly the level of government services supplied to Druze (and Circassian) citizens and settlements, and to make such services equal to those provided to Jewish settlements in their region.

There has been a great improvement in the area of environmental health, both in the preparation of a master plan and in executing the plan. Every Druze village has a family health clinic, and health bureaus provide services to school-age children. In general, the Ministry of Health finances these services even when no fee is collected.

In the area of education, most Druze youth tend to take the easy way out and find a job with one of the security services, and refrain from contending with either high school or higher education. This has led to a slow but continual regression in the education of the community in comparison with other communities. In 1983, only 3% of Druze families had someone with an academic degree, compared with 4.3% among Muslim families, 8.3% among Christian families, and 13.4% among Jewish families. The relatively tiny number of those who go on to higher education is due to the Druze families' poor economic situation, early marriage (customary in this community), or restrictions on girls leaving the village. There is a strong desire to advance education among Druze youth; however, there are important questions regarding the place of Druze identity and heritage in the modern era. The following opinions summarize the two basically different stands on the issue taken by members of the community.

A Druze Minister of the Knesset, S̲āliḫ T̲arīf, argued that the spiritual identity of the community does not bother him.

> In my opinion, the matter of identity is not at all important for educated people with intellectual ability. Heading my list are the opportunities for the advancement of education in all areas in the Druze sector. The challenge that faces us is increasing the supply of academics – doctors, engineers, psychologists, and so on – in order to be able to compete successfully for government tenders and important places of work.[3]

A senior Druze pedagogue, Fā'iz 'Azzām, has expressed a different view:

> The fate and character of the Druze community for generations to come will not be determined or shaped only by achievements in education, technology, or economics. They will be determined foremost by the cultivation of the community's spiritual values, whose existence and uniqueness are to be preserved, and these will characterize the community's identity and the nature of its relations with the world around it. I do not belittle the importance and value of educational achievements, higher education, or economic development, which form the basis for the honorable existence of every group in our world. . . . Without spiritual values, however, we can say that the "operation was a success, but the patient died." We healed the body, but we lost the soul . . . I would like my son to be an engineer; but by the same token, I want him to be a good Druze and a good person, honest, moral, modest, faithful to his community and to his country.

In 'Azzām's opinion, the Druze community in the future will face the danger of assimilation and being submerged in the majority culture in which it lives "if we do not succeed in time to provide suitable answers to the challenges that modernization places before us."[4]

An important area in which Druze have complaints about the government's treatment of them relates to economics and employment. At the time of the establishment of the State of Israel, agriculture was the principal occupation of the Druze. Because of land expropriations, it is claimed, agriculture was neglected – in any case, obsolete methods were used to till the soil – and the men started to turn to regular service in the security forces as a source of livelihood. Yūsūf Qablān, an attorney and (at the time of writing) head of the Bayt Jann local council, expresses serious concern over this phenomenon, which he says might break down in an era of peace, forcing many Druze to leave the armed forces and other security agencies.

The percentages of the main communities in Israel in different occupations in 1983 are shown in table 9.1. In view of these statistics, Yūsuf Qablān urges the government to develop industry in Druze villages in order to provide sources of livelihood and occupation. He implores the government, too, to advance commercial and business entrepreneurship through grants-in-aid and standing loans; to develop internal tourism in the villages; and to increase the integration of youths and graduates in government service and employment. The present situation, in his opinion, constitutes "a very difficult trap" that might bring about large-scale unemployment and even crime. The table shows, too, and very strikingly, that the Druze community lags far behind in the field of education. This, he believes, is also related to the difficult economic situation in which the Druze find themselves, and therefore he calls on the government to increase financial aid to Druze so that they can pursue their education.

Table 9.1 Occupations of Israeli communities, 1983 (in percentages)

Occupation/Community	Jews	Muslims	Christians	Druze
Academics	9.6	2.5	6.7	2.3
Free Professions	10.3	7.6	10.0	10.1
Managers	8.8	0.6	1.8	1.5
Clerks	13.2	3.6	7.2	4.8
Sales Personnel	9.1	7.2	8.6	4.3
Services	7.9	10.4	7.4	12.9
Agriculture	3.7	8.3	2.1	6.5
Industry	33.9	42.1	46.7	38.4
Other	3.6	17.8	9.5	19.1

10

Strayers and Those who Return to the Fold

Religious Conversions of Druze in Israel[1]

In the fifty years between 1952 and 2002, there were 145 cases of Israeli Druze who turned away from the precepts of their religion and left the Druze faith (to be called those who "strayed").[2] This straying took two forms: either a formal act of religious conversion, or setting up a family with a non-Druze spouse, this latter being an act of serious religious significance no less than conversion, and at times even more so. The religions to which these Druze converted are as shown in table 10.1.

Table 10.1 Religions to which Druze converted

"Target Religion"[3]	No. of Cases	%
Islam	63	43.5
Judaism	55	38
Christianity	13	9
Baha'i	2	1.5
Unknown	12	8
Total	145	100

The 145 who strayed may be classified into sub-groups having common "straying" characteristics:

- 32 converted in a formal religious act and became Muslims because of purely political motives;[4]
- 54 converted in order to avoid religious differences in the family that they had established with a non-Druze spouse;
- 59 strayed by setting up a dual-religion family, whether through a civil marriage or by living together without a formal marriage.

Of the total population of those who strayed, at least 65 (45%) are known to have returned to their original faith, either by a formal act of reconversion or by dissolving the family framework with the non-Druze partner. These will be called "those who returned to the fold." In the later years of our survey, in fact, this return accelerated, apparently because of the intervention of Druze Religious Court judges.

Settlements of Origin, and Destination of "Strayers"

Table 10.2 Breakdown by settlement origin of the 145 who left the fold

Region	Settlement	No.
The Carmel (al-Karmil)	Dāliyat al-Karmil	11
	'Isifyā	17
Western (al-Sā<u>h</u>il) and Lower Galilee	Jūlis	7
	Yarkā	18
	Abū Sinān	4
	Kafr Yāsīf	1
	Shefar'am (Shafā'amr)	15
The Galilee (al-Shāghūr)	Sājūr	7
	Rāma	15
	'Ayn al-Asad	1
	Mughār	12
Upper Galilee (al-Jabal)	Bayt Jann	13
	Jathth	2
	Yānūḫ	0
	Peqi'in (Buqay'a)	3
	Kafr Sumay'	5
	Kisra	1
	Ḫurfaysh	4
Golan Heights (Ha<u>d</u>abat al-Jūlān)	Majdal Shams	3
	Mas'ada	1
	'Ayn Qinya	1
	Buq'āthā	0
	Unknown	4
Total		145

A comparison of the frequency of the phenomenon in any one settlement in relation to the size of the Druze population in that settlement shows four striking exceptions: More than 13% of the Druze population of Israel live in the village of Dāliyat al-Karmil, but the scope of the straying phenomenon here is only 7.5% of all such cases. The opposite trend marks the neighboring village of 'Isifyā, which has only 7% of the Israeli Druze population, but can count 12% of the conversions out of the Druze faith. A similar phenomenon is revealed in Shefar'am. This city has 5% of all Israeli Druze, but the "straying" rate here is 10%. The most striking asymmetry is found in Rāma, where the Druze constitute 2.5% of the town, but the scope of straying stands at fully 10%.[5]

The explanation for these phenomena apparently lies in the mixed population that occupies Shefar'am and Rāma, where Druze constitute, respectively, a fifth and a quarter of the population. (In Rāma, more than 50% are Christians, and the rest Muslims.) As for 'Isifyā, it turns out that most of the converts have their origins in Syria, a fact that influences their way of life socially and religiously.

The Druze community has a decidedly negative view of those who stray. Consequently, converts are forced to leave their home village and to exile themselves to distant, non-Druze villages. This is especially the case when the defection involves marriage to a non-Druze wife.

An investigation showed that certain settlements are preferred as destinations. Foremost among these are Greater Haifa, Jerusalem, and Karmiel. There have been cases in which those who strayed preferred to live in Muslim villages. Some converts, in fact, have migrated to villages in Samaria and Judea, and a very few went even further, emigrating to Canada and the United States.

Strayers and Straying, 1977–1982

In the studies of the 145 cases of straying recorded between 1952 and 2002, the period 1977–1982 was exceptional in that it saw 40 such cases. This wave apparently was related to the debate among the Druze public at that time concerning the national and religious identity of the Druze. One manifestation of this debate was a letter sent by two Druze brothers to the Ministry of Defense on May 23, 1977, in which they defined themselves as "Palestinian Arabs . . . Muslims, Druze,"[6] and therefore requested exemption from compulsory army service.

In the end, the matter came up before the courts.[7] The two brothers asked the Supreme Court, sitting as the High Court of Justice, and the Haifa District Court to instruct the Ministry of the Interior to change the Nationality entry on their identification cards from "Druze" to "Arab."

The District Court, on February 15, 1979, rejected the request, stating that the two brothers had not come to court "innocently and with clean hands."[8]

"Straying" toward Judaism

Fifty-five of the 145 cases of straying (or 38% of the total) were toward Judaism. These divide into two categories:

(a) Thirty-two percent of the cases were full religious conversions, following which there was generally a marriage with a Jewish female partner in a Jewish religious ceremony;
(b) Sixty-eight percent of the cases were family frameworks created with Jewish women, whether through a civil marriage ceremony or by openly living together.

Of these relationships, 32 percent were unstable. More than 40 percent of the cases that were set up without a religious conversion broke up. There were only two divorces among the Druze who had converted to Judaism. This divorce rate is characteristic of a traditional society, even when a dual religious past is not involved.

Another interesting finding was that in almost all cases of "straying to Judaism," the Druze party was forced to abandon his original residence. Generally the couple then went to a predominantly Jewish destination: In greater Tel Aviv, Haifa, southern region of the country, the northern district, and in Judea–Samaria. Only three couples continued to live in a Druze settlement. For very obvious reasons, no mixed couple chose to live in an Arab/Muslim village.

"Straying" in the Direction of Islam

Islam was the target religion for 63 of the 145 cases of straying (43.5%). These are divided into three categories:

(a) Fifty-one percent of the cases became Muslims because of political motives, and they inspired by a leftist political Druze body called "The Druze Initiative Council."
(b) Forty-three percent of the cases converted because of marriage to a Muslim spouse.

(c) Six percent of the cases set up a family with a Muslim wife without becoming Muslim or without a formal act of marriage.

Becoming Muslim from political motives

In those cases of Druze becoming Muslim from political motives, they did so with the declared or implied intention of escaping army service. An important characteristic of this group is the especially young age of those who converted – on average, 20.9 years old, compared with the average age of the entire group of those who strayed, 30.5 years. It is interesting to note that most of those who strayed in the direction of Islam are related in one way or another.

Another characteristic that unites these particular political strays is that they refrained from leaving their residences and moving away from the Druze concentrations despite having converted in a formal religious act in a *Shar'ī* court. Perhaps, though, the most important characteristic is that after a period of time, 75 percent of the young adults appealed to the Druze Religious Court to be accepted back into their community. Their return to the fold generally came about close to the date of their discharge from the army or when they were about to marry a Druze girl.

Six did not return to the Druze community, though their motives for converting had been political. These six either had not married yet, or had strayed after marrying a Druze girl who did not convert to Islam.

The intentions of this group who strayed in the direction of Islam may be learned from verdicts handed down by the Druze Religious Court when any of them sought to return to the community. Thus one characteristic verdict held that the youth's act had been undertaken

> from personal motives, without any deep thought . . . The appellant expressed his sorrow for what he had done . . . said he had not left his [Druze] faith, and that his had been a gratuitous act (*ḥibr 'ala waraq*), and nothing more. He continued to be a Druze in his blood, his thinking, and in his heart. . . . He did not go to the mosque and did not keep any strictures of the religion that he had joined [Islam] . . .[9]

In another case, the young Druze explicitly declared to the court his motive for becoming a Muslim:

> It became clear to this court that the appellant . . . did not at all change his place of residence . . . and that the purpose of his act was to avoid army service; but he failed in this and was forced to serve in the IDF, and now has been discharged from the army . . .[10]

Within the group whose motives for conversion were defined as political, there were 10 residents of Yarkā. This was no coincidence, for the (pro-Arab) Druze Initiative Committee conducts widespread activity in this settlement and serves as a source of inspiration for those defined as "political strays" and others like them, who promote the committee's views.

The Druze Initiative Committee

The Druze Initiative Committee (*Lajnat al-Mubādara al-Durziyya*) was set up in 1972 by a group holding Arab nationalist opinions. Some of the members were Raqaḫ (the Israel Communist Party at the time) party activists. Chairing the committee in its early years was Shaykh Farhūd Farhūd of Rāma, who had been among the founders of the committee and was considered its spiritual father. Since 1981, Shaykh Jamāl Muʻaddī of Yarkā has been serving as chairman.

This body's tenets state that the Druze community is an inseparable part of the Palestinian people and of the Arab nation. Therefore, it must work to abrogate compulsory conscription and to encourage refusal to serve in the army. From time to time, the committee airs complaints about the government's neglect of the community in matters of finance, land expropriations, and other rights. In recent years, the committee has emphasized activities relating to Judea, Samaria, the Gaza Strip, and the Golan Heights. One of its platforms calls for an end to "trampling on the good name of the Druze as criminals of the Israeli occupation and to exploiting Druze soldiers for oppressive military actions against the sons of the Palestinian people."[11] Shaykh Muʻaddī demanded that the spiritual head of the community and its leaders "act in concert to defend the community's honor and demand the cessation of campaigns of incitement and scheming against it and the withdrawal of Druze soldiers from the occupied territories."[12]

The *intifāḏa* was also stressed in committee activity. At a gathering in December 1989, there was a loud call for "the success of the *intifāḏa*, now one year since the establishment of the Palestinian state and on the occasion of its [the *intifāḏa*'s] entering its third year." Similarly there was condemnation of the "occupation's terrible criminals."[13] Muʻaddī, in an interview at the end of 1990, welcomed the *intifāḏa*, "which has created the Palestinian state and the heroes of the stone, who have decided to do away with the occupation at any cost."[14]

At an assembly that took place in Umm al-Faḫm on June 22, 1990, Shaykh Jamāl Muʻaddī, in answer to a question about the Druze's affinity to the Arab people, told the audience that he demanded "the cancellation of compulsory service for the Arab-Druze community because we are part of the Arab-Palestinian nation. We are an inseparable part of this people, and we support the struggle of our people for freedom and independence.

Compulsory army service which is imposed on Druze youth is nothing but a scheme devised by the local Arab reactionary powers and the authorities." He contended, further, that "hundreds of Druze youth refuse to serve in the army, and many have been imprisoned for that reason."

In September 1990, Shaykh Jamāl Mu'addī lectured on the Gulf crisis. At a meeting of the Initiative Committee held on September 8, the Shaykh condemned "the imperialist attack on Arab states and their treasures" and pointed to the need to solve the crisis in an internal Arab context.[15] At the end of the meeting, a decision was taken to demand "the withdrawal of imperialist forces from the Gulf region and to lay stress on the importance of solving the crisis in a peaceful way and in an internal Arab framework." That meeting condemned the "barbarous activities of the occupation in the occupied state of Palestine" and extended greetings "to the *intifāḏa* and its heroes on the occasion of the thousandth day of its outbreak." Calls were made for increased solidarity with those carrying out the *intifāḏa*. The inhabitants of Druze villages were urged to give them material assistance.

The Druze Initiative Committee carried on with its struggle against compulsory military service. On December 30, 1990, it coordinated with MK Muḫammad Naffā' the organization of a demonstration opposite the Prime Minister's office.[16] Speakers at this demonstration, who included among others the poet Samīḫ al-Qāsim, Shaykh Jamāl Mu'addī, and MK Muḫammad Naffā', emphasized that the demonstration was against the compulsory service law, which was "a loathsome law that stood in complete contradiction to all Arabs . . . and was a degrading attempt to dissociate the Druze from the Arabs."[17]

The desire of the Initiative Committee to strengthen so far as possible the affinity of the Druze to the Arab nation was manifested in protracted, bitter activity against the idea of teaching Druze pupils about their community's history as a valuable "Druze heritage," so as to strengthen their special consciousness as Druze. From time to time, the committee would recruit clerics, parents' committees, and other bodies to support its stand.[18]

Marriages with Muslim spouses

The last group of those who strayed toward Islam is a group of men including six women who overtly converted in order to marry a Muslim. What is striking about this group is the relatively mature age of those who strayed. Like Druze who converted to marry Jewish women, the average age of this group is 30.

Another prominent characteristic is the very short time between their conversions and their marriages, and before the couples leave to settle in a non-Druze area. Following is a breakdown of the settlements to which these couples moved: 13 went to mixed settlements; two moved to Muslim villages; and four stayed in their villages of origin. (The place of residence of the other couples is not known.)

Women who "Strayed"

One of the most striking findings arising from the statistics collected was the tiny number of straying women and the rare instances of a Druze woman marrying a non-Druze man. The Druze attitude toward Druze women who "marry out" is one of complete hostility. The act is not only a serious infringement of the religion, it also arouses feelings of contempt and humiliation, which the woman's family is unable or unwilling to bear.

Of the 145 known cases of straying, six involved women, all of whom went in the direction of Islam. Two of the women converted because of social–religious pressures. Three other Druze women underwent conversion because they wanted to return to their former Druze husbands, from whom they had been divorced; since Druze law forbids taking back a divorced woman, these couples had no choice but to convert.[19]

The last case involved a young girl from Jabal al-Durūz in Syria who converted and married a Muslim man. In order to escape the hostile environment, the couple moved to one of Israel's large cities in the pre-State period. A young Israeli Druze who knew about the woman was seized with religious zeal and forced the man to give his wife a divorce; he then married the Druze woman himself. The Druze Religious Court deliberated on the woman's status and that of her offspring at length, and its verdict lavished praise on the behavior of the new husband.[20]

"Straying – Returning to the Fold"

A conspicuous finding was the return of 65 of those who went astray (45%), whether after a period of but one day or a span of thirty years. As table 10.3 shows, 30 of these returned to the Druze community after establishing a family with non-Druze women and even producing offspring.[21] Of particular note is the fact that two-thirds of the families that broke up were Druze–Jewish families.

It should be stressed that the dissolution of a family framework in such a case meant not only dissociation from the non-Druze partner, but a declared commitment to break off all contact even with joint offspring.

Table 10.3 Those who returned to the Druze community after an intermarriage

Religion of Spouse	After Religious Marriage	After Civil Marriage	After Living Together	Total
Muslim	7	—	1	8
Jewish	3	14	2	19
Other	1	2	1	4
Total	11	16	4	31

Attitude of the Druze faith to those who stray and those who return to the fold

The Druze faith stresses the uniqueness of the Druze, who have gained what no other believers have been privileged to achieve: a serene view of the divinity, who assumes the image of a human being. The Druze are allocated extra-special rights – not earned by non-Druze. The privilege of being counted among the members of this faith is given only to someone born to a Druze father and mother. No Druze can ever free himself of this:

> Whoever is born a Druze – will die a Druze, and any act of deceit, fraud, or estrangement toward his community cannot change this fact, because the Druze religion is immutable and incontrovertible (*al-dīn al-durzī la yaqbal al-taghyīr wal-tabdīl*).[22]

Offspring of strays who return to the fold

As was mentioned above, even the offspring of Druze who marry non-Druze cannot be counted among the members of this faith – neither with regular status or with a lower status. In this regard, it makes no difference whether the mixed marriage involves a male or female non-Druze.[23]

The attitude toward a dual-religion family and the status of the offspring have been discussed several times and in different circumstances at both levels of the Druze Religious Courts. In 1979, the subject came up in regard to the rights of the offspring of a non-Druze woman who had been the common-law wife of a Druze killed in a road accident. She appealed to the court on her own behalf and that of her five children, to recognize her and her children as heirs of the deceased. The *Qāḏī*, Shaykh Nūr al-Dīn Ḫalabī, rejected her request, arguing that

> What transpired to the appellants [the woman and her children] will serve as a lesson to every "lover" (heaven forbid) or woman, regardless of her religion, not to marry except with a proper marriage contract and in a marriage bond that is recognized religiously and officially . . . Such a [non-

> proper] marriage can only end in tragedy and misfortune for the unfortunates, who have committed no sin.[24]

The court rejected the woman and children's request and placed the blame on the parents, including the woman, "who should have anticipated these consequences."[25]

The *Qāḏī* was also asked about the idea of a common-law wife and ruled that, according to Druze custom and law, such a relationship was tantamount to prostitution (*zina*), and that because the fruit of such a relationship is the result of a deed that contradicts the foundations of the Druze faith and because the decisions of the Druze Religious Court are committed to the fundamentals of the Druze religion, therefore it [the court] cannot recognize the illegal fruit or results of anti-religious actions or make any decision on their behalf.[26]

In 1986 and 1987, the subject came up again for decision, and *Qāḏī* Na'īm Hinū took a similar stand. He condemned the common-law phenomenon in the sharpest terms, holding that this relationship was nothing but "the gratification of animal appetites,"[27]

> which blinds one's eyes and leads [the Druze male] to serious sin [*kabīr*], contradicting custom and the noble Druze tradition. . . . A relationship with a woman without a legal marriage contract is considered harlotry . . . and this court cannot give recognition to such relations.[28]

The most serious incident brought before the court dealt with a Druze man who abandoned his wife and children and lived in common-law marriage with a non-Druze woman. The affected Druze wife turned to the Druze court, which granted her request for a divorce and awarded her far-reaching material rights in regard to their joint property. In reasoning the court's verdict, the *Qāḏī* said, among other things:

> The husband's deed is worthy of punishment, considering the social dangers and ruination of the family unit inherent in the act: deserting children and in effect making them orphans, ruining the woman's purity [*'afāf al-mar'a*], her innocence, her dignity, her glory, and her nobility. . . . Protecting the family from prostitution is a basis on which the wholeness of society and home and the children's happiness is built. . . .There is here [in the husband's action] contempt and violation of the sanctity of marriage and family relations.[29]

Druze religious law makes almost no distinction between a Druze who sets up a family with a non-Druze woman by way of marriage (religious or civil) and one who sets up a family in a common-law relationship. Still, one can sense that the attitude toward a family that is not established through marriage is much more severe. The first incidence of a mixed marriage between a Druze man and a non-Druze woman and the fate of their offspring being brought before a Druze court was in 1977, when four of the offspring of this marriage requested that they be recognized as Druze.[30] In a precedent-making decision, signed by all *Qāḏī* members of the two Religious Appeals Courts, the request was rejected outright.[31] The decision reads as follows:

1 The Druze community is known for its tolerance (*tasāmuḫ*) toward and love of all mankind. Its tenets call for brotherhood and cooperation with all communities and religions for the general good.
2 From the time of its establishment to the present time, the Druze community has lived for the preservation of its fundamentals, its religion, its independence, and its very existence thanks to the devotion of its sons to their values and religion.
3 Since its establishment, the Druze community has condemned and rejected any intervention on anybody's part in its internal and religious affairs. Similarly the Druze community has invalidated all mixed marriages in order to preserve the unity of the community, its religious fundamentals, and its continued existence.
4 In recent years, to our great sorrow, there has been an increase in mixed marriages between members of the Druze community and members of other communities. If, heaven forbid, this situation continues, it might bring great damage to the Druze community. Therefore, we must act to put an end to marriages of this sort, and to their increasing number, for the good of the Druze community.
5 The Druze community cannot recognize as Druze children who are born from a marriage involving a non-Druze partner. We see their fathers and mothers as those who have brought this crime upon them.[32]

The anger of the Druze leadership was vented on the intelligentsia (lawyers, academics, and so forth) who had dared argue that the Druze faith was a branch of Islam, and some of whom, on the basis of that contention, had even become Muslims or had married Muslim women and produced Muslim offspring. Dr Sulaymān Bashīr, a prominent figure in this group, viewed himself as an Arab-Muslim even while still a Druze[33] and for several years had tried to convince others of this idea.[34] After some ten years he decided to return to the fold, divorced his Muslim wife, and expressed deep sorrow for his past acts, to the Druze Religious Court.[35]

Policy of the Druze Leaders toward Straying

The picture that emerges from the statistics about Druze who have strayed from their religion is similar, in effect, to the general process that is occurring in this area in the Western world today: a questioning of the role of religion in a modern society.

In Western society, religious uniqueness is becoming more and more blurred. In contrast, there has been at times a strengthening of nationalist foundations (which is not our concern here). A pattern has been created of departing from the religious collective, even at times without the individual undergoing an overt act of conversion. The process begins with the discovery of indifference, conscious or not, toward religious values, and continues with a gradual isolation from particularist values, leading to assimilation within the majority culture. In the Western world, a new type of dual-religious family has been growing, and marriage can be a mark of identification, as it were, representing one's belonging to a specific group, its tradition and culture, or one's dissociation from it.

Very generally speaking, a similar process may be distinguished among the Druze. On the one hand, the data points to a very restricted rate of "straying." On the other hand, the community in Israel has been recently experiencing unfamiliar phenomena: scores of cases of full acts of religious conversion and scores more of family frameworks being formed with a non-Druze partner. It should be stressed that the cases presented here concern a minority group comprising only 1.7 percent of the Israeli population, but one known for its seclusion, religious orthodoxy, and spiritual immunity.

An interesting phenomenon discovered in the course of this study relates to the "target religion" of Druze conversions. On the face of it, one might think that because Jews represent the majority culture in Israel, the number of strays to Judaism would be much larger than that to Islam, a religion toward which the Druze faith bears some animosity. Nevertheless, almost half the cases of Druze conversions to another religion were to Islam. Several factors may account for this:

1 The young Druze who stray are not entirely familiar with their religion and its hostility toward Islam.
2 The "majority culture" in their eyes is the Arab-Muslim culture, for they speak its language and are familiar with it from the environment in which they live – their home, leisure, education, and work – much more than with Jewish culture.
3 In contrast to Muslim society, there is a natural tendency among Jews

بسم الله الرحمن الرحيم .

الحمد لله رب العالمين . والشكر لصفيه الهادي الامين .

في اليوم الخامس والعشرون من شهر شباط سنة ١٩٩٠ الف وتسعمائة وتسعون . عُقِدَ اجتماع عام
للقرى الاربعه في مجلس مجدل شمس من شيوخ وشباب روحانيين وزمنيين لأجل التمسك
بدياناتنا المُقدّسة الشريفه . والمحافظة على عروبتنا ووطنيتنا الاصيلة النزيهه . ومن هذا
المنطلق الكريم يجب علينا المحافظة على طهارة الاعراق صوناً من براثن الفساد والنفاق وبراءة
من العصيان والإباق . وصولاً وارتقاء لمكارم الاخلاق . والتي تصح بها الانساب يوم العرض والحساب .
وإعلاماً أيها الاخوان ان طائفتنا الكريمة التي هي نبراساً للشهامة والكرامة . والمُثل العُليا
لسائر الامم . ولهذا أُوجب علينا جميعاً ان نحذر مكائد الهفوات والزلات . ونُحرِّم كما هو
مُحرَّم ونُحلِّل كما هو مُحلَّل . وقراراً من كافة سكان القرى الدرزيه مجدل شمس . بقعاثا . مسعده .
عين قنيه . بإنزال العقاب الشديد على كل مَنْ يقترن بإمرأة اجنبيه غير درزيه مِنَ الابوين
يكون مقاطعاً دينياً واجتماعياً . ومطروداً من القُرى الدرزيه مع نسله المشبوه مدى الحياة .
ويكونوا الاهل اعني الوالد والوالده ملزومون بطرده وحرمانه من وصيَّة ارث وغير ذلك مدى الحياة .
وكل من يخالف هذا البيان من الوالد والوالده والأقارب والمجتمع بأسره تحرم المُعامله معه .
ويُعاقب دينياً واجتماعياً . فالحذر الحذر والعياذ بالله من هذا الانزلاق والتمويه الذى هو
عار على راكب هواه . وغضب عليه من باريه ومجتمعه . لأننا بعون الله متماسكين ومُتعاونين
دفاعاً عن انفسنا وكرامتنا تمسكاً بنسبنا العريق وأصلنا الشريف وعروبتنا الاصيله
وحفاظاً على ابنائنا واجيالنا القادمه .
وفي الختام نضرع بالتوسل والابتهال الى الله بان يهدينا جميعاً الى السبيل القويم .

الهيئة الدينيه والزمنيه في قرى هضبة الجولان
مجدل شمس . بقعاثا . مسعده . عين قنيه .

Proclamation Against Mixed Marriages

The resolution adopted by the Druze leadership of the Golan Heights calls for excommunicating anyone who marries a non-Druze. The assembly at which the proclamation was issued took place on February 25, 1990. Severe sanctions, in the form of social, religious, and economic ostracism, were imposed for anyone who violated this stricture.

to refrain from personal communication with Arabs (or with those who appear to be Arab), for nationalistic reasons.

The number of Druze women who stray is negligible, a phenomenon that does not match the parallel process occurring in Western society. It should be recalled that this is a society that does not encourage exogamy, and that such a woman is exposed to threats of excommunication and even harsher punishments.

Alongside these examples of conversions and the sharp reactions on the part of the Druze leadership toward the various cases of straying, there should be added an important document published in 1991 by the religious and secular leadership of the four Druze villages on the Golan Heights: Majdal Shams, Mas'ada, Buq'āthā, and 'Ayn Qinyā. In a proclamation distributed among residents of the Golan, the local leaders called for "preserving the purity of origins (*ṯahārat al-a'rāq*) . . . so that the lineage (*nasab*) will not be harmed on judgment day (*yawm al-'arḏ wal-ḫisāb*)."

The proclamation continues with a threat to anyone who marries a woman both of whose parents are not Druze and states that those who belittle this injunction "will be cast off religiously and socially and expelled from the Druze villages along with their offspring for all the days of their lives." Parents are urged to expel such a person and to remove him from all rights of succession and inheritance forever.

These threats certainly had their effect on the Golan Druze, as did the rigid stance of the Druze spiritual leaders in Israel toward their constituents. Still, it is difficult to point to an actual attempt on the part of the spiritual leadership to cope with the problem through education for specific Druze identity. Indeed, the matter of developing "Druze heritage" as a means of strengthening this special consciousness among Druze youth has met with apathy, if not hostility, on the part of Druze spiritual leaders.

Part IV

Laws Governing Personal Status

11

Laws of Personal Status of the Druze in Israel, Lebanon, and Syria: Implementation in Practice

The source of the Druze law of personal status is Lebanese, having been approved by Lebanon's parliament on February 24, 1948. It had been prepared by a special committee appointed for this purpose, composed of religious figures, *Qāḏīs-madhhab*, [1] members of parliament, and jurists, all of them Druze. The law is based in essence on pronouncements by al-Amīr al-Sayyid 'Abd Allāh al-Tanūkhī, who lived in the early fifteenth century.

Until the formulation of the law, matters of personal status were adjudicated in the Lebanese *madhhab* courts according both to Druze custom and tradition and to Islamic law (*sharī'a*). These sources were not, however, kept in any compendium that could be relied upon when quickly needed. In the absence of suitable instructions on matters to do with personal status, the members of the committee were aided by Druze law and custom as well as by the Ottoman Family Rights Law (*qānūn ḫuqūq al-'ā'ila*) of 1917 and Islamic *sharī'a* laws on the subject, especially those of the Ḫanafī school.

The Druze Religious Council and the *Qāḏī madhhab* of the Druze Religious Courts in Israel "adopted" this law on November 2, 1961, but with several emendations, two of which were of supreme importance:

(a) The pronouncement that divorces were conditional on the *Qāḏī*'s verdict was annulled, and the law now stated that a divorce came into force as soon as the husband announced, in the presence of witnesses, that he was divorcing his wife, even before the *Qāḏī* had issued a ruling.[2]

(b) Where the law makes no explicit ruling on personal status, the original pronouncement, that the court must rule according to the laws of the Ḫanafī School of Islam and all other laws that do not contradict Islamic law, was abolished. Instead, the new law held that the court would rule according to "the laws that were customary among the Druze community in Israel and according to other court rulings."[3] The law is very comprehensive, dealing as it does with marriage and divorce, bridal price and alimony, the upkeep of children and guardianship, absent persons and those whose status has been revoked, wills and inheritance, paternity, and consecrated property. In general, it may be said that the law is very liberal, even compared with the family laws of the most advanced states in the Middle East.

Although there is much similarity between this law and Muslim family laws, there are also significant differences, and precisely in areas considered the most important, such as the minimum marriageable age,[4] bigamy,[5] taking back one's divorced wife,[6] a woman's right to terminate the marriage,[7] the waiting period (*'idda*),[8] several laws in the area of wills and inheritance,[9] and others.[10]

The present chapter used the following sources:

A. Layish, *Marriage, Divorce and Succession in the Druze Family*, Leiden 1982;
J. N. D. Anderson, "The Personal Law of the Druze Community," *Die Welt des Islams*, N.S. II, No. 5, 1/2 (1952);
N. Dana, *The Druse, A Religious Community in Transition*, Jerusalem 1980;
_______, *Ha-Druzim*, Ramat Gan 1998;
Ḫalīm Taqī al-Dīn, *Qaḏā' al-Muwaḫḫidīn al-Durūz*, Beirut 1979;
Sajī' Yūsuf al-A'war, *Al-Aḫwāl al-Shakhṣiyya al-Durziyya 'Ilman wa-Ijtihādan* [Beirut], 1983;
S. D. Goitein and A. Ben-Shemesh, *Ha-Mishpat ha-Muslemi bi-medinat Israel*, Jerusalem, 1957.

The rest of this chapter details the main components of this law and how its directives are implemented in practice, as reflected in the verdicts of the Druze Religious Courts. These conclusions rely principally on verdicts handed down in Israel by the Druze Religious Court of first resort in 1983, 1988, and 1998 as well as on more than one thousand marriage certificates, most of them from 1998.[11]

Marriageability (*Ahliyyat al-Zawāj*)

The law on Druze personal status sets forth that the marriage bond is valid if the bridegroom (*khāṭib*) is at least 18 years old and the bride, 17 years old.[12] The original Lebanese law gave the *Qāḏī-madhhab* the authority to allow the marriage of an adolescent girl (*murāhiqa*) who was 15 years old, relying on a physician's opinion as to her physical maturity and after receiving her guardian's consent to the marriage.[13] Israel's marriageable-age law of 1950, however, does not give this authority to the *Qāḏī-madhhab*.[14] The Personal Status Law forbids the marriage of a male minor (*ṣaghīr*) under the age of 17 and a female minor under the age of 16, or of anyone who is mentally handicapped (*ma'tūh*) or has a venereal disease, leprosy, or an advanced case of tuberculosis. The law also obligates the *Qāḏī-madhhab* to ascertain the medical fitness of the couple before allowing them to marry.[15] An investigation of this latter point, though, showed that it is not always strictly adhered to; so far as we know, this is also the situation in Lebanon.

Forbidden Marriages (*Al-Zawāj al-Mamnū'*)

Marriage with another man's wife, or with a woman during the waiting period (*'idda*)[16] following divorce or the death of her husband, is forbidden and void.[17] Polygamy (*ta'addud al-zawjāt*) is also forbidden; and if someone takes a second wife, this second marriage is nullified.[18] By the same token, the marriage of a man with someone within the forbidden degree of consanguinity (*maḥram*)[19] is prohibited and void, as is marrying someone related through marriage (*muṣāhara*).[20]

The Marriage Bond (*'Aqd al-Zawāj*)

The marriage is effected by an explicit offer (*ījāb*) and expression of consent (*qabūl*) on the part of the two people concerned, in the presence of witnesses, and the registering of the marriage in a contract (*'aqd zawāj*) signed by the couple and the witnesses.[21] The marriage enters into force from the time the ceremony is conducted. Weddings are performed by marriage registrars (*ma'zūn*) appointed by the *Qāḏī-madhhab* in each region.[22] Investigation shows, however, that there are actually a number of stages in the marriage proceedings: engagement (*khuṭba*), which enables the intended couple to become acquainted without creating a legal or religious bond between the two sides; the marriage bond itself (*'aqd*), creating a legal and religious knot, as it were, binding the couple, though the bride still does not go to live with her husband in their joint home until after another wedding ceremony (*ishhār al-'urs*);[23] finally the fulfilling of certain agreed-on terms on the part of the groom, whereupon the wife goes to their home and normal marriage relations commence between the couple, including his right to have intimate relations (*ijtimā‘* or *muqāraba*) with her.

An examination of some 800 marriage certificates issued in 1998 showed that there were ten cases of double marriages, where a brother and sister from one family marry a sister and brother from another family. It is impossible, however, to determine with any certainty whether these were exchanges (*tabādul al-zawjāt*) in order to save paying the bridal price.[24] On the other hand, it turns out that the marriage of cousins and endogenous marriages have not lessened over time, but in fact increased, perhaps because of the expansion of the *ḫamūla* framework.

Marriage Laws and their Consequences (*Aḫkām al-Zawāj*)

With the signing of a valid marriage contract, the laws of inheritance apply to the two parties, as do various laws mutually obligating the couple. Thus the husband, starting from this date, is required to pay the immediate bridal price (*mahr mu‘ajjal*)[25] to his wife, and to sustain her. The husband must treat his wife with affection (*ḫusn muṣāhara*) and equality (*musāwāt*).[26] At the same time, upon receiving the immediate bridal price, the woman is expected to obey her husband, including going to live in his house, provided that it is a legal dwelling place (*maskan shar‘ī*). [27] She is also obliged to go with him even if he wishes to move to another settlement, provided there is no serious legal obstacle to doing so.[28] The woman is not entitled to demand the deferred bridal price (*mahr mu’ajjal*) in advance of: (1) a divorce, with her not being at fault; (2) the death of her spouse.[29]

The Bridal Price (*Mahr*)

The "bridal price" is an amount of money due the wife following the marriage bond; its level is recorded in the marriage contract. In the absence of such a record, the *Qāḏī-madhhab* sets the proper amount. Payment of the bridal price may be deferred in whole or in part.[30]

The bridal price is divided into two: an immediate or advance sum (*mahr mu‘ajjal*) and a later amount (*mahr mu’ajjal*). The former is an ancient custom,[31] and there are those who give it only symbolic value. The level of the later bridal price is set by agreement; it becomes due on the death of the husband or if there is a divorce. Its principal purpose is to serve as economic security for the widow or divorcee. Where the divorce or death occurred after the couple's union (*ijtimā‘ ṣaḫīḫ*), the woman gains the full amount of the bridal price. If the marriage was not consummated, she has the right to only half the amount.[32] If the intended marriage breaks up after the engagement stage, then if it is the man who calls things off, he cannot reclaim gifts that he has already given his former fiancée; but if it is the woman who has had second thoughts, then she must return what she has received from him or pay its equivalent in money if the gift has been damaged.[33]

Maintenance Support (*Nafaqa*) to Wife

The husband must maintain his wife and children with food (*ṯa'ām*), clothing (*kiswa*), lodgings (*maskan*), medical care (*taṯbīb*), and household help (*khidma*) for a woman of rank (*dhāt karāma*). If he is prevented from working or she cannot work because of her status, the amount of maintenance is set by agreement or by the *Qāḏī*'s decision, but may be changed in accordance with a change in the couple's circumstances.[34]

If the husband is unable to support his wife or refuses to do so, the *Qāḏī* may permit the wife, at her request, to borrow money to cover the cost of her maintenance, starting from the day she makes the request. Sums borrowed will be debited to the husband's account.[35]

Should the husband go missing without having arranged support for his wife, the *Qāḏī* may permit her, at her request, to borrow money against the husband's account. If the woman has a family member who would have been responsible for her support were she not married, he must lend her money, and can sue the husband to recover the amount. If the lender is a stranger to the family, he has the choice of demanding the sum from the husband upon the latter's return, or recovering it from the woman when she has the ability to repay. If the missing husband has capital, or claim to an outstanding debt against another person, the *Qāḏī* can call on those assets for the woman's support.[36] A debt that accumulates from maintenance sums ordered by the *Qāḏī* is not canceled in the event of divorce or death.[37]

Dissolving the Marriage (*Mufāraqāt*)

The original Lebanese law stated that the bond of marriage is untied when the divorce verdict is pronounced by the *Qāḏī-madhhab*.[38] This dictum in effect represents an amendment, since the husband's arbitrary ability to divorce his wife has been withdrawn and made conditional on a *Qāḏī-madhhab*'s verdict in the framework of legal proceedings.

Members of the Druze Religious Council in Israel held that the Lebanese legislation contradicts Druze religious law, according to which a wife is immediately forbidden to her former husband if he has divorced her in front of trustworthy witnesses. They decided, therefore, to amend the law in line with Druze religious law, going as far as to state that whoever "does not do this, transgresses the religious prohibition and offends the honor of the community."[39] The new law further states that once the court has issued a divorce verdict, the woman is proscribed to her former husband for life.[40] This represents one of the most prominent differences between Druze and Islamic law. According to the latter, the husband can take back his wife within the waiting period (*'idda*),[41] either by an explicit expression or even by suggestive behavior. The idea of *taḫlīl* in Islam, according to which a divorced woman may remarry her first husband after having been married to someone else in between, is completely foreign to Druze religious law.

Before the *Qāḏī-madhhab* declares the marriage dissolved (*tafrīq*), he must appoint mediators (*ḫakam*) to try to get to the bottom of the conflict and convince the couple not to divorce. If divorce is unavoidable, then the *Qāḏī-madhhab* may so rule.[42] If he finds that the dissolution is the fault of the woman, her right to the later bridal price is forfeited; if the husband is at fault, the man must pay the bridal price in whole or in part, according to the degree of guilt of each party.[43] If material damage (*'uṯl wa-ḏarar*) has been caused to one of the couple, the *Qāḏī-madhhab* will rule on appropriate compensation separately from any decision on payment of the later bridal price.

It should be noted that in contrast to Islamic law, the Druze woman can turn to the Druze court to demand an end to her marriage. She can do so on the following grounds, among others: if her husband is infected with an illness that does not permit them to have relations, such as impotence, leprosy, syphilis, chronic dementia; if he is accused of prostitution; if he is sentenced to ten years or more in prison, and he serves at least five consecutive years; or if he disappears or is absent for a protracted period, so that there is no opportunity to collect maintenance from him.[44]

An examination of Druze Religious Court files shows, somewhat surprisingly, that the Druze woman has indeed exploited her right to initiate divorce proceedings, in fact relatively more often than have Druze men. This fact emerges from the data in files from the years 1983, 1988, and 1998:

(a) 41 divorce files were examined for 1983: 36 of the cases were presented to the court by mutual agreement, one was at the husband's initiative, and four were at the wives'.[45]

(b) 73 proceedings were investigated for 1988: 61 of them were brought by mutual agreement, four at the husbands' initiative, and eight at the wives'.
(c) 85 cases were examined for 1998: 64 were presented to the court by mutual consent, nine at the husbands' initiative, and 12 at the wives'.

As a general average, then, women initiated 12 percent of the divorce proceedings in the courts, whereas men brought only 7 percent of the cases. The overwhelming majority of the cases (more than 80%) were referred to the Druze courts by mutual consent of the couple after the formulation of a divorce agreement regulating both family and monetary matters. It is only natural that these files did not specify the cause of the divorce.

In those instances where a man initiated the divorce proceedings, the following reasons were cited against the wife: improper performance of housework; disloyalty;[46] immorality;[47] hostility toward the husband's parents when sharing a common household;[48] rebelliousness;[49] and others.[50]

The reasons for a woman's initiating court action to break up the marriage were: incompatibility; not living up to obligations; improper behavior; physical abuse; being forced to use drugs; not consummating the marriage; hostitlity on the part of the husband's family;[51] impotence of the husband;[52] abandoning her for another woman (not a Druze);[53] husband's use of drugs and leaving a drug clinic before being rehabilitated;[54] and others.[55]

There were at least ten cases, regardless of who initiated the proceedings, in which the *Qāḏī-madhhab* levied a heavy fine on the husband for harming his wife materially and morally (*'uṯl wa-ḏarar māddī wa-ma'nawī*).[56] A striking phenomenon connected with the divorces action is that the majority of proceedings were started even before the couple had begun to live together.[57] In other words, if the engagement had lasted a little longer, it would have ended before the wedding contract (*'aqd*), thereby obviating the necessity for a divorce to bring an end to the relationship, since the couple would have learned of their incompatibility at an earlier stage. *Qāḏī* Shaykh Na'īm Hinū discussed this point in one of his judgments:

> The stage of engagement, preceding the marriage bond, is known and constitutes a preparatory period intended for each of the couple to examine his and her ability to live with one's spouse and to see in the other a life's partner – for raising a family and for a lifetime social framework. There is a common mistake among the youngsters of the community – to conduct the marriage ceremony already on the day of the engagement, giving insufficient time for an engagement . . .[58]

An investigation of the phenomenon showed that haste in conducting a wedding stemmed in the main from material interests: a couple is entitled to receive state benefits, especially for housing, that far surpass those given to a single person. Age is another factor: the age of most of those marrying coincides with the age for compulsory army service, and the benefits given to a married soldier are more than those for to bachelor.

The Waiting Period (ʻIdda)

Following divorce or widowhood there is a waiting period before a woman can remarry, in order to make sure that she is not pregnant, or if she is and a child is born, to determine who the father is. This waiting period lasts four months, from the day of the divorce when the marriage bond is dissolved through legal proceedings (*faskh*), or from the day the husband dies.[59] There is no need for a waiting period if there was no union (*khalwa, ijtimāʻ*) and no realization of the marriage bond (*dukhūl, muqāraba*).[60] The waiting period for a pregnant woman lasts until she gives birth or miscarries.[61] A husband is required to maintain his divorced wife during this period; however, a widow, whether pregnant or not, is not entitled to support during the waiting period.[62]

In practice, the *Qāḏī* in most cases releases the woman from the waiting period. An examination of 150 relevant Druze court files from 1988 and 1998 showed the following: in 125 cases (or more than 80%), the court freed the woman from the waiting period; in 75 percent of these instances, the couple never even reached the stage of living together and the "wife" was still living in her father's house.[63] In the other instances in which the woman was released from waiting, the couple declared that they had ceased to share the conjugal bed and the woman declared that she knew for certain whether or not she was pregnant.[64]

Maintenance of Children (*Ḫiḏāna*)

The mother is thought to be the most appropriate person to keep and rear her children so long as she is married and able to do so; in other words, being mature (*bāligha*), healthy in spirit (*ʻāqila*), trustworthy (*amīna*), healthy in body, and not married to someone of forbidden consanguinity (*maḫram*) in relation to her minor offspring.[65] If she does not fulfill these conditions, her right to keep her children is forfeited in favor of, in the following order: her mother, the mother of her father, sisters of the child, and daughters of the sisters.[66] Maintenance for the children falls on the father.[67] The mother's hold over her children ends at the age of nine for a girl, and seven for a boy. Whereupon the father is obliged to take in this child.[68] So long as the mother keeps the child, the child stays in her place of residence. If the person caring for the child is not the mother, that person is not allowed to move the child other than to the father's house.[69]

An investigation of the relevant files shows that there were several cases in which minors were removed from their mothers and handed over to other family members: a grandmother (the father's mother),[70] a grandfather,[71] a brother,[72] and so forth.[73] Each of these cases involved a woman who had married for the second time with a man who was within the forbidden consanguinity in relation to her minor offspring.

There are a number of explanations accounting for this abrogation of the woman's legal right to keep her children in these instances: the danger of their neglect by the mother owing to this second marriage; a relationship between the woman and her second husband that is considered immoral from the point of view of the minors; family pressures on the woman regarding property issues; and others. These reasons, despite their importance, do not constitute reasonable cause in every case, since there seems no sense in embarking on this path when a male child or children are concerned. Or is there *any* reason for such a sweeping course of action when the issue is not related to property rights?

Qāḏī Shaykh Na'īm Hinū raises another justification for transferring minors from the mother's care: these minors are entitled to a well-grounded family education, and this can be given only, in his opinion, by the males in the father's family; the alternative, in this view, is the risk of exposing the children to an unrooted life.

Maintenance Support (*Nafaqa*) to Children

The father is responsible for the sustenance of his minor children as well as those of his children who are unable to support themselves, until such time as they become mature and can do so if they are boys, or become married if they are girls.[74] If the father dies or finds himself without the means to support his children, then responsibility for their maintenance falls on the mother. If she, too, cannot support the children, then the obligation is that of their relatives in accordance with the line of succession or entitlement to the inheritance.[75]

Should the father go missing and leave behind property or have a debt owed to him, the *Qāḏī* may order this property to be used to cover the cost of child support. If he is not owed anything, then money for child support may be borrowed against his account.[76]

Responsibility for the financial support of indigent parents and grandparents falls on a well-to-do son, regardless of age or condition.[77] If he has insufficient income to support them, he must expend on them the amount it would cost him if they were to join his household.[78] The responsibility for members of the family who are without means falls on those *with* means, following the order of their right to inherit.[79]

Guardianship (*Wilāya, Wiṣāya*)

The father is the guardian of his minor children as well as of his mentally-ill adult children. He is allowed, on this basis, to manage his minor or mentally ill children's property – so long as his behavior is without fault and he is trustworthy. If not, the *Qāḏī* has the right and even the obligation to appoint another guardian, who is allowed to cancel any proceedings conducted by the father in relation to the minor.[80]

A man or woman who has agreed to be appointed guardian while the person who appointed him is still alive is not permitted to renege on the appointment after the latter dies.[81] If he is notified of the appointment after the appointer's death, he can refuse to accept the guardianship, but must so inform the *Qāḏī,* who will then appoint someone else.[82] When a minor becomes an adult he is entitled to demand from his guardian an account of all the latter's activity.[83]

The *Qāḏī* will determine the unfitness of a demented person, a mentally ill person, a wastrel, or a simpleton, and appoint them a guardian. This determination must be based on medical accounts or testimonies and made only after the *Qāḏī* has met the person involved and heard their case or plea.[84]

Missing Persons (*Mafqūd*) and Trusteeship (*Qayyim*)

If a man or woman's whereabouts are unknown, and it is not known whether he is dead or alive, he is considered as missing.[85] If, before his absence, he left an agent to manage his affairs and maintain his property, the latter must do so and is not allowed, without the *Qāḏī*'s permission, to undertake any act that would lessen the value of the missing person's property.[86] In the absence of such an agent, the *Qāḏī* will appoint a trustee for the property.[87]

A person who has been missing for ten years will be decreed dead by the *Qāḏī* following a thorough investigation, and his estate will be divided among those of his heirs who are alive on the date of the judgment.[88] Should the missing person return within two years of the announcement of his being considered dead, all his estate will be returned to him. If he returns after two years, he will receive back only what remains of the estate, though he will receive compensation for the rest.[89]

Lineage/Paternity (*Nasab*)

The shortest pregnancy period is 180 days, and the longest 300 days.[90] A child who is born less than 180 days after the marriage ceremony will be considered the husband's only if the husband recognizes it as such – that is, accepts paternity, explicitly or implicitly.[91] It should be noted that Druze law does not recognize bastardy. There are a number of court files relating to a child born to a woman who had relations with a foreigner while still married to her legal husband; the court discussion revolved only around the question of the baby's lineage/paternity without ascribing any defect at all to the child's religious–legal status.[92]

Wills (*Waṣiyya*) and Inheritance (*Irth*)

A will is the handing over of property as a gift and becomes valid only after the death of the testator.[93] Consequently, a person can, in his lifetime, amend his will or cancel it altogether.[94] A condition of the validity of the will is that the testator be mature, be in control of his senses, be free and able to receive gifts.[95] It is permissible to will one's estate, in whole or in part, to an heir who is a family successor or to a person who is not such an heir,[96] or even to someone who is not from the Druze community.[97]

If a person wills his property to someone and the latter dies before the former, then the heirs of the deceased will inherit his share so long as the testator did not introduce any subsequent changes in the will. This is also the law in the case of the death of one of the family heirs prior to the death of the one who willed his assets.[98] In the absence of a will, the estate will be divided according to Druze custom.[99]

One of the most striking phenomena reflected in the Druze court files is the great many concessions made by women. Here are a few figures: of 23 cases of inheritance in 1988 that were examined, the daughters gave up their rights in 15 cases; in five of the cases, the widows joined them in giving up their share of the inheritance in favor of the sons; in the eight other cases, the daughters did not concede their share.[100] Of 60 cases of inheritance in 1998 that were investigated, in only 16 cases was there no concession on the part of female heirs. The widows themselves generally joined their daughters in forgoing the inheritance.

This phenomenon of female heirs giving up their share of an estate so that the males can inherit is perplexing, for it is an explicit distortion of the testator's wishes. In 21 cases involving wills in 1998, six women with inheritance rights conceded the share willed to them in favor of male heirs.[101] In 1988, 10 will files were examined, and in half the cases the women surrendered their rights to the men. There are a number of hypotheses to account for this phenomenon:

1. Males, being the principal breadwinners in the Druze patriarchal society, are thought to be entitled to receive the lion's share of the property.
2. Concession (*tanāzul*) on the part of the female heirs is sometimes done under pressure.
3. *Qāḏī* Shaykh Na'īm Hinū is of the opinion that these concessions signify an improved economic situation that marginalizes the issue of the female heirs' share of the inheritance. Moreover, Druze society, according to past tradition, views the man as the owner of the family property.[102]

Sacred Trusts (*Awqāf*)

In regard to consecrated property, the law states that one should operate according to the law's concerning sacred trusts and also according to long-standing, existing tradition, Druze custom, and other relevant laws.[103]

The Personal Status Laws of the Druze in Syria

In contrast to Lebanon and Israel, Syria has no special legislation detailing the laws of personal status of the Druze. This is a direct result of the status of Druze in that country, where they are in effect considered Muslims. The (general) law of personal status (*qānūn al-aḫwāl al-shakhṣiyya*), which was enacted in 1953, does state marginally that certain laws included in the legislative Act will not apply to the Druze. The Act has more than 300 articles. Article 307 specifies certain subjects for which a different law from the general one applies to Druze: these relate to prohibitions against polygamy and taking back a divorced wife, certain matters of wills and inheritance, and other matters.

It should be noted that significant changes were made in the Druze religious juridical system in 1959. The number of Druze *Qāḏī* positions was reduced to one, and appeals against this *Qāḏī*'s decisions were to be made before a non-Druze panel. The appointment of the Druze *Qāḏī*, too, was to be made by the ruling civilian authorities without any regard to the Druze spiritual leadership.

Following is a translation of the wording of Article 307, along with several comments.

Legislative Order No. 59 of September 17, 1953

Article 307 of the Personal Status Laws states: Anything that contradicts these laws will not apply to the Druze community:

1 The *Qāḏī* will verify the eligibility of the two partners to a marriage and its validity prior to its taking place.[104]

2 Polygamy is forbidden.[105]

3 Laws relating to cursing (*li'ān*)[106] and to nursing (*riḏā'*)[107] will not apply to members of the community.

4 Should a man marry a young girl under the assumption that she is a virgin and find that she is not: if he knew this before their union, he is not entitled to request the return of any of the bridal price, or *mahr*, or the needs of the bridal veil (*jihāz*). If he did not know until after their union, he has the right to receive back half of the *mahr* if he wishes to keep it in his possession or to demand all of it and also the prenuptial gifts he gave her if it is proven that the absence of virginity was caused by an act of prostitution and he wants a divorce. Should the husband make a false accusation that he found his wife not to be a virgin and (therefore) he wants to divorce her, she is entitled to retain the *mahr* and the bridal veil needs that she received.

5 If a woman is found guilty of prostitution, her husband has the right to divorce her and to take back the *mahr* and whatever remains of the bridal veil needs. If a man is adjudged to be a prostitute, his wife is entitled to demand a divorce and to take all her later *mahr*.[108]

6 A divorce is not valid except on the basis of a *Qādī*'s decision.[109]

7 A divorced woman may not be returned to live with the man who divorced her.

8 A will is to be executed for the benefit of the heir or other inheritor, according to the measure of a third and more than a third.[110]
9 If offspring die before the death of the testator, the offspring [of the former] will inherit in their place, and their share will be taken as if he they were alive.

General Syrian Law of Jurisdiction No. 56 of 1959

Article 10 (2): Matters of personal status of the Druze community will be adjudicated by a *Qāḏī Shar'ī* of that community, who will be appointed by a presidential order in accordance with the recommendation of the Syrian Minister of Justice, and provided that the conditions required for a *Qāḏī* are fulfilled.

Appeals against a verdict that is handed down will be made to the Appeals Court within a short time thereafter and on the basis of the rules that are customary in appeals relating to a verdict by *Qādīs Shar'ī.*

The Druze Court of Appeals will be abolished, and its members will serve in a department to be called "The Department for Religious Laws of the Druze Community." Each of them will be given proper compensation.

Afterword

The three large concentrations of Druze in the world – in Syria, Lebanon, and Israel – differ from one another in their behavior, identity, status, and relationships with non-Druze.

Numerically the largest concentration is in Syria; but the unique Druze religious identity of this population appears to be in an accelerated process of erosion. The situation in Lebanon is different in that the authorities are not working toward an intentional blurring of this special identity, and therefore the identity crisis is less sharp. Nevertheless, it should be emphasized that the very openness and freedom that this community enjoys have created the same feelings toward Lebanon's other religious groups and cultures. This is manifested in the Druze's living among them, mixing with them, and even marrying them to an ever greater extent than in the past, especially in the region of Beirut and its suburbs.

In Israel, which contains the third largest Druze concentration in the Middle East, this population is characterized by a consolidated religio-community particularism whose patterns have been determined in the course of several generations. Owing to the nationalist Israeli–Arab confrontation, the Druze in Israel have become an ideological prize, competed for by Israelis and Arabs alike. The Israeli perception, representing the majority, affects to a greater extent the outlook of the Druze in Israel, especially that of the elite group, the *'uqqāl.* There are, however, visible cracks in this perception, particularly among the younger generation. These "cracks" are manifested in different ways, as discussed in chapter 10, but all have a link to the crisis of identity that young Druze are experiencing today.

The modern era has created a revolution among Druze in all three countries – not only in the realm of technology, but also in the inner consciousness of the new generation, who are increasingly mobile and likely to abandon the village for non-agricultural pursuits. The new roads to and within the villages, the electricity, educational institutions, and other developments are all bringing this community closer to the twenty-first century, along with values that at times contradict the traditional patterns Druze have lived by for hundreds of years.

The influence of these changes appears principally in four religious–social areas: (a) the type of settlements where Druze live; (b) the nature of the leadership; (c) the status of women; and (d) the establishment of families with spouses who are not part of this community.

One of the most striking aspects defining the modern era is the widening dispersal of the Druze population. Until fairly recently, the world knew only of an almost uniform type of Druze settlement, marked by its mountain setting and the absence of non-Druze. Although this type of settlement still exists, we witness more and more the dispersal of this group, which has intermixed increasingly within the religiously varied population.

Another striking sign of the modern era is the community's leadership in each of the three large concentrations. Until a few generations ago, the religious figures of the community generally dealt with the whole complex of topics that preoccupied the population, including "secular" issues such as politics, economics, the military, and others. In those few cases where these were separated from religious issues, and various personalities were appointed to deal with them, the preferred status of the religious leader (*shaykh dīn*) was maintained over that of the "secular" leader (*shaykh zamanī, shaykh dunyawī*).

Another area of change is in the age of the leadership, which today is much younger, and their level of education, which is much higher and broader.

All these differences are noticeable even in the Druze population of Israel, which has tended to be less forward-looking – perhaps stemming from the respect accorded to the aged head of the community, Shaykh Amīn Ṭarīf, who had led this community for two generations prior to his death. Nonetheless, one can distinguish intensified efforts to fill the vacuum created with the Shaykh's passing. Among those trying to compete for the leadership are not only religious figures from his family, but other religious figures, as well as members of the free professions, activists in municipal and parliamentary affairs, retired army officers, and others.

The traditional leadership allowed only limited circles to engage in public activity. Today, however, one can discern a minor revolution taking place in the Druze political leadership in Israel. In the Knesset, one no longer meets people like Shaykh Jabr Mu'addī, the late Shaykh Labīb Abū Rukn, or Shaykh Sāliḥ Khunayfis. Their place has slowly been taken by members of the younger generation who have had a general education and live a modern way of life. This process, moreover, has made inroads at the municipal level, too. Parliamentary activists are no longer connected to ethnic lists, but belong to the general parties with none of the traditional Eastern symbols.

One of the most interesting expressions of this revolt among young Druze concerns the status of women. It is true that the personal status of the Druze woman is incomparable to other societies in the Middle East. She is not threatened by disaster; she expects her husband to relate to her in accordance with her status; she has equality in several important personal areas, including the possibility of turning to the court for a divorce. It should be recalled, however, that severe social limitations are placed on her, such as the restriction on leaving the village unaccompanied, even for the purpose of education or work. A whole array of demands are made of her that do not accord with modern society, such as the prohibition against developing social relations that are not strictly linked to marriage, or being forbidden to drive a vehicle, or to learn in a mixed-gender educational institution, or to study nursing. She is also prohibited from other "modern" activities (such as going to a coffee shop alone, driving or going to cinema) that seem to contradict the philosophy of traditional Druze society.

The intensification of Druze involvement with non-Druze has confronted this society with a problem that was unknown in the past: the setting up of religiously mixed families. There are very many instances of "straying" in Syria and Lebanon, and to a certain extent also in Israel. The question arises, therefore: Are these isolated cases, providing an answer for one individual or another, or are they signs of a general phenomenon that will only increase with time?

The points of contact between the young Druze and the external world are multiplying in all areas of life: employment, social activities, culture, education, and others. Because the Druze lack nationalistic values outside the religious sphere – they have no affinity to a national Druze territory, no Druze language, etc. – and because even their religious particularism cannot serve as a spiritual dam for most of the community, since the majority do not participate in the religious assemblies and do not share the *'uqqāl* experiences, reason suggests that the crisis of identity will worsen.

It should be made clear that most adult Druze, including religious figures, do not discern this process at all, and perhaps therein lies the root of the problem. Mixed marriages or conversions, for example, are considered exceptional deviations, an expression of the personal crisis of an individual. They are not viewed as indications of a "natural" process that might intensify and put the Druze way of life at risk, as is happening in the two larger Druze concentrations in the Middle East.

In Syria, which has the world's largest Druze population, the apathy of the community itself is significant. This apathy suits the tendencies of the country's Ba'th authorities: blurring the religious identity of its citizens and strengthening general nationalistic feelings.

In Lebanon, one sees various and contradictory reactions in the three large Druze collectives. In the Ḫās̱bayyā region there is great sensitivity to such deviations, and religious leaders have been working hard to strengthen the spiritual foundations of Druze youth. Particularly active in this regard is the al-Bayyāḏā religious center in the town of Ḫās̱bayyā. In the al-Shūf region, the attitude is less zealous and more "realistic." Druze leaders, such as Walīd Junblāṯ, are married to non-Druze women and the community does not view them as "traitors." The situation is completely different in Beirut and the 'Aleh sector, where mixed marriages between Druze men and non-Druze women and, to no small extent, of Druze women to non-Druze men, are frequent. This is similar to the situation in the Druze diasporas in the United States, Argentina, Brazil, Australia, Canada, and elsewhere.

Amazingly, it is in Israel, with the smallest Druze concentration in the Middle East, that religious discipline has been well maintained, at least up to now, so that intermarriage is less widespread than in Syria or Lebanon. There are two principal reasons for this:

1 The religious leadership managed in the past to maintain its authority over the whole Druze population and to instill in it an awareness that they should have qualms about marrying non-Druze, even to the extent of expressing repugnance at such an idea.
2 The young Druze have gained, in the framework of the state education system, a familiarity with the community's values through the study of "Druze heritage." These studies are the outcome of conclusions reached by two committees that investigated the subject in the 1980s.

In regard to the second reason, reservations have from time to time been expressed about the "Druze Heritage" course both by religious figures, who fear "deviation" resulting from learning the secrets of the religion in the framework of the "Heritage" subject, and by Arab nationalists, Druze and non-Druze, who fear that learning the subject will sharpen the differences between Druze and Arabs.

The Druze religion, as we have seen, constitutes a strong, almost exclusive foundation uniting the Druze. The trouble is that the religion is a secret one both for the Druze themselves and, all the more so, for non-Druze. In this context, the principle of *taqiyya* should be recalled, one of whose declarations states:

Our Lord commanded that we hide behind the prevailing religion, be it what it may: with Christians, to behave as Christians; with Muslims, to behave as Muslims, and so forth; for our Lord, *al-Ḥākim bi-Amrihi*, said: when one of the nations overcomes you, follow it, but preserve me in your hearts. What does this refer to? In external, not inward behavior.[1]

وتكثر فيكم البلايا والامتحانا
فاصبروا على الامتحان تنالوا المغفرة
والاحسان وصونوا الحكمة عن
غير اهلها ولا تمنعوها المستحقها
فان من منع الحكمة عن
اهلها فقد دنس امانته
ودينه ومن سلمها الى غير
اهلها فقد تعدى اتباع الحق
بيقينه فعليكم بحفظها
وصيانتها عن غير اهلها
والاستتار بما لم الحق عند اهله
ولا

ولا تنكشفوا عند من غلبت
عليه شقوته وجهله فانتم
ترونهم من حيث لا يرونكم وانتم
بما في ايديهم عارفون وعلى ما الفوه
من زخرف قولهم مطلعون وهم
عما في ايديكم غافلون وعما
اقتبستموه من نور الحكمة محجوبون
لقد اخرسوا ونطقتم وابكموا
وسمعتم وعموا وابصرتم وجهلوا
وعرفتم فاحمدوا المولى سبحانه
على ما افاض عليكم من طر

Maintaining Religious Secrecy

The Druze religious texts include words of encouragement for the faithful along with an instruction to maintain the secrecy of the religion. This directive says, in part: "An Obligation to Keep the Writings of the Religion Secret: Hardships and persecutions will multiply for you. Gird up your loins with patience in order to be worthy of forgiveness and loving-kindness. Guard the wisdom (books) [a reference to *Kutub al-Ḥikma*] from those who are not worthy of it and do not withhold it from anyone who merits it. . . . Do not expose yourselves to anyone whose evil nature and ignorance overcome him, for [by doing so] you watch them without having the ability to look deeply into them. The words of their law are familiar to you, while their knowledge lacks what is in your hands, and they are removed from the light of wisdom that rests with you. . . ."

Indeed, this idea has greatly helped the Druze people to preserve its existence for a thousand years, in particular by presenting themselves as Muslims, for their religion is far from Islam. The *juhhāl*, who are not part of the religious elite, have not the tools to discern between truth and what is offered as "truth," and are tempted to think at times that the Druze faith is part of Islam. We find, then, that the basis of *taqiyya*, which is meant to offer protection to Druze from the machinations of strangers, especially Muslims, has become a stumbling block and an impediment for many of this community, and even encourages drawing closer to Islam.

In 1982, in conversation with the spiritual leader of the Druze community of Lebanon, the late Shaykh Muḫammad Abū Shaqrā, I expressed amazement that in all his pronouncements, both written and spoken, he describes the Druze as Arab-Muslims, for in doing so he sows confusion among the younger generation. Somewhat taken aback, he replied: "You are right. We find ourselves with a sensitive problem."

It is not impossible that along with the decrease in the standing of the religion, Druze identity will grow, with the development of nationalistic characteristics. Indeed, little by little, a community heritage has been developing. At its base is the stress on a knowledge of Druze history, important sites related to their history, their social particularism, faith, popular beliefs, the special status of Druze women, and so forth. Similarly, Druze youngsters who are without religious knowledge (the *juhhāl*) can identify with the faith by participating in open religious ceremonies, such as the assemblies at Ayyām al-'Ashr, the Nabī Shu'ayb celebrations, and so forth.

Nonetheless, the desire arises again and again among the younger generation to gain a deeper familiarity with and knowledge of their religious values as a spiritual manifestation of their particularism.

The difficulty in exposing the religion to the entire Druze community certainly exists. Nevertheless, a real danger is also revealed: What hundreds of years of persecution of this community did not manage to do, a few score years of openness to the outside world may well succeed in doing.

One Druze intellectual who understood this was Yūsuf Naṣr al-Dīn of Dāliyat al-Karmil. His anger once welled up at the burial of a Druze who had been murdered by a Muslim terrorist, when the usual prayer over the dead was recited in its traditional Muslim version. He exclaimed: "From the day I became an adult, I have been living with a double identity. At fateful ceremonies in a person's life – marriage and death – we dress up as Muslims even though we have no affinity or closeness to Islam . . . We have forgotten that we have a religion of our own, with our own values and tradition." His conclusion: "I insist that we return to ourselves and adopt the sublime heritage and values of the Druze."[2]

Chronology

996–1021	Reign of the Fatimid Khalifate of al-Ḫākim bi-Amr Allāh in Egypt
1017–1021	The *Kashf* period – divine revelation
1017–1043	Opening of the Druze faith to new believers
11th–15th c.	Tanūkh Dynasty
1187	Battle of Ḫiṯṯīn; the Druze fought alongside the Muslims against the Crusaders
1260	Battle of 'Ayn Jālūt (near Nazareth); the Druze fought on the side of the Mamelukes against the Tartars
1417–1479	Lifespan of Jamāl al-Dīn 'Abd Allāh al-Tanūkhī (al-Amīr al-Sayyid)
1445–1505	Lifespan of Jalāl al-Dīn al-Suyyūṯī, one of the senior Muslim sages of all time
16th–17th c.	Ma'n Dynasty
1516–1544	Reign of Fakhr al-Dīn al-Ma'nī I, in the Shūf Mountains
1572–1635	Lifespan of Fakhr al-Dīn al-Ma'nī II, who ruled most of the territory of Lebanon as well as parts of Syria and Palestine; was murdered by the Ottomans
1640	Death of Shaykh Maḫmūd Abū Hilāl (al-Shaykh al-Fāḏīl)
17th–18th c.	Shihāb Dynasty
1711	Battle of 'Ayn Dāra in the Shūf Mountains between the Tanūkhs and the Shihābs (Qays) and the Ma'ns (Yaman); the Yamanī faction was beaten (*Madhbaḫat 'Ayndāra*)
1704–1753	Lifespan of Shaykh 'Alī Fāris
End of 18th c.	Withdrawal of the appellation *Jabal al-Durūẕ* (Druze Mountain) from Mount Lebanon and its transfer to Mount Ḫawrān in Syria because of the intensive migration to the latter, 1840–1860
	Series of bitter confrontations between the Druze and the Maronite Christians in and outside Lebanon; these reached a peak in 1860
1850–1884	Leadership of Muḫammad Maḫmūd Ṯarīf, as spiritual leader of the Druze in Palestine
1884–1928	Leadership of Ṯarīf Muḫammad Ṯarīf, as spiritual head of the Druze in Palestine
1925–1927	Revolt against the French led by Sulṯān (Pasha) al-Aṯrash (who died in 1982)

1951	Death of Nazīra Junblāṯ, important female Druze leader in Lebanon
1917–1977	Lifespan of Kamāl Junblāṯ (who was murdered)
1893–1993	Lifespan of Shaykh Amīn Ṭarīf, who from 1928 served as spiritual head of the Druze in Palestine/Israel

Appendix

Arabic Original of the Laws of Personal Status in Lebanon and Israel

A. *Marriageability*
B. *Forbidden Marriages*
C. *The Marriage Bond*
D. *Marriage Laws*
E. *Bridal Price*
F. *Maintenance*
G. *Dissolving the Marriage*
H. *The Waiting Period*
I. *The Maintenance of Children*
J. *Maintenance Support*
K. *Guardianship*
L. *Missing and Trusteeship*
M. *Lineage/Paternity*
N. *Wills and Inheritance*
O. *Sacred Trusts*

A. *Marriageability*

الفصل الاول

في أهليـــة الــزواج

المادة ١ ــ يجوز الخاطب على أهلية الزواج باتمــامه الثامنة عشرة والمخطوبة بإتمامها السابعة عشرة من العمر •

المادة ٢ ــ لقاضي المذهب أن يأذن بالزواج للمراهق الذي أكمــل السادسة عشرة من عمره ولم يكمل الثامنة عشرة إذا ثبت لديــه طبياً أن حالــه يتحمل ذلك ، على أن يكون اذن القاضي موقوفاً على إذن ولي المراهق •

المادة ٣ ــ لقاضي المذهب أن يأذن بالزواج للمراهقــة التي أكملت الخامسةعشرة من العمر ولم تكمل السابعة عشرة إذا ثبت لديه طبياً أن حالها يتحمل ذلك وأذن وليها •

المادة ٤ — إذا أذن القاضي بزواج المراهق والمراهقة بدون إذن الولي حق لكل من المراهق والمراهقة أن يطلب فسخ الزواج في مدة ستة أشـهر تبتدىء من تاريخ بلوغ السـن المبينة في المادة الاولى •

المادة ٥ — لايجوز لاحد أصلا أن يزوج الصغير الذي لم يتم السادسة عشرة والصغيرة التي لم تتم الخامسة عشرة •

ولا يجوز تزويج المعتوه ولا المعتوهة ولا المريض ولا المريضة بعـلة من العلل السارية وهي الامراض الزهرية والجذام والتدرن الرئوي في طور النمو •

وعلى القاضي أن يستثبت قبل الاذن بالزواج سلامة الزوجين من العته والعلل السارية بتكليفهما ابراز شهادة صحية من طبيب قانوني ويجوز الاعتراض على هـذه الشهادة لدى القاضي وقراره بشأنها قابل لطرق المراجعة •

المادة ٦ — إذا طلبت الكبيرة التي يتراوح سـنها بين السابعة عشرة والحادية والعشرين أن تتزوج بشـخص فالقاضي يبلغ ذلك لوليهـا ، وإذا لم يعترض الولي في مدة خمسة عشر يوماً من تاريخ تبليغه أو اعترض ورؤى اعتراضه في غير محـله ، أذن القاضي بزواجهما •

المادة ٧ — الولي في الزواج هو العصبة بنفسه على الترتيب ويشترط أن يكون مكلفاً ، فلا ولايـة للصبي والمجنون والمعتوه على أحد أصلا •

المادة ٨ — إذا لم يكـن لطالب الزواج ولي أو كان وليـه غير حائز الاهلية القانونية فيقوم بالولاية القاضي أو من يسـتنيبه لهـذه الغايـة •

B. *Forbidden Marriages*

الفصل الثاني

في من هو ممنـوع زواجـه

المادة ٩ ــ عقد الزواج على مزوجة الغير أو معتدته ممنوع وباطل.

المادة ١٠ ــ ممنوع تعـدد الزوجات فلا يجوز للرجل أن يجمع بـين زوجتين وإن فعل فزواجه من الثانية باطل .

المادة ١١ ــ لا يجوز لاحد أن يعيد مطلقته .

المادة ١٢ ــ تزوج النساء ذوات الرحم المحرم برجل بينه وبينهن قرابة نسبية ممنوع وباطل. والنساء المذكورات أربعة أصناف:

١ ــ أم الرجل وجداتـه .

٢ ــ البنات والحفيدات .

٣ ــ الاخـوات وبنـات الاخـوة والاخـوات مطلقاً وحفيداتهن .

٤ ــ العمات والخالات مطلقاً .

المادة ١٣ ــ تزوج النساء بالرجل الذي بينه وبينهن مصاهرة ممنوع وباطل . والنساء المذكورات أربعة أصناف :

١ ــ زوجات الابناء والحفدة .

٢ ــ أمهات الزوجات وجداتهن مطلقاً .

٣ ــ زوجات الآباء والاجداد .

٤ ــ بنات الزوجات وحفيداتهن .

C. *The Marriage Bond*

الفصل الثالث

في عقــد الــزواج

المادة ١٤ ــ يتم عقد الزواج بالايجاب والقبول من الفريقين في مجلس العقد بحضور شهود، ويجوز أن يكون الشهود من أصول وفروع الخاطب والمخطوبة على أن لا يقــل عددهم عن الاربعــة ويجب أن يتم العقد كتابة وان يوقعه الزوجان وشهودهما ، وإذا تعذر حضور أحد الزوجين مجلــس العقد يجوز أن يوقعه عنه وكيل مفوض بموجب وكالة خطية مصدق عليها من المختار أو ممن يقوم مقامه على أن يذكر في التوكيل قيمــة المهر أو يترك تعيينــه لرأي الوكيل وعلى أن يضم هذا التوكيل الى العقد •

المادة ١٥ ــ الايجاب والقبول في الزواج يكونان بالالفاظ الصريحة وكذلك في الخطبة واشارة الاخرس تقوم مقام العبارة•

المادة ١٦ ــ لا يكون عقــد الزواج صحيحاً إلا إذا أجراه القاضي أو من أنابه عنــه لاجرائــه •

المادة ١٧ ــ يعين القاضي مأذونا أو أكثر لاجراء عقد الزواج في كل ناحية أو بلدة حسب الاقتضاء وليس للمأذون أن يجري العقد قبل أن يحصل على إذن خطي خاص من القاضي بذلك•

المادة ١٨ ــ بعــد أن ينظم المأذون العقد يرســله الى القاضي لاجل المصادقة عليه وتســجيله ويسري مفعول هــذا العقد اعتباراً من تاريخ حصولــه •

المادة ١٩ ــ على القاضي أن يسجل هذه العقود في سجل مخصوص ممهورة صفحاته من قبله ومرقمة بالتسلسل• ويعاد العقد الى صاحبــه خلال شــهر على الاكثر من تاريخ ايداعه المحكمة المذهبية لتســجيله •

D. *Marriage Laws*

الفصل الرابع

في احكام الزواج

المادة ٢٠ ـ يلزم مهر الزوجة ونفقتها الزوج منذ اجراء العقد الصحيح ويثبت بينهما حق التوارث •

المادة ٢١ ـ ليس للزوجة حق المطالبة بالمؤجل من المهر قبل حلول أحد الاجلين الطلاق أو الوفاة •

المادة ٢٢ ـ تجبر الزوجة بعد استيفاء المهر المعجل واجراء عقدالزواج الشرعي على الاقامة في بيت زوجها إذا كان مسكناً شرعيا وكذا على الذهاب معه إذا أراد الذهاب إلى بلدة أخرى ولم يكن هنالك مانع جدي • والمسكن الشرعي هو المسكن الذي يمكن أن يسكن فيه أمثال الزوجين •

المادة ٢٣ ـ الزوج مجبر على حسن معاشرة زوجته ومساواتها بنفسه والزوجة مجبرة أيضاً على إطاعة زوجها في الحقوق الزوجية المشروعة •

E. *Bridal Price*

الفصل الخامس

في المهر

المادة ٢٤ ـ المهر هو المال الذي يجب بالزواج ويترتب على الزوج للزوجة بمجرد العقد الصحيح عليها ويعين مقداره بعقد الزواج ، وإذا لم يعين مقدار المهر في العقد يحكم القاضي بمهر المثل •

المادة ٢٥ ـ يجوز تعيين وتأجيل المهر كلا أو بعضا •

المادة ٢٦ ـ لكل من الخاطب و المخطوبة أن يرجع عن الخطبة من غير أن يلزمه شيء • أما فيما يتعلق بهدايا الخطبة فاذا كان

الرجوع من جهة الخاطب فلا يجوز له أن يسترد شيئا مما قدمه للمخطوبة سواء أكان باقيا وقت رجوعه أم لم يكن. وإن كان الرجوع من جهة المخطوبة وجب عليها أن ترد كل شيء قدمه الخاطب لها ، فان كان قائما ردته بنفسه وان كان قد هلك في وقت رجوعها ردت مثله أو قيمته ما لم يكن بينهما شرط فيعمل به .

المادة ٢٧ ـ إذا توفي أحد الزوجين أو وقع الطلاق بينهما بعد الاجتماع الصحيح يلزم المهر بكامله ، أما إذا وقع الطلاق أو الوفاة قبل الاجتماع الصحيح يسقط نصف المهر .

F. *Maintenance*

الفصل السادس

في النفقة

المادة ٢٨ ـ النفقة هي ما ينفقه الانسان على عياله وزوجته ويشمل الطعام والكسوة والسكنى والتطبيب وخدمة الزوجة ذات الكرامة أو العاجزة أو المريضة وهي لازمة الاداء بتراضي الفريقين أو بحكم القاضي .

المادة ٢٩ ـ بعد تقدير النفقة يجوز زيادتها أو انقاصها بحسب تغيير الاثمان أو تبدل حال الزوجين يسراً أو عسراً .

المادة ٣٠ ـ إذا امتنع الزوج الحاضر عن الانفاق على زوجته وطلبت الزوجة النفقة فالقاضي يقدر النفقة حسب حال الفريقين اعتباراً من يوم الطلب وله أن يأمر باعطائها سلفة عن المدة التي يعينها .

المادة ٣١ ـ إذا عجز الزوج عن الانفاق على زوجته وطلبت الزوجة النفقة فالقاضي يقدر النفقة اعتباراً من يوم الطلب على أن تكون ديناً بذمة الزوج ويأذن للزوجة أن تستدين باسمه.

المادة ٣٢ ــ إذا ترك الزوج زوجته بلا نفقة واختفى أو تغيب بذهابه لمحل بعيد أو فقد فالقاضي يقدر النفقة اعتباراً من يوم الطلب بعد إقامة البينة على الزوجية والغيبة وعلى كونه مفقوداً وبعد تحليف الزوجة بأن الزوج لم يترك لها نفقة وبأنها غير مطلقة ويأذن للزوجة عند الحاجة بالاستدانة باسم الزوج .

المادة ٣٣ ــ إذا أذن القاضي للزوجة المعسرة بالاستدانة عملا بأحكام المواد السابقة واستدانت من قريب تلزمه نفقتها فلهذا القريب حق الرجوع على الزوج فقط . أما إذا استدانت من غريب فللدائن الخيار في أن يطالب الزوج أو الزوجة.

المادة ٣٤ ــ إذا كان للزوج الغائب مال بيد الغير أو بذمته وأقر المؤتمن أو المديون بالمال الذي بيده أو بذمته أو أنكر ذلك واثبتت الزوجة أمام المحكمة المدنية المختصة فبعد أن تقيم الزوجة البينة بالزوجية وتحلف اليمين على أن الزوج لم يترك لها نفقة وبأنها غير مطلقة يقدر لها النفقة من ذلك المال أو من ريعه أو من ثمنه اعتباراً من يوم الطلب .

المادة ٣٥ ــ لا يسقط المقدار المتراكم من النفقة المقدرة قضاء أو رضاء بالطلاق أو بوفاة أحد الزوجين .

المادة ٣٦ ــ إذا تركت الزوجة بيت زوجها بدون سبب مشروع أو كانت في بيتها ومنعت زوجها من الدخول إليه قبل طلب نقلها لبيت آخر تسقط نفقتها مدة دوام هذا النشوز .

G. *Dissolving the Marriage*

الفصل السـابع

فـي المفـارقات

المادة ٣٧ ــ **ينحل عقد الزواج بالطلاق حالاً، أمام شهود ثقات •**

المادة ٣٨ ــ **لا تحل للرجل مُطلقته ابداً بعد وقوع الطلاق بينهما حسب المادة ٣٧ •**

المادة ٣٩ ــ إذا ظهرت للزوجة السالمة من عيوب المقـاربة قبل أو بعد الزواج أن زوجها مصاب بعـلة لا يمكنها معها مساكنته بلا ضرر كالجذام والبرص والزهري وما شابهها فلها أن تراجع القاضي وتطلب التفريق • فإذا كانت العلة غير قابلة الشفاء فيحكم القاضي بالتفريق في الحال وإذا كان من أمل بزوال العلة فيؤجل القاضي التفريق سنتين على أن يقرر في الحال الفصل المؤقت بين الزوجين ، وإذا لم تزل العلة خلال هذه المدة ولم يرض الزوج بالطلاق وأصرت الزوجة على طلبها يحكم القاضي بالتفريق • أما العاهات كالعمى والعرج فليست سـبباً للتفريق •

المادة ٤٠ ــ إذا كان الزوج مصاباً بالعنـة فللزوجة أن تطلب التفريق متى ثبت طبياً أن هذه العنة غير قابلة للشفاء •

المادة ٤١ ــ إذا جن الزوج بعد عقد الزواج وراجعت الزوجة القاضي طالبة التفريق فالقاضي يؤجل النظر بالطلب مدة سنة وإذا لم يزل الجنـون في خلال هـذه المدة وأصرت الزوجة حـكم بالتفريق •

المادة ٤٢ ــ للزوجين أن يفسخا عقد الزواج بالتراضي ويتم هذا الفسخ باعلانه بحضور شاهدين أمام القاضي الذي يصدر حكماً به •

المادة ٤٣ ــ إذا حـكم على الزوج بجريمة الزنا فللزوجـة أن تطلب التفريق وإذا حكم على الزوجة بجريمة الزنا وطلقها زوجها لهذه العلة يسقط عنه مؤجل المهر •

المادة ٤٤ ــ إذا حكم على الزوج بعقوبة الحبس لمدة عشر سنوات فأكثر وقضى منها في السجن خمس سنوات متتالية كان للزوجة أن تطلب التفريق في ختام هذه المدة .

المادة ٤٥ ــ إذا اختفى الزوج أو تغيب مدة ثلاث سنوات وتعذر تحصيل النفقة منه فالقاضي يحكم بالتفريق بطلب الزوجة .
أما إذا تيسر تحصيل النفقة فلا يجاب طلبها إلا إذا مر على الغيبة خمس سنوات بدون انقطاع وإذا حكم على الزوج الحاضر بالنفقة وتعذر تحصيلها منه مدة سنتين فللزوجة أيضاً أن تطلب التفريق .

المادة ٤٦ ــ إذا حكم بفسخ زواج امرأة لغيبة الزوج وتزوجت بآخر ثم ظهر الزوج الاول فظهوره لا يوجب فسخ الزواج الاخير .

المادة ٤٧ ــ إذا وقع نزاع أو شقاق بين الزوجين وراجع أحدهما القاضي يعين القاضي حكماً من أهل الزوج وحكماً من أهل الزوجة وإن لم يكن بين أهلهما من توفرت فيه أوصاف الحكم اختار القاضي حكماً من غير أهلهما .

المادة ٤٨ ــ على الحكمين أن يتعرفا أسباب الشقاق بين الزوجين وأن يجتهدا في اصلاح ذات البين وإذا لم يمكن التوفيق بينهما وكان القصور والاصرار من جهة الزوج يفرق القاضي بينهما ويحكم للزوجة بكامل المهر المؤجل أو ببعضه ، وإذا كان من جهة الزوجة يحكم القاضي باسقاط المهر المؤجل كلا أو بعضاً وللقاضي أن يحكم في كلا الحالين على غير المحق من الزوجين بما يستحق الآخر من عطل وضرر .

المادة ٤٩ ــ إذا ظهر للقاضي أن الطلاق لا يبرره سبب شرعي يحكم للزوجة بالعطل والضرر علاوة على مؤجل المهر على أن يؤخذ بعين الاعتبار الضرر المعنوي والمادي .

H. *The Waiting Period*

الفصل الثامن

في العدة

المادة ٥٠ ـ مدة العدة أربعة أشهر تبدأ من تاريخ الطلاق أو التفريق أو وفاة الزوج وعدة الحامل تنتهي بالوضع أو بسقوط الجنين •

المادة ٥١ ـ لا تلزم العدة إذا وقع الطلاق أو الفسخ قبل الاجتماع والمقاربة •

المادة ٥٢ ـ تبدأ العدة من تاريخ وقوع الطلاق أو الفسخ أو وفاة الزوج وإن لم تطلع الزوجة على الوفاة •

المادة ٥٣ ـ تجب نفقة العدة للمرأة المطلقة على زوجها ولا تجب للمرأة التي توفي زوجها سواء كانت حاملا أم غير حامل •

I. *The Maintenance of Children*

الفصل التاسع

في الحضانة

المادة ٥٤ ـ الام أحق بحضانة الولد وتربيته حال قيام الزوجية وبعد الفرقة إذا اجتمعت فيها الاهلية المطلوبة •

المادة ٥٥ ـ يشترط في الحاضنة أن تكون بالغة عاقلة أمينة صحيحة الجسم قادرة على تربية الولد وصيانته وأن لا تكون متزوجة بغير محرم للصغير ولا فرق في ذلك بين الام وغيرها من الحاضنات •

المادة ٥٦ ـ إذا تزوجت الحاضنة أماً كانت أم غير أم بزوج غير محرم للصغير سقط حقها في الحضانة وانتقل إلى من يليها في الاستحقاق من الحاضنات فان لم توجد مستحقة أهلا للحضانة فلولي الصغير أخذه ومتى زال المانع يعود حق الحضانة للحاضنة المستحقة .

المادة ٥٧ ـ حق الحضانة يستفاد من قبل الام فيعتبر الاقرب فالاقرب من جهتها ويقدم المدلي بالأم على المدلي بالأب عند اتحاد المرتبة قرباً. فاذا ماتت الام أو تزوجت بقريب أو لم تكن أهلا للحضانة ينتقل حقها الى أمها فان لم تكن أو كانت ليست أهلا للحضانة تنتقل الى أم الاب وان علت عند عدم أهلية القربى ثم لاخوات الصغير وتقدم الأخت الشقيقة ثم الاخت لأم ثم الاخت لاب ثم لبنات الاخوات بتقديم بنت الاخت لابوين ثم لام ، ثم لخالات الصغير وتقدم الخالة لابوين ثم الخالة لام ثم لاب ثم لبنت الاخت لاب ثم لبنات الاخ كذلك ثم لعمات الصغير بتقديم العمة لابوين ثم لام ثم لاب ثم خالات الام ثم خالات الاب ثم عمات الامهات والاباء بهذا الترتيب .

المادة ٥٨ ـ إذا فقدت المحارم من النساء أو وجدت ولم تكن أهلا للحضانة تنتقل للعصبات بترتيب الارث فيقدم الاب ثم الجد ثم الاخ الشقيق ثم الاخ لاب ثم بنو الاخ الشقيق ثم بنو الاخ لاب ثم العم الشقيق ثم العم لاب فاذا تساوى المستحقون للحضانة في درجة واحدة يقدم أصلحهم ثم أكبرهم سنا .

المادة ٥٩ ـ إذا لم توجد عصبة مستحقة الحضانة أو وجد من ليس أهلا لها فلا تسلم اليه المحضونة بل تدفع لذي رحم محرم ويقدم الجد لام ثم الاخ لام ثم ابنه ثم العم لام ثم الخال لابوين ثم الخال لاب ثم الخال لام ولا حق لبنات العم والعمة والخال والخالة في حضانة الذكور ولهن الحق في حضانة الإناث ولا حق لبني العم والعمة والخال والخالة

في حضانة الاناث وانما لهم حضانة الذكور فان لم يكن
للانثى المحضونة إلا ابن عم كان للقاضي أن يوليه حضانتها
إن رآه صالحاً وإلا سلمها لامرأة ثقة أمينة •

المادة ٦٠ ــ أجرة الحضانة غير بدل النفقة وكلها تلزم الاب أن لم يكن
للصغير مال فان كان له مال فلا يلزم أباه منها شيء
إلا أن يتبرع •

المادة ٦١ ــ إذا كانت أم الطفل هي الحاضنة له وكانت مطلقة أو
متزوجة بمحرم للصغير أو معتدة له فلها الاجرة وان لم
يكن للحاضنة مسكن تمسك فيه الصغير الفقير فعلى
أبيه سكناهما وان احتاج المحضون الى خادم وكان أبوه
موسراً يلزم به وغير الام من الحاضنات لها الاجرة •

المادة ٦٢ ــ إذا أبت أم الولد ذكراً كان أم أنثى حضانته مجاناً ولم
يكن له مال وكان أبوه معسراً ولم توجد متبرعة من
محارمه تجبر الام على حضانته وتكون أجرتها ديناً على
أبيه ولها أن تستدين باذن القاضي إذا كانت معسرة •

المادة ٦٣ ــ إذا وجدت متبرعة أهل للحضانة من محارم الطفل وكان
الاب موسراً ولا مال للصغير فالام وان طلبت أجرة أحق
من المتبرعة أما اذا كان الاب معسراً وللصبي مال أو لا
مال له تخير الام بين امساكه مجاناً ودفعه للمتبرعة فان
لم تخير امساكه مجاناً ينزع منها ويسلم للمتبرعة وللام
رؤية الولد وتعهده واذا كان الاب موسراً وللصبي مال
وكانت المتبرعة غريبة فلا يدفع اليها الصبي بل يسلم لامه
بأجرة المثل ولو من مال الصغير •

المادة ٦٤ ــ تنتهي مدة حضانة الصبي عند اتمامه السنة السابعة من
العمر وتنتهي مدة حضانة الصبية عند اتمامها السنة
التاسعة • ويجبر الاب على أخذ الولد • فاذا لم يكن
للولد أب أو جد يدفع للاقرب من العصبة إذا كان صبياً
أما الصبية فلا تسلم لغير محرم فان لم يكن عصبة يترك
المحضون عند الحاضنة إلا اذا رأى القاضي غيرها
أولى له منها •

المادة ٦٥ ــ يمنع الاب من إخراج الولد من بلد أمه بلا رضاها مادامت حضانتها فان أخذ المطلق ولده منها لتزوجها بغريب ولم يكن لـه حاضن غيرها جاز لـه أن يسافر بـه الى أن يعود حق أمه أو من يقوم مقامها في الحضانة •

المادة ٦٦ ــ ليس للام المطلقة أن تسـافر بالولد الحاضنة له من بلد أبيه الى بلـد بعيد بغير اذن أبيه وليـس لغير الام من الحاضنات بأي حال نقل الولد من محل حضانته إلا بإذن أبيه أو اذن القاضي اذا لم يكن لـه أب •

J. *Maintenance Support*

الفصل العاشـر

في النفقة الواجبـة للابناء على الاباء

المادة ٦٧ ــ تجب النفقة بأنواعها الثلاثة على الاب لولده الصغير الفقير سـواء أكان ذكراً أم أنثى الى أن يبـلغ الذكر حـد الكسب ويقدر عليه وتتزوج الانثى •

المادة ٦٨ ــ تجب على الاب نفقـة ولده الكبير الفقير العـاجز عن الكسـب لعاهة تمنعه عن الكسب ونفقة الانثى الكبيرة الفقيرة ما لم تتزوج •

المادة ٦٩ ــ لا يشارك الاب أحد في نفقة ولده ما لم يكن معسـراً عاجزاً عن الكسب فيلحق بالميت وتسقط عنه النفقة وتجب عندئذ على من تجب عليـه نفقة الابن في حالـة عدم وجود الاب •

المادة ٧٠ ــ يتوجب على الام قبل سائر الاقارب الانفاق على ولدها حال عسـر أبيه وان كان الابوان معسرين ولهما أولاد

يستحقون النفقة يؤمر بها الأقرب إن كان موسراً ويجبر عليها ويكون انفاق القريب ديناً على الاب المعسر يرجع به إذا أيسر سواء أكان المنفق أماً أو جداً ام غيرهما .

المادة ٧١ ــ إذا كان أبو الصغير الفقير معدماً وله أقارب موسرون من أصوله فان كان بعضهم وارثاً له وبعضهم غير وارث وتساووا في القربى والجزئية يرجح الوارث وتلزمه نفقة الصغير فان لم يتساووا في القربى والجزئية يعتبر الاقرب جزئية ويلزم بالنفقة وان كان أصوله وارثين فنفقته عليهم بقدر استحقاقهم بالارث .

المادة ٧٢ ــ إذا كان أقارب الطفل الفقير المعدم أبوه بعضهم أصولا وبعضهم حواشي فان كان أحد الصنفين وارثاً والآخر غير وارث يعتبر الاصل لا الحاشية ويلزم بالنفقة سواء أكان هو الوارث أم لا فان كان كل من الاصول والحواشي وارثاً يعتبر الارث وتجب عليهم النفقة على قدر انصابهم في الارث .

المادة ٧٣ ــ إذا كان الاب غائباً وله أولاد ممن تجب نفقتهم عليه وله مال عندهم أو مال مودع عند أحد أو دين عليه وكان المال منقولا فللقاضي أن يحكم بالانفاق عليهم منه أما إذا كان مال الغائب عقاراً فلا يباع منه شيء للنفقة بل يؤذن بالاستدانة عليه لنفقة الاولاد .

المادة ٧٤ ــ لا يجب على الاب نفقة زوجة ابنه الصغير الفقير إلا اذا ضمنها وانما يؤمر بالانفاق عليها ويكون ديناً له يرجع به على ابنه إذا أيسر .

في النفقة الواجبة للابوين على الابناء وفي نفقة ذوي الارحام

المادة ٧٥ ــ تجب على الولد الموسر كبيراً كان أم صغيراً ذكراً أم أنثى نفقة والديه وأجداده وجداته الفقراء .

المادة ٧٦ ــ المرأة المعسرة المتزوجة بغير أبي الولد نفقتها على زوجها لا على ولدها انما إذا كان زوجها معسراً أو غائباً وولدها من غيره موسراً يؤمر بالانفاق ويكون ديناً له يرجع بـه على زوجها إذا أيسر أو حضر •

المادة ٧٧ ــ لا تجب على الابن نفقة والـده الفقـير إلا إذا كان الابن كسوباً والاب عاجزاً عن الكسـب والام المحتاجة بمنزلة الاب العاجز عن الكسب وان كان للابن الفقير عيال يضم أبويه المحتاجين الى عيـاله وينفق على الكل ولا يجبر على اعطائهما شـيئاً على حدة •

المادة ٧٨ ــ إذا كان الابن غائباً وله مال مودع عند أحد أو دين عليه فللقاضي أن يفرض منه النفقة لابويه الفقيرين ولو أنفق المودع الوديعـة أو المدين الـدين على أبوي الغائب بـلا اذنه أو بغير أمر القاضي يضمن للغائب ما أنفقه ولا رجوع لـه على أبويـه •

المادة ٧٩ ــ لا عبرة للارث في وجوب النفقة المترتبة على الابنـاء للوالدين بل تعتبر الجزئية والقرابة لتقديم الاقرب فالاقرب •

المادة ٨٠ ــ تجب النفقة لكل ذي رحم محرم فقير على من يرثـه من أقاربه الموسرين ولو صغيراً بقدر ارثـه منه •

K. *Guardianship*

الفصل الثاني عشر

في الولايـة

المادة ٨١ ــ للاب ولو مسـتور الحال الولايـة على أولاده الصغار والكبار غير المكلفين ذكوراً وإناثاً في النفس وفي المال ولو كان الصغار في حضانة الام وأقاربهم •

المادة ٨٢ ــ إذا بلغ الولد معتوهاً أو مجنوناً تستمر ولاية أبيه عليه في النفس وفي المال وإذا بلغ عاقلا ثم عته أو جن عادت عليه ولاية أبيه بحكم القاضي •

المادة ٨٣ ــ إذا كان الاب عدلا محمود السيرة أو مستور الحال أميناً على حفظ المال فله التصرف والتجارة بالمعروف من مال الصغير •

المادة ٨٤ ــ إذا باع الاب الحائز الاوصاف المذكورة في المادة السابقة شيئاً من أموال ولده المنقولة أو غير المنقولة أو اشترى له شيئاً أو أجر شيئاً من ماله بغبن فاحش أقام القاضي وصياً لطلب ابطال عقد البيع أو الايجار ولا يتوقف

الابطال على الاجارة بعد البلوغ • وإذا أدرك الولد قبل انقضاء مدة الاجارة الصحيحة فليس له نقضها • أما عقد الشراء فينفذ على الولي لا على ولده •

المادة ٨٥ ــ إذا كان الاب فاسد الرأي سيء التدبير أو محكوماً جزائياً بعقوبة تمنعه لمدة طويلة من القيام بأعباء الولاية فلا يجوز له بيع مال الصغير وان كان فيه انفعية للصغير إلا باذن من القاضي •

المادة ٨٦ ــ إذا كان الاب مبذراً متلفاً مال ولده غير أمين على حفظه فللقاضي أن ينصب وصياً وينزع المال من يد أبيه ويسلمه الى الوصي ليحفظه •

المادة ٨٧ ــ لا يجوز للاب شراء مال ولده لنفسه ولا بيع ماله لولده ولا رهن ماله من ولده أو ارتهان مال ولده من نفسه ولا اقراض مال ولده أو أقتراضه الا أن يأذن القاضي بذلك ويقيم وصياً لاجراء العقد ولا يجوز للاب في مطلق الاحوال هبة شيء من أموال الصغير ولو بعوض •

في الوصايـة

المادة ٨٨ ــ الوصي هو الشخص الذي أقامه غيره مقامه ليتصرف في تركته بعد وفاته أو أقامه القاضي إذا كانت هناك داعية اليه • فالوصي نوعان : وصي مختار يعينه الموصي حال حياته ، ووصي منصوب يعينه القاضي •

المادة ٨٩ ــ من أوصي اليه فقبل الوصاية في حياة الموصي لزمته وليس لـه الخروج عنهـا بعـد موت الموصي إلا لأسـباب موجبـة يقرها القاضي •

المادة ٩٠ ــ من أوصي اليه بغير علمه فله الخيار بعد موت الموصي إن شاء قبل الوصاية وإن شاء ردها وعليه في حالة الرد أن يعـلم القاضي بذلك •

المادة ٩١ ــ تجوز الوصاية الى الزوجة والام وغيرهما من النساء والى أحد الورثـة أو غيرهم • ويجوز جعـل الام أو غيرها مشـرفة مع وجود الوصي •

المادة ٩٢ ــ يشترط في الوصي المختار أن يكون قد أتم الثامنةعشرة وفي الوصي المنصوب أن يكون قد أتم الحادية والعشرين من عمره ، ويشترط في الوصي المختار كما يشترط في الوصي المنصوب أن يكون عاقلا أميناً حسـن التصرف حائزاً جميع الحقوق المدنيـة •

المادة ٩٣ ــ إذا لم يكن الوصي المختار حائزاً الاوصاف المذكورة في المادة السابقة فللقاضي أن يعزلـه ويسـتبدله •

المادة ٩٤ ــ ليس للقاضي عزل الوصي المختار إذا كان عدلا قادراً على القيام بالوصاية وان كان عاجزاً يضم اليه غيره أو يستبدله وان قدر بعد ذلك يعيده وصياً •

المادة ٩٥ ــ للقاضي عزل الوصي متى تثبت لديه خيانته •

المادة ٩٦ ــ يعتبر قاصراً من لم يتم الثامنة عشرة من عمره ذكراً كان

أم أنثى وينصب عليه وصي إن لم يكن له ولي أو وصي مختار •

المادة ٩٧ ـ متى بلغ القاصر السن المذكورة في المادة السابقة ترتفع عنه الوصاية حكماً وتسلم اليه أمواله •

المادة ٩٨ ـ لا تبرأ ذمة الوصي بتسليمه الى القاصر أمواله إذا بلغ وكان مجنوناً أو معتوهاً أو ذا غفلة أو ذا سفه • ولا يصح التسليم في مثل هذه الاحوال إلا للوصي الذي ينصبه القاضي •

في تصرفات الوصي

المادة ٩٩ ـ واجبات الوصي المحافظة على أموال القاصر وتنميتها بقدر الامكان •

المادة ١٠٠ ـ للوصي أن يتصرف في منقولات القاصر كافة وان لم يكن للقاصر حاجة بثمنها على أن يستأذن القاضي بذلك •

المادة ١٠١ ـ ليس للوصي بيع غير المنقولات من أموال القاصر إلا بمسوغ من المسوغات الشرعية الآتية :

١ ـ أن يكون في بيع العقار خير للقاصر بأن يباع بأكثر من بدل مثله •

٢ ـ أن يكون على الميت دين لا يمكن ايفاؤه إلا من ثمن العقار •

٣ ـ أن يكون في التركة وصية مرسلة (مطلقة) ولا عروض فيها ولا نقود لنفاذها منها فيباع من العقار بقدر ما يلزم لتنفيذ الوصية •

٤ ـ أن يكون القاصر بحاجة للنفقة وليس له نقود أو عروض •

٥ ـ أن تكون نفقاته وما يترتب عليه من أموال أميرية يزيد على غلاته •

٦ ــ أن يكون العقار آيلا الى الخراب ولم يكن للقاصر نقود تمكنــه من الترميم •

المادة ١٠١ ــ ليــس للوصي بيــع غير المنقولات من أموال القاصر إلا بمســوغ من المسوغات الشرعية الآتية :

١ ــ أن يكون في بيع العقار خير للقاصر بأن يباع بأكثر من بدل مثــله •

٢ ــ أن يكون على الميت دين لا يمكن ايفــاؤه إلا من ثمن العقــار •

٣ ــ أن يكون في التركة وصيــة مرسلة (مطلقة) ولا عروض فيها ولا نقود لنفاذها منها فيباع من العقار بقدر ما يلزم لتنفيذ الوصيــة •

٤ ــ أن يكون القاصر بحــاجة للنفقة وليس لــه نقود أو عروض •

٥ ــ أن تكون نفقاته وما يترتب عليه من أموال أميرية يزيــد على غلاتــه •

٦ ــ أن يكون العقار آيلا الى الخراب ولم يكن للقاصر نقود تمكنــه من الترميم •

المادة ١٠٢ ــ تشترط اجازة القاضي لنفــاذ عقد البيع بأحد المسوغات الشرعية المذكورة في المادة السابقة • ولا يجوز للقاضي أن يمنح الاجازة إلا بعد إجراء تحقيق دقيق يثبت المسوغات الشرعية المشــار اليها •

المادة ١٠٣ ــ على الوصي مختاراً كان أم منصوبا أن ينظم قبل مباشرة أعمال الوصاية وبمعرفة من ينتدبه القاضي لتحرير التركة بياناً بأموال القاصر من منقول وغير منقول وان يعرضه مرفقا بالمستندات لمصادقة القاضي عليه •

المادة ١٠٤ ــ على الوصي المختار أو المنصوب أن يقدم في ختــام كل سنة حساباً الى القاضي بدخل القاصر وخرجه واذا امتنع بعد انذاره عد مقصراً وعزل •

المادة ١٠٥ ــ لا يجوز للوصي أن يبيع ماله للقاصر أو أن يشتري لنفسه أو ان يبيع لاحد أصوله أو فروعه مال القاصر •

المادة ١٠٦ ــ لا يجوز للوصي قضاء دينه من مال القاصر ولا اقراضه واقتراضه ولا رهن ماله عند القاصر ولا ارتهان ماله •

االمادة ١٠٧ ــ ليس للوصي أن يوكل غيره بما يجوز له عمله بنفسه في مال القاصر إلا باذن من القاضي فيما خلا التوكيل بالخصومة والمرافعة ، وللوصي عزل الوكيل •

المادة ١٠٨ ــ إذا أقام الميت وصيين أو اختارهما القاضي فلا يجوز لاحدهما أن ينفرد في التصرف إلا في الاحوال الآتية :

١ ــ تجهيز الميت •

٢ ــ الخصومة عن الصغير •

٣ ــ المطالبة بالديون لا قبضها •

٤ ــ قضاء ما عليه من ديون ثابتة بحكم أو بسند رسمي •

٥ ــ تنفيذ وصية معينة لفقير معين •

٦ ــ شراء ما لا بد منه للصغير من حاجيات •

٧ ــ قبول الهبة •

٨ ــ رد العارية والودائع الثابتة •

٩ ــ رد ما اغتصبه الميت بعد الحكم بالغصب •

١٠ ــ بيع ما يخشى تلفه من المحصولات •

المادة ١٠٩ ــ إذا أقام الموصي وصيين فقبل أحدهما الوصاية ورفض الآخر فللقاضي أن يضم اليه غيره •

المادة ١١٠ ــ ليس اوصي الام أن يتصرف في شيء مما ورثه الصغير من تركة غير تركة أمه •

المادة ١١١ ــ ليس للوصي أن يبريء غريم الميت من الدين ولا أن يحط منه شيئاً إلا باذن القاضي •

المادة ١١٢ ــ للوصي أن يصالح عن دين الميت ودين اليتيم اذا لم يكن لهما بينة وكان الغريم منكراً ويشترط في ذلك موافقة القاضي •

المادة ١١٣ ــ للوصي أن يصالح عن الحق المدعى به على الميت أو اليتيم إذا كان هذا الحق ثابتاً بصك رسمي أو بحكم قضائي •

المادة ١١٤ ــ لا يصح اقرار الوصي بدين أو عين أو وصية على الميت •

المادة ١١٥ ــ إذا قضى الوصي ديناً على الميت بلا بينة مستفادة من صك رسمي وبلا قضاء القاضي أو بلا تصديق الورثة الكبار فيما يتعلق بحصتهم فعليه الضمان •

المادة ١١٦ ــ متى كبر الصغير فله محاسبة الوصي والوصي مجبر على التفصيل وعليه البينة اذا لم تكن النفقة قد أذن بها القاضي أو حاسب بها الوصي •

المادة ١١٧ ــ إذا مات الوصي مجهلا مال الموصى عليه فالضمان في تركته ويستوفى عيناً اذا وجد فيها أو ديناً ممتازاً اذا كان مستهلكا وذلك قبل توزيع التركة •

المادة ١١٨ ــ على الوصي أن يسلم للموصى عليه ماله تحت اشراف القاضي أو من ينيبه عنه •

Interdiction

في الحجر ومفاعله

المادة ١١٩ ــ يحجر القاضي على المجنون والمعتوه والسفيه وذي الغفلة ويقيم عليه وصياً بعد أن يتحقق من ذلك بالشهادة والتقارير الطبية أو بأحدهما حسب مقتضى الحال •

المادة ١٢٠ ــ اذا حجر القاضي على من ذكر يعلن للناس سبب الحجر •

المادة ١٢١ ــ يشترط حضور الشخص المطلوب الحجر عليه أمام القاضي

وإذا تعذر ذلك فعلى القاضي أن ينتقل لاستماعه عند الاقتضاء •

المادة ١٢٢ ـ لا تعتبر تصرفات المجنون قبل الحجر وبعده وانما تصح تصرفاته قبل الحجر في حالة افاقته •

المادة ١٢٣ ـ لا تعتبر تصرفات المعتوه وذي الغفلة قبل الحجر وبعده الا اذا كان لهما فيها نفع محض •

المادة ١٢٤ ـ تصرفات السفيه قبل الحجر جائزة ونافذة أما تصرفاته بعد الحجر واعلانه فغير معتبرة فيما عدا الزواج والطلاق والانفاق على من تجب عليه نفقتهم والوصية في سبيل الخير ان لم يكن له وارث •

المادة ١٢٥ ـ لا تسلم الى المجنون أو المعتوه أو السفيه أو ذي الغفلة أمواله بعد زوال الحجر الا بحكم من القاضي يفيد زوال هذا السبب •

L. *Missing and Trusteeship*

الفصل السادس عشر
في المفقود والقيم عنه

المادة ١٢٦ ـ المفقود هو الغائب الذي لا يدري مكانه ولا تعلم حياته ولا وفاته •

المادة ١٢٧ ـ اذا ترك المفقود وكيلا قبل غيابه لحفظ أمواله وادارة مصالحه فلا ينعزل وكيله بفقده إلا إذا ظهرت خيانته أو تقصيره ولا تنزع الورثة المال من يده وليس للوكيل تعمير عقارات المفقود إذا احتاجت الى تعمير الا باذن القاضي•

المادة ١٢٨ ـ اذا لم يكن المفقود ترك وكيلا ينصب عنه القاضي قيماً لحفظ أمواله وأخذ غلاته وريع عقاراته وقبض ديونه التي أقر بها غرماؤه •

المادة ١٢٩ ــ يشترط في تعيين القيم ما يشترط في تعيين الوصي •

المادة ١٣٠ ــ للقيم أن يبيع باذن القاضي ما يتسارع اليـه الفساد من أموال المفقود المنقولة ومن أمواله غير المنقولة ما يكون آيلا الى الخراب اذا لم يكـن للغائب نقود تمـكن من الترميم • ويحفظ القيم الثمن بمعرفـة القاضي ليعطيه للمفقود إذا ظهر حيـاً أو لمن يسـتحقه من ورثته بعد الحـكم بموتـه •

المادة ١٣١ ــ للقيم أن ينفق من مال المفقود على من تجب عليه نفقته وعلى ما يقتضيه حفظ أموال المفقود •

المادة ١٣٢ ــ للقاضي أن يأذن للقيم بالخصومة عن المفقود •

المادة ١٣٣ ــ على القيم أن يقدم في نهاية كل سنة حساباً الى القاضي بدخل المفقود وخرجه واذا امتنع بعد انذاره يعد مقصراً ويعـزل •

المادة ١٣٤ ــ يحكم القاضي بموت المفقود الذي يغلب عليه الهلاك بعد انقضاء عشر سنوات من تاريخ فقده أما في الاحوال التي لا يغلب فيها الهلاك فيترك أمر المدة التي يحـكم بموت المفقود بعدها الى القاضي وذلك بعد التحري عنه بجميع الطرق المؤدية إلى معرفة ما إذا كان المفقود حياً أو ميتاً ولا يجوز أن تقل هذه المدة عن عشر سـنوات •

المادة ١٣٥ ــ بعد الحكم بموت المفقود بالصورة المبينة في المادة السابقة تقسم تركته بين ورثته الموجودين وقت الحكم على أنه لا يحق لهم التفرغ عن شيء من الارث قبل مضي سنتين على اكتساب الحكم بالوفاة الدرجة القطعية •

المادة ١٣٦ ــ إذا عاد المفقود أو تبين أنه لا يزال حياً بعد الحكم بموته فالباقي من ماله في أيدي ورثتـه يسترده عيناً وما ذهب منه يطالب بثمنه بتاريخ التصرف بـه •

M. *Lineage/Paternity*

الفصل السابع عشر

فـي النسـب

المادة ١٣٧ ــ أقل مدة الحمل مائة وثمانين يوماً وأكثرها ثلاثمائة يوم.

المادة ١٣٨ ــ إذا ولدت الزوجة حال قيام الزواج الصحيح ولداً لتمام مائة وثمانين يوماً فصاعداً من حين عقده ثبت نسـبه من الزوج وان جاء به لاقل من مائة وثمانين يوما منذ تزوجها فلا يثبت نسبه منه الا اذا أقر به صراحة أو دلالة .

المادة ١٣٩ ــ إذا نفى الزوج الولد المولود لتمام مائة وثمانين يوماً من عقد الزواج فلا ينتفي الا اذا نفاه في غضون شـهر من تاريخ الولادة اذا كان حاضراً ومن تاريخ علمه بالولادة إذا كان غائبـاً .

المادة ١٤٠ ــ لا ينتفي نسب الولد في الاحوال الآتية :

١ ــ إذا نفاه الزوج بعد مضي الوقت المبين في المـادة السـابقة .

٢ ــ إذا نفاه بعد الاقرار به صراحة أو دلالة .

٣ ــ اذا نزل الولد ميتاً ثم نفـاه .

٤ ــ اذا نفاه بعد الحكم بثبوت نسبه شرعياً .

المادة ١٤١ ــ اذا ولدت المطلقـة أو المتوفي عنها زوجها ولدا لاقل من ثلاثمـائة يوم من وقت الطلاق أو الوفـاة يثبت نسب ولدهـا . أما إذا جاءت بـه لأكثر من ثلاثماية يوم فلا يثبت نسـبه .

المادة ١٤٢ ــ اذا ادعت الزوجة الولادة وجحدها الزوج أو أنكر تعيين الولد تثبت الولادة كما يثبت تعيين الولد بشهادة القابلة ومن حضر على الولادة من النسوة .

المادة ١٤٣ ــ يثبت نسب الولد إذا ولد لاقل من ثلاثماية يوم من وقت الفرقة اذا كان الزوج أو الورثة قد أقروا بالحبل أو كان الحبل ظاهراً غير خاف •

المادة ١٤٤ ــ لا يثبت عند الانكار النسب لولد زوجة ثبت عدم التلاقي بينها وبين زوجها من جهة العقد ولا النسب لولد زوجة أتت به بعد ثلاثماية يوم من غيبة الزوج عنها •

N. *Wills and Inheritance*

الفصل الثامن عشر

في الوصية والارث

المادة ١٤٥ ــ الوصية تمليك مضاف الى ما بعد الموت بطريق التبرع•

المادة ١٤٦ ــ يشترط لصحة الوصية كون الموصي بالغاً عاقلا مختاراً أهلا للتبرع والموصى به قابلا للتمليك بعد موت الموصي•

المادة ١٤٧ ــ لا تنفذ الوصية اذا كانت تركة الموصي مستغرقة بالدين الا اذا أبرأه الغرماء أو أجازوا الوصية •

المادة ١٤٨ ــ تصح الوصية بكل التركة أو ببعضها لوارث أو لغير وارث•

المادة ١٤٩ ــ يحرم الموصى له مما أوصي له به اذا أقدم على قتل الموصي عمداً أو قصداً •

المادة ١٥٠ ــ تجوز الوصية في جميع سبل الخير •

المادة ١٥١ ــ اختلاف الدين والملة لا يمنع صحة الوصية •

المادة ١٥٢ ــ يملك الموصى له الموصى به بوفاة الموصي مصراً على وصيته ما لم يرد الموصى له الوصية • فاذا ردها يوزع نصيبه من الوصية بحسب العرف الدرزي •

المادة ١٥٣ ــ للموصي أن يرجع عن الوصية كلها أو بعضها وان يدخل عليها أو يبدل فيها ما يشاء •

المادة ١٥٤ ـ إذا هلك الموصى به في يد أحد ورثة الموصي بدون تعديه فلا ضمان عليه أما إذا استهلكه فيكون ضامناً له •

المادة ١٥٥ ـ اذا توفي أحد الموصى لهم قبل الموصي ولم يعدل الموصي وصيته قبل وفاته فان كان للموصى له المتوفي وارث يعود نصيبه لورثته حسب العرف وان لم يكن له وارث فيعود نصيبه الى الاحياء من ورثة الموصي •

المادة ١٥٦ ـ إذا توفي الموصي والموصى له في وقت واحد ولم يثبت أيهما توفي قبل الآخر فتصبح الوصية من حق ورثة الموصى له أما إذا لم يكن للموصى له وارث فتوزع الوصية بين ورثة الموصي بحسب العرف الدرزي •

المادة ١٥٧ ـ إذا أوصى الموصي قبل الزواج ثم تزوج ورزق ولداً أو أوصى بعد الزواج ولم يكن له ولد ثم رزق ولداً تبطل وصيته هذه وتوزع تركته حسب العرف الدرزي أما إذا لم يرزق ولدا فتنفذ الوصية بعد أن يعطى الزوج أو الزوجة الفرض الشرعي من التركة •

المادة ١٥٨ ـ للموصي الخيار حيال حياته بتصديق وتسجيل وصيته لدى قاضي المذهب •

والوصية المسجلة قابلة للتنفيذ بلا حكم من القاضي•

أما الوصية غير المسجلة فلا تنفذ الا بعد صدور حكم القاضي بصحتها •

المادة ١٥٩ ـ على الموصى لهم أو أحدهم أن يراجع القاضي بطلب الحكم بصحة الوصية في مدة سنتين من تاريخ وفاة الموصي وان لم يفعل سقط حقه بالمطالبة بالوصية • ولا تسري أحكام المدة المذكورة بحق القاصر والغائب والمعتوه •

تحفظ الوصية الاصلية لدى القاضي ويعطى صاحب العلاقة نسخة مصدقة عنها •

المادة ١٦٠ ـ يجوز للقاضي أن ينيب عنه أحد رجال الدين لتنظيم أو تصديق الوصية وعلى المستناب أن يرفعها الى القاضي للتسجيل إذا طلب الموصي ذلك •

المادة ١٦١ ـ اذا كان الموصي في بلاد أجنبية يمكنه المصادقة على وصيته لدى المرجع الرسمي المختص في تلك البلاد ولا تنفذ الوصية في اسرائيل الا اذا أعطيت الصيغة التنفيذية من قاضي المذهب وفقاً للاصول المرعية لتنفيذ الاحكام الاجنبية في الاراضي الاسرائيلية •

المادة ١٦٢ ـ تسجل الوصية في سجل القاضي ويوقع الموصي امضاءه في السجل بحضور القاضي وشهود الوصية أو شاهدين منهم على الاقل ويوقع الشهود امضاءاتهم في السجل مع الموصي ثم يصدق القاضي المعاملة المجراة أمامه وتذيل النسخة المحفوظة بيد الموصي بعبارة التصديق الواردة في السجل •

المادة ١٦٣ ـ إذا كان الموصي أمياً فتؤخذ مصادقته على وصيته لدى القاضي بوضع بصمة ابهامه في السجل بعد أن يتلو عليه القاضي مضمون الوصية بحضور شهودها أو بحضور شاهدين منهم على الاقل •

المادة ١٦٤ ـ يجوز ابقاء الوصية مستورة وفي هذه الحالة يوضع الموصي وصيته ضمن غلاف يختمه في الشمع الاحمر بحضرة القاضي وبخاتم المحكمة ويوقعه مع القاضي وأربعة شهود ثم ينظم القاضي محضراً بذلك ويدرج في سجل الوصايا وتعطى صورة مصدقة عنه لصاحب العلاقة ويحفظ الغلاف المختوم المحتوي على الوصية لدى القاضي•

المادة ١٦٥ ـ بعد وفاة الموصي يفتح الغلاف بحضور ذوي العلاقة وتتلى الوصية بحضورهم وتسجل في سجل الوصايا وتحفظ لدى القاضي ويعطى لذوي العلاقة صورة مصدقة عنها •

المادة ١٦٦ ــ إذا شاء الموصي استرجاع وصيته المستورة لرجوعه عنها أو لتعديلها فينظم القاضي محضراً بهــذا الشأن يوقعه القاضي والموصي وشــهود العقد •

المادة ١٦٧ ــ إذا طلب أحد من ذوي العلاقة إصدار حكم بالوفاة وحصر الارث فعلى القاضي أن يحــكم بتوزيع التركة وفقــاً للوصية المنظمة والمصدقة وفقاً لهــذا القانون وعند عدم الوصية توزع التركة بحســب العرف الدرزي •

المادة ١٦٨ ــ في حال الوفاة من غير وصية أو في حال بطلان الوصية توزع التركة بحســب العرف الدرزي •

المادة ١٦٩ ــ يرجع في مسائل الإرث إلى أحكام العرف الدرزي فان الفرع المتوفي قبل وفاة مورثه تقوم فروعه مقــامه وتأخذ نصيبه كما لو كان حيــاً •

O. *Sacred Trusts*

Endowments

الفصل التاسع عشر

فــي الاوقــاف

المادة ١٧٠ ــ يرجع في حكم الوقف ولزومه واســتبداله واســتغلاله والولاية عليه وتعيين مستحقيه وتوزيع ريعه الى صكوك الوقف أو التعــامل الجاري منذ القِــدَم وإلى العرف الدرزي والقوانين النافذة •

المادة ١٧١ ــ في جميع المســائل الداخلة في اختصاص قاضي المذهب والتي لم يرد عليها نص خاص في هــذا القانون يطبّق القاضي المشار اليــه الاحكام المتبعة لدى أبناء الطائفة الدرزية في اســرائيل وجميع النصوص القانونيــة •

Arabic Original of Personal Status Laws of the Druze in Syria

المرسوم التشريعي رقم ٥٩

الصادر في ١٧/٩/١٩٥٣

قانون الاحوال الشخصية

ان رئيس الجمهورية

بناء على احكام الفقرة الاولى من المادة ١٢٤ من الدستور

رسم مايلي

المادة (١)

يطبق اعتباراً من ١/١١/١٩٥٣ اليوم الاول من شهر تشرين الثاني عام الف وتسعمائة وثلاث وخمسين قانون الاحوال الشخصية المرفق بهذا المرسوم التشريعي .

المادة (٢)

يلغى اعتباراً من التاريخ المذكور قانون حقوق العائلة الصادر بتاريخ ٢٥ تشرين الاول عام ١٣٣٣ وسائر القوانين والارادات السنية والمراسيم التشريعية والقرارات التي تخالف قانون الاحوال الشخصية او لا تأتلف مع احكامه

المادة (٣)

ينشر هذا المرسوم التشريعي ويبلغ من يلزم لتنفيذ احكامه ويودع نسخة منه لدى مكتب مجلس النواب حين انتخابه .

رئيس الجمهورية

اديب الشيشكلي

المادة (٣٠٧)

لا يعتبر بالنسبة لطائفة الدرزية ما يخالف الاحكام التالية

أ — يتثبت القاضي من اهلية العاقدين وصحة الزواج قبل العقد

ب — لا يجوز تعدد الزوجات.

ج — لا تسري احكام اللعان والرضاع على افراد الطائفة.

د — اذا تزوج شخص بنتاً على انها باكر ثم ظهر انها ثيب فان كان عالماً بذلك قبل دخوله بها فليس له حق المطالبة بشيء من المهر او الجهاز، وان لم يعلم ذلك الا بعد الدخول بها فله استرجاع نصف المهر اذا اراد ابقاءها في عصمته وله استرجاع كامل المهر والجهاز اذا تبين ان فض البكارة كان بسبب الزنا واراد تطليقها.

اذا اساء الزوج معاشرة زوجته وثبت ذلك وطلبت التفريق منه كان لها ان تستبقي ما قبضته من مهر وجهاز.

هـ — اذا حكم على الزوجة بالزنا فللزوج تطليقها واسترجاع ما دفعه من مهر وما بقي من جهاز.

اذا حكم على الزوج بالزنا فللزوجة طلب التفريق واخذ كامل مهرها المؤجل.

و — لا يقع الطلاق الا بحكم القاضي وبتقرير منه

ز — لا يجوز عودة المطلقة الى عصمة مطلقها

ح — تنفذ الوصية للوارث ولغيره بالثلث وباكثر منه

ط — ان الفرع المتوفى قبل وفاة مورثه تقوم فروعه مقامه ويأخذ نصيبه كما لو كان حيا

المادة (٣٠٨)

يطبق بالنسبة الى الطوائف المسيحية واليهودية ما لدى كل طائفة من احكام تشريعية دينية تتعلق في الخطبة وشروط الزواج وعقده، والمتابعة والنفقة الزوجية ونفقة الصغير وبطلان الزواج وحله وانفكاك رباطه وفي البائنة (الدوطة) والحضانة

Notes

1 *The Druze Faith and Its Believers*

1 The name al-Ḫākim bi-Amr Allāh means "the ruler by command of the Lord."

2 The Druze believe that their faith was in existence long before the 11th century, and that it was only revealed (*kashf*) and propagated in the later period. They also thus explain the existence of prophets they consider "Druze," even though these lived and worked thousands of years earlier, such as Nabī Shu'ayb.

3 Ironically despite this negative image, members of this sect are called by his name: Durzī or Darazī in the singular, and Durūz in the plural. Druze believers choose to be identified by one of two other terms: Muwaḫḫidūn, or those who unify, monotheists; or Banū Ma'rūf (al-Ma'rūfiyyūn), meaning the righteous people or those with the (true) knowledge (of God).

4 According to Druze belief, various figures began to propagate the faith at the start of al-Ḫākim's rule: Abū al-Khayr Salāma ibn 'Abd al-Wahhāb, Abū 'Abd Allāh Muḫammad ibn Wahab al-Qurashī, Abū Ibrāhīm Muḫammad ibn Ismā'īl al-Tamīmī, and Ḫamza ibn 'Alī, who began his preaching in 1017 and disappeared in 1021.

5 It was a Christian Arab tribe in origin that adopted Islam in the second half of the eighth century.

6 Al-Amīr al-Sayyid is known as the person who consolidated and interpreted (*sharaḫa*) the scriptures of the Druze religion (*Kutub al-Ḫikma*).

7 The Ma'n tribe's origins go back to Iraq; with the spread of Islam, they wandered westward and settled, among other places, in the vicinity of Beirut and the Shūf Mountains.

8 There is a view among Druze that the Shihāb emīrs indeed had been Druze even though their external behavior did not always so testify. This behavior is explained on the basis of the *taqiyya* doctrine (the principle of survival, which will be discussed later on).

9 Theoretically this ancient war between these tribes has no real affinity to the internal Druze wars. On the Qays–Yaman tribal wars, see, for example, Y. Shimoni, *'Arveh Eretz-Israel* (Tel Aviv, 5707–1947), pp. 16–17 (Hebrew).

10 From 1947 to 1949, the Syrian parliament numbered 14 Christian representatives, four Alawites, and three Druze. In 1953, all representation of the sect

was entirely erased. See S. Saleh, *Toldot ha-Druzim* (Bar-Ilan University Press and Ministry of Defense, Ramat Gan, 5749–1989), p. 181 (Hebrew).

11 At first, al-Shīshaklī found refuge in Lebanon. In 1960, he went to Brazil. There he was murdered by a Syrian Druze on September 22, 1964.

12 Afterwards, Ḫāṯūm again came into conflict with the Syrian regime, following which he went into exile in Jordan. He was executed by the Syrian authorities on June 26, 1967.

13 Saleh tells of the positive stance that Shaykh ʻAbd Allāh Khayr took toward the Jews, in contrast to the negative position of the Ṯarīf family. These conflicting positions created ferment, which came to a head during the Nabī Shuʻayb celebrations on April 25, 1934. (See Saleh, *Toldot ha-Druzim*, p. 198 ff.) Among those who preferred cooperation with the Arab side were the Mukhtars of the villages of Dāliyat al-Karmil and ʻIsifyā.

14 In time, the Abū Rukn family's aid was also expressed in two additional areas: purchase of weapons for the Yishuv and collecting useful information on what was going on in the region.

15 Besides the material damage and religious slurs and worse that the Druze had experienced at the hands of the rebels, they also suffered personal assaults; thus in early 1939, Shaykh Ḫasan Khunayfis, among the Druze leaders of Shefarʻam, was murdered.

2 *Fundamental Principles of Faith and the Druze Tradition*

1 See chapter 1 of *ha-Druzim* by Nissim Dana (Bar-Ilan University Press, 1998), (Hebrew).

2 Kamāl Junblāṯ (Lebanon) indeed notes: "The Druze neither accept anyone nor permit anyone to abandon the religion"; but in his opinion, "the gates will be opened to new believers in the year 2000" (K. Junblāṯ, *Hādhihi Waṣiyyatī*, Beirut, 1978, p. 50). Despite this, there is a pervasive tradition among the Druze that claims that the Junblāṯ family is of Kurdish origin and joined the sect hundreds of years after the "locking of the gate"! It will yet be noted that the son of Kamāl Junblāṯ, Walīd, one of the two heads of Druze factions in Lebanon, twice married non-Druze women – an act which gravely defies Druze religion. Chapter 10 elaborates upon the phenomenon of intermarriage among the Druze in Israel and the different religious questions that this raises.

3 Saleh, *Toldot ha-Druzim*, p. 183.

4 *Ibid.*, p. 31. Regarding the creation of the world, Saleh said that God revealed himself seventy-two times to his creations, only ten of which were in any way described in the religious texts. The first revelation is called *al-ʻAlī al-AʻLa* (the Supreme Almighty) and occurred where Jerusalem is now located. Between this revelation and the second revelation, 343 million years transpired. At the beginning of this period, God created the universe and all that is in it with simplicity and in an orderly manner.

5 *Ibid.*, p. 33. In Druze faith, there are five cosmic fundamental principles (*Ḫudūd*): general sense (*al-ʻAql al-Kullī*), the comprehensive soul (*al-Nafs al-Kulliyya*), the word (*al-Kalima*), the early arrival (*al-Sābiq*), and the arrival that follows (*al-Tālī*). Saleh explains that each of these fundamentals was revealed

in the form of a human being in different periods from the time of Creation and all were revealed together during the period of the rule of al-Ḫākim bi-Amr Allāh.

6 Benjamin Metudela, *Mass'ot Binjamin,* photo-print (The Hebrew University, Jerusalem, 1965), p. 19. Metudela proceeds to attribute marital customs to the Druze that are unfounded.

7 In Druze terminology, reincarnation is called *Taqammuṣ*. A. Najjār, *Mabhhab al-Durūẓ wal-Tawḫīd* (Cairo, 1965), p. 62, defines reincarnation thus: "The human body is the clothing of the soul. . . . Upon a man's death, his soul is transferred to the body of a baby, indiscriminate of sex, race, or location. . . . The number of souls neither increases, nor decreases . . . Reward and punishment for the soul are invoked over multiple incarnations." On reincarnation, see also Dana, *ha-Druzim*, p. 34.

8 Aside from these seven prophets, the Druze recognize other prophets, among them the prophets mentioned in the scriptures of the three monotheistic religions. Muḫammad ibn Ismā'īl was the seventh Shī'īte Imām; he died young in the year 762 and is considered, as stated, the founder of the Ismā'īliyya sect. Regarding Ismā'īliyya, see H. Lazarus-Yaffe, *Peraqim be-Toldot ha-Aravim ve-ha-Islam* (Tel Aviv, 1970), pp. 183, 189–90.

9 This is not a simple matter according to Druze faith, since a prophet does not marry.

10 Najjār, *Banū Ma'rūf fī Jabal Ḫawrān,* p. 148.

11 See chapter 1, note 2.

12 There are those who call the *'uqqāl* by the name *ṯā'i'ūn*. The wise men of the *'uqqāl* who learn by heart all of the Epistles are called *al-Khattāmiyya*, and among them are those who live apart from Druze society. Many of them are concentrated in Khalwāt al-Bayyāḏa in the village of Ḫāṣbayyā in southern Lebanon. Their turbans (*laffa*) are elongated and arranged differently from the turbans of others (*laffa Mukalwasa*).

13 *Khalwa* – the Druze "house of prayer." The precise translation of this word is the "place of solitude."

14 Friday is sanctified more than the other days of the week in the eyes of the Druze, though they do not impose any additional limitations nor forbid working. It is called *al-Jum'a al-'Aẓima* (the Great Friday), and Monday is considered *mubārak* (blessed).

15 Religious persons who have been excluded from the *'uqqāl* circle owing to a grave transgression are no longer entitled to read the religious scriptures with the *'uqqāl*, and the commentaries (*sharḫ*) on the scriptures alone have to suffice for them. These persons are called *sharrāḫūn.*

16 For more on the religious status of women, see the section, "The Religious Status of Women."

17 The role of the *Sā'is* is generally passed on by inheritance in certain families. The appointment is determined by the religious person in the particular house of prayer.

18 Regarding Ṣūfism, see Lazarus-Yaffe, *Peraqim be-Toldot ha-Aravim ve-ha-Islam*, pp. 316–32.

19 A stranger is permitted to visit the *khalwa* when a religious gathering is not taking place. There are regions in which the place of gathering is called *Majlis*.

20 According to the assumption of S. Falāẖ, the ban on smoking was invoked at the beginning of the Ottoman period, based on motives of economic origin; excessive smoking at the time, which reached the religious members of the community, as well, and the addiction to it, resulted in smokers having to pay a special tariff. See S. Falāh, *ha-Druzim be-Israel*, MA thesis submitted to the Hebrew University of Jerusalem, 1962.

21 The commonly used invocation is "Subẖāna man qassama al-Arzāq wa-lam yansa min fadlihi aẖad" (Praised be He who distributes food, and of Whose grace no man is deprived).

22 This is generally the way in which the request is phrased: "Atlubu safu khātirikum" (Grant me of your pure spirit). The joining of an *'uqqāl* is called *Istilām al-Dīn* (accepting the religion), and the new member declares that he accepts the Druze faith with all of his heart and avoids other beliefs (*mithāq walī al-zamān*). Falāẖ discusses "Questions of Code," according to which one can check if a particular person is indeed an *'āqil*. He is asked, for example: Are you familiar with the alypsa (*ihlīlaj*) plant? What is the name of the Sultān of China? Are you familiar with *ẖijāz* and *najrān*? (Falāẖ, *ha-Druzim be-Israel.*, p. 59). The accusation that the Druze worship a calf is fallacious, and it could be that the reason for this accusation is related to a possible phonetic confusion between the word, *'Aql*, and the word, *'Ijl*.

23 Saleh, *Toldot ha-Druzim,* p. 49. For more about relations between men and women, see sections "Engagement, Marriage, and Divorce," and "Status of Women and Education of Children."

3 *Holidays, Festivals, and Holy Places*

1 The Nabī Shu'ayb festivities are considered *ziyāra* – a visit to a holy site. See below, note 6. It warrants mention that the members of the sect are divided on the question of their religious connection to the *'īd al-Fitr* (festival of breaking the fast), observed by the Muslims at the conclusion of the month of *Ramadān*. Nonetheless, even those who do attribute religious importance to it, attribute a different significance to it than do the Muslims; for the Druze do not fast during *Ramadān*.

2 About Nabī Shu'ayb, see the *Qur'ān,* Chapter 7 (*Sūrat al-A'rāf*), verse 58 ff; Chapter 11 (*Sūrat Hūd*), verse 84 ff; Chapter 26 (*Sūrat al-Shu'arā'*), verse 177 ff. Also compare the reports in the Book of Exodus, Chapter 2; Genesis, Chapter 19.

3 This place is mentioned in the book, *Riẖlat ibn Jubayr* by Muẖammad ibn Jubayr (1145–1217), who visited there in 1185. It is also mentioned in the book, *Mu'jam al-Buldān* by Yāqūt al-Ḫamawī (died 1229). Muẖammad ibn Battūtā (1303–77) writes in his book, *Tuẖfat al-Nuzzār fi Gharā'ib al-Amsār wa-'Ajā'ib al-Asfār,* that "in Tiberias there is a mosque, known as the mosque of the prophets, where the grave of Shu'ayb is, he should rest in peace; and his daughter, the wife of Moses, she should rest in peace." Rabbi Samuel Ben

Samson, who visited there at the beginning of the thirteenth century, claims that he saw two graves, identified as those of Joshua and of Jethro.

4 The *Maqām* was registered under the name of the High Muslim Council (*al-Majlis al-Islāmī al-A'la*) among the Muslim holy sites. The Druze objected to this step, and the conflict was brought to the High Commissioner for determination. The British Mandate in Palestine terminated before the High Commissioner had issued a decision on this issue.

5 According to the late Shaykh 'Abd Allāh Khayr, only the religious leaders gathered inside the *Maqām*, but over time April 25th became the day of mass congregation of all members of the sect, including those who are not among the *'uqqāl*. Therefore, the *'uqqāl* made a practice of coming a day earlier or a day later for their religious gathering. The newspaper, *Lisān al-Ḥāl,* in issue #1880 of October 16, 1889 (page 3), published in Lebanon, mentions the 25th of April as the date of the celebrations that year. I will take this opportunity to acknowledge the help of the late Shaykh Salmān Ṭarīf, who was of great help to me with this research; among other things, he made this issue of the newspaper available to me. The date of the Nabī Shu'ayb celebrations and the date of the Festival of the Sacrifice are determined by different calendars; therefore, the time periods between them are inconsistent. In 1996, both holidays fell on the same date!

6 It should be emphasized that the celebrations at the *Maqām* Nabī Shu'ayb are not considered a holiday (*'īd*), but rather a visit to a holy site (*ziyāra*), and the greeting on such an occasion is "*ziyāra maqbūla*" or "*ziyāra mubāraka*" (a blessed visit), whereas the customary greeting on a religious holiday is "*kull 'ām wa-antum bi-khayr*" (Happy New Year).

7 Zebulun and the rest of the sons of Jacob are recognized as prophets and their graves are holy to the members of the Druze sect. According to tradition, Sabalān spent his time in this cave interpreting the Druze religious books. The swearing of people to honesty is also done at other sites that are holy to the members of the sect.

8 The site in Haifa is also referred to as al-Qabr al-Gharbī (the western grave), as opposed to the site at the village of Yāsīf, referred to as al-Qabr al-Sharqī (the eastern grave). The sites are places where Elijah the Prophet was said to stay, not literal graves, the term employed in popular usage. II Kings 2: 11.

9 I Kings 18: 20–21. Regarding the tradition of making a sacrifice at Maḫriqa, see S. Falāḫ, *Toldot ha-Druzim be-Yisrael* (Jerusalem, 1974).

10 II Samuel: 15–16.

11 See chapter 1, section "The Beginning of the Sect."

12 It has already been noted that the ideal to which the religious Druze is to aspire is the *ṣūfī* lifestyle of grace. In the story about Sitt Sha'wāna, as in many other stories, it is customary in Druze tradition to bring an example of this kind of lifestyle from the early history of the Sons of Israel (*Banū Isrā'īl*). In general, there is a belief among the Druze that there is a connection between them and the ten lost Tribes.

13 There are some other places that the Druze have sanctified in one way or another for their being connected with the lives of important religious person-

alities. It should be emphasized, however, that this is not real sanctification, as the Druze religion absolutely forbids attributing holiness to sites or objects.

14 Adjacent to the *Maqām* are two graves, considered by the local residents to be the tombs of two brothers (*Qabr al-Akhkhayn*) who loved each other dearly. Many tales were told about them in the cultures of different peoples.

4 *The Druze Faith in Relation to Non-Druze*

1 *Rasā'il al-Ḥikma* or *Kutub al-Ḥikma* (Epistles of Wisdom, the term for the Druze religious texts; hereafter, Epistle), *Mithāq walī al-Zamān,* Epistle 5. This Epistle is considered one of the most important in the *Kutub al-Ḥikma.*

2 Actually, the burial ceremony is conducted in accordance with the Islamic ritual, including the reciting of the opening chapter of the *Qur'ān* (*Sūrat al-Fātiḥa*) and turning to face in the direction of Mecca. This city as well as *Ka'ba* and the Muslim holy well of *Zamzam* are explicitly mentioned in the burial prayer (*Ṣalāt al-Janāza* or *al-Ṣalā 'Ala al-Mayyit*). See *Ṭuqūs al-Muwaḥḥidīn, Iṣdāq al-Waṣiyya wa-Ṣalāt al-Janāza, Maktab Mashyakhat al-'Aql* (Beirut, 1961).

3 The two testimonies (*al-shahādatān*) are the belief that there is no God other than *Allāh* and that Muḥammad is his (last) messenger.

4 This religious ruling (*fatwa*) was published in *Majallat al-Ḍuḥa al-Durziyya*, Sec. 12, Lebanon, December 1968, as well as 'A. Najjārr, *Banū Ma'rūf fī Jabal Ḥawrān* (Damascus 1914), p. 150. This source has it that *Imām Jāmi' al-Azhar*, Muḥammad Shaltūtī, declared in the newspapers on August 1, 1959, that al-Azhar University sent *'Ulamā'* to become better familiar with the Druze sect, and that the Druze are "monotheistic, Muslims, and believers."

5 M. al-Zu'bī, *Al-Durūz Ẓāhiruhum* wa-*Bāṭinuhum* (Beirut, 1972), pp. 10–12. Subsequently, he even maintained that "whoever doesn't think so is influenced by political motives." *Ibid.*, pp. 20–1.

6 Jalāl al-Dīn al-Suyyūṭī (1445–1505) lived in Egypt and was considered the most prolific writer on Islam. Among his outstanding compositions are *Jam' al-Jawāmi'* and *Tafsīr al-Jalālayn,* a comprehensive commentary on the *Qur'ān* that he wrote together with his teacher Jalāl al-Dīn al-Maḥallī.

7 The *fatwa,* which will be further discussed below, can be found in the National Library in Jerusalem, the Institute for Manuscripts (MS. AP. AR. No. 152), entitled "*Al-Sayf al-Maslūl 'Ala Ahl al-Tanāsukh wal-Ḥulūl min al-Durūz wal-Tayāmina*" (the sword drawn against the Druze and the *Tayāmina,* who believe in reincarnation).

8 *Dār al-Islām* – a term for the countries in which Islam rules. Lazarus-Yaffe, *Peraqim be-Toldot ha-Aravim ve-ha-Islam* (Tel Aviv, 5731–1970), p. 85.

9 *Qur'ān,* Chapter 9 (*Sūrat al-Tawba),* verse 29; Lazarus-Yaffe, *Ibid.,* p. 77.

10 Najjār, *Banū Ma'rūf fī Jabal Ḥawrān*, wrote extensively about the Druze faith. Likewise, for this subject, it is necessary to refer to the following studies: S. Saleh, *Toldot ha-Druzim*; S. Makārim, *Aḍwa' 'ala Maslak al-Tawḥīd – al-Durziyya* (Beirut, 1966); M. 'Anan, *al-Ḥākim bi-Amr Allāh wa-Asrār al-Da'Wa al-Faṭimiyya* (*al-Ḥakim bi-Amr Allāh* and the Secrets of the Fatimic Emissary Missions), *Dār al-Nāshr al-Ḥadith* (Cairo, 1937); S. De Sacy, *Exposé de la Religion des Druses* (Paris, 1836); D. R. W. Bryer, "The Origins of the Druze Religion," *Der Islam*,

52 (1975), 53 (1976); A. Yāsīn, *Al-'Aqīda al-Durziyya* (The Druze Faith), (Paris, 1985). One of the important sources presented in Yāsīn's book (and it appears that this is a fictitious name and that the publisher is a Maronite-Christian from Lebanon) is "Risālat Kashf al-Ḫaqā'iq" of al-Amīr al-Sayyid Jamāl al-Dīn 'Abd Allāh al-Tanūkhī (1417–1479; hereafter, *Kashf*), which, according to him, includes more than 1,000 pages. For obvious reasons, it is with extreme caution that we have related to the book *Al-'Aqīda al-Durziyya* as well as to the quotes presented therein from Risālat Kashf al-Ḫaqā'iq. It warrants mention that the booklet that was published by the same writer, Ta'līm al-Dīn al-Durzī (hereafter, *Ta'līm*), is a list of questions and responses by means of which the Druze becomes familiar with important principles of the faith. A copy of such a list can be found in the National Library in Jerusalem, the Institute for Manuscripts (AR. #185). In this study, we have also used a similar list published by Yāsīn.

11 The changes in the attitude of al-Ḫākim did not occur in a distinct, marked manner, but rather as part of an ongoing process, and therefore the periods indicated are not defined with rigid boundaries.

12 T. D. Al-Maqrīzī, *Kitāb al-Sulūk li-Ma'rifat al-Mulūk* (Cairo, 1939), Part 4, pp. 73, 158–60, according to 'Anān, *al-Ḫākim bi-Amr Allāh*, p. 76.

13 *Ṣalāt al-Tarāwīḫ* – an optional prayer recited on the nights of the month of *Ramaḏān*.

14 *Ṣalāt al-Ḏuḫa* – an optional prayer recited close to the time of sunrise.

15 This is a particular offense to the Christians, for whom wine is part of their ritual.

16 'Anān, p. 77.

17 *Al-khamīs* is an optional prayer that was primarily included on Thursdays by the righteous Muslims (Ikhwān al-Ṣafā).

18 Two years later (1010), the same decrees were proclaimed anew regarding these three prayers, as well as with regard to the addition to the morning call to prayer, but only for a very short time. It is also known that during the same year, al-Ḫākim took an active part himself in the *Al-Ḏuḫa* prayer "as no *khalīfa* had done before him." In the year 1010, this decree was reactivated. See 'Anān, *al-Ḫākim bi-Amr Allāh*, p. 78.

19 From 1008–1011, ordinances on restrictions were published each year.

20 Such incidents occurred primarily during the years 1007, 1010, and 1013.

21 Among other things, edicts were published in 1007 forbidding ceremonies related to the Epiphany, and the procession opening the week prior to Easter (Palm Sunday) during which participants carry palm branches in memory of Jesus' entrance into Jerusalem as described in the Book of John 2 and thereafter. Likewise, reservations were expressed with regard to the ceremony of transmitting "The Holy Fire" at the Church of the Holy Sepulcher in Jerusalem by the Greek Orthodox. One explanation is that this was done because al-Ḫākim viewed this ceremony as idolatry.

22 According to Y. Anṯāqī, *Ta'rikh* (Beirut, 1905–1909), p. 196, al-Ḫākim ordered the destruction of the Church of the Holy Sepulcher to its foundations. There are sources that attribute this to a later time, to 1010.

23 *Nawāqīs* – a percussion instrument, made of metal or wood, which Christians in the East played to call to prayer.

24 In an order from 1012, it was stated that Christians must wear heavy wooden crosses around their necks, and Jews were required to wear a wooden stamp (*qarāmī*) of similar measure and weight around their necks.

25 Epistle 6, which was composed in 1017 (408 to the *hijra*), states that several years earlier, al-Ḫākim had already halted the tradition whereby Egypt gave an expensive *kiswa* every year to cover the *Ka'ba* structure in Mecca, where the black stone (*al-Ḫajar al-Aswad*) is located.

26 Ḫamza ibn 'Alī, the ideologist and major propagator of the new religion, clarified in Epistle 41 that there was no longer a need for the commandments of Islam or the holiday of the Festival of the Sacrifice (*'īd al-Aḏḫa*), because of the fact that from the year 408 (to the *hijra*), a new age began with the "revelation" of al-Ḫākim as God. The divinity of al-Ḫākim "was hidden" in the year 1018 (408 to the *hijra*), defined as "the year of the test" (*sanat miḫna*), in order to see who among the believers in the unique religion were doing so by will, and who by force. The divinity returned and was revealed anew in the year 1019 (410 to the *hijra*) for a period of time of approximately three years until the disappearance of al-Ḫākim, Ḫamza, and other messengers in the year 1021.

27 Epistle 36 and 58.

28 *Ibid.*, 72.

29 *Ibid.*, 71.

30 *Ibid.*, 12.

31 Muḫammad ibn Ismā'īl was the seventh *Shī'ite Imām*, considered the founder of Ismā'īliyya.

32 See *Kashf* according to Yāsīn, *Al-'Aqīda al-Durziyya*, p. 74.

33 Epistle 64.

34 Epistle 68.

35 *Kashf,* pp. 93–4, according to Yāsīn, *Al-'Aqīda al-Durziyya,* p. 74.

36 Epistle 6. In the Druze faith, the *Sunnī* Muslims are referred to as *Ahl al-Ẕāhir* or *Ahl al-Tanzīl*; he who has brought down (*nazala*), the heavenly book (the *Qur'ān*) to them, and they are required to exhibit its external significance (*ẕāhir*). As opposed to them, the *Shī'a* Muslims are referred to as *Ahl al-Bāṯin* or *Ahl al-Ta'wīl* – those who profess the inner (*bāṯin*), allegorical (*ta'wīl*) significance of the *Qur'ān*, owing to the hidden internal significance that they attribute to the *Qur'ānic* text. The Druze are sometimes referred to as *Ahl Qā'im al-Zamān*, meaning the people that believe in al-Ḫākim, or *Ahl al-Tawhīd*, meaning the believers in the unity of God.

37 The prophet of Islam is described in the most negative manner. Epistles 56, 57, 60, 62, and 71. In Epistle 71, the story is recalled of the Jew who said to Muḫammad: "Raise yourself up above the ground and then we will believe in you." Thus, according to this same story, the true plot of Muḫammad – to confiscate the Jews' estates – was exposed.

38 Bahā' al-Dīn al-Muqtana was among the founders of the Druze faith. See Dana, *ha-Druzim*, p. 15; and at greater length in Saleh, *Toldot ha-Druzim*, p. 33 and onwards. *Ta'līm*, Questions 113 and 115.

39 *Qur'ān,* Chapter 2 (*Sūrat al-Baqara*), verse 143; Epistle 71.
40 *Ibid.*, Chapter 17 (*Sūrat al-Isrā'),* verse 1.
41 For the commandments regarding the *Ḥajj*, see Lazarus-Jaffe, *Peraqim be-Toldot ha-Aravim ve-ha-Islam,* p. 99 and onwards; Epistle 71.
42 In Epistles 53 and 55, the Christians are often referred to as *Ahl al-Ta'Wīl*, a name also frequently used in reference to the *Shī'ītes*. It should be noted that these two epistles, together with Epistle 54, almost entirely address Christianity.
43 Epistle 54; regarding the claim that the Jews killed the prophets, see *Qur'ān,* Chapter 2 *(Sūrat al-Baqara*), verse 61; Chapter 3 (*Sūrat āl 'Umrān*), verses 12, 21, 181; Chapter 4 (*Sūrat al-Nisā'*), verse 155, and more.
44 Epistle 54. Jesus is accompanied by different derogatory descriptions.
45 Reference to them is made in Epistles 72, 76, 78, and 80.
46 Epistle 72.
47 There are additional references to the Jews and the founding fathers of the Jewish people; Epistle 80 highlights the image of Abraham and his war against idolatry.
48 *Qur'ān* , Chapter 61 (*Sūrat al-Ṣaff*), verse 6.
49 *Ibid.*, Chapter 106 (*Sūrat Quraysh*), verse 3.
50 Epistle 6.
51 *Qur'ān*, Chapter 9 (*Sūrat al-Tawba*), verse 119; Epistle 10.
52 *Ibid.*
53 *Ibid.*, 53. The many quotes from the New Testament found in the writings of al-Ḥākim led De Sacy to infer that Bahā' al-Dīn was Christian. See De Sacy, *Exposé de la Religion des Druses.*
54 See the New Testament, The Gospel According to John, 9, 4, where it is stated, "In another day, the night will come . . ." Epistles 53 and 54.
55 *Ibid.*, 52.
56 The New Testament, The Gospel According to Matthew, 2, 15; and see Hosea 11, 1; Epistle 55.
57 *Ibid.*, 23, 34–6. Epistle 55.
58 *Ibid.*, 20, 25 and onwards. *Ta'līm*, Questions 87–97.
59 Epistle 54–5.
60 *Ta'līm*, Question 29.
61 The biblical sources are generally quoted with reasonable precision, while at times there are digressions from the biblical formulation. It is claimed, among other things, that there is reference to the "messiah" in the Books of Joshua, Isaiah, Jeremiah, Ezekiel, Michael (Micha?), Daniel, and Malachi. Epistle 72.
62 Deuteronomy 33:2.
63 Isaiah 42:9.
64 *Ibid.*, 43:18–19. Later in the "quote" it is stated, " You shall come upon them and kill them," the implication being that a struggle occurs between the religion of unity with God and the other religions.
65 *Ibid.*, 40:3.
66 Compare with Psalm 149. Later, a selection of verses from Psalm 18 is

presented (verses 17, 27, 39), attributed to al-Ḫākim: "He saved me from my fierce enemy, from foes too strong for me . . . For you will save a poor nation . . . I will pursue my enemy and will not return until the last of them are crushed and will not be able to rise; they lay fallen at my feet."

67 According to Jeremiah 18, Isaiah 66:3, Amos 5:21, etc. In contrast to what appears in the Druze text, there is no consideration of this subject in the book.

68 Epistle 3. It is noteworthy that there are many epistles in which there are references to the Jews. The outstanding ones are 3, 13, 56, and 72.

69 See above, notes 6–7.

70 *Qur'ān,* Chapter 9 (*Sūrat al-Tawba*), verse 29.

71 In this regard, see *Qur'ān,* Chapter 7 (*Sūrat al-A'rāf*), verse 157.

72 Epistle 13. In Epistle 72, it is claimed that al-Ḫākim knew Arabic, Aramaic, and even Hebrew, and that he had abundant evidence to negate the religion of the Jews.

73 Exodus 3:1–2.

74 Exodus 19. Another revelation of God to Moses – in the wind – is mentioned in the Druze source, and one can make the connection between this and that which is related in Numbers 11.

75 Epistle 56. The attitude of the Druze faith to the tribes of Israel is interesting: there is a distinction between the nine tribes and half of the tribe that "deviated from the way of unity" and remained in Egypt, and among them the "half of the tribe of Samuel(!)," and the other two and a half tribes "clean from transgression" who entered the Land of Israel. Epistle 72.

76 *Al-Jāliya* tax is the tax imposed on non-Muslims. It was determined that the tax, the amount of which will be elaborated upon below, would be annual and mandatory for "the elderly, the young, women, youth, and babies in the cradle." Epistles 9 and 16.

77 Epistle 35; *Ta'līm*, Questions 12 and onwards.

78 Epistle 16, as well as Epistles 9 and 19.

79 Epistle 57. This perspective is not consistent throughout "*Kutub al-Ḫikma.*"

80 *Ta'līm*, Question 14.

81 *Ibid.*, Question 110.

82 *Ibid.*, Question 21.

83 *Ibid.*, Question 116.

84 *Ibid.*, Question 120.

85 Epistle 55. Bryer, "The Origins of the Druze Religion," p. 251, notes that the tax is 3 dinars!

86 See A. M. Majid, *Al-Ḫākim bi-Amr Allāh, al-Khalīfa al-Muftara 'alayhi* (Cairo,1959) who interprets this as "the color of the moon." Bryer, "The Origins of the Druze Religion," p. 251, thinks that the color is gray. The Jews are also referred to as "*nawāṣ̱ib.*"

87 Epistle 16.

88 *Ta'līm*, Questions 121–2. Later, there is reference to the fate of idol worshippers: they, like grass, will dry up and will be scattered in the wind. Question 123. He argues that "the monotheistic sect (i.e., the Druze) show the way in [observing] the Qur'ānic commandments" (p. 215).

89 Despite this, there are sources, such as Najjār, *Mabhhab al-Durūz wal-Tawḫīd*, that do claim that there is a strong tie between the Druze religion and Islam.
90 Epistle 33. In a similar manner, it is stated in Epistle 42: "Remain silent rather than speaking, and guard the sword of the tongue with the razor." This idea is also expressed in Epistles 34, 39, 42, 98, 99, 103, and more.
91 Epistle 34.
92 Epistle 74. See *Kashf*, p. 42, according to Yāsīn, *Al-'Aqīda al-Durziyya*, pp. 107–8.
93 *Ta'līm*, Question 110 and onwards. Bryer, "The Origins of the Druze Religion," p. 261, expresses the thought that this method of adopting the religion of the ruling environment (*taqiyya*) outwardly was not yet practiced at the time of Ḫamza, but rather began during the period of Bahā' al-Dīn.
94 Ṣalāt al-Janāza 'Ala al-Mawta, *Ta'līm*, Questions 29, 30, and 87.
95 Epistle 67.
96 *Ibid.*, 10.
97 *Ibid.*, 17.
98 In the source: "*Al-Da'wa irtafa'at wa-ughliqa al-bāb wa-kafara man kafara wa-āmana man āmana.*" *Ta'līm*, Question 103.
99 *Ta'līm*, Questions 34–5. In order that it be possible to prevent the "infiltration" of strangers and their joining the Druze religion, means were determined for recognizing a true Druze by presenting him with specific questions that have specific responses known only to those who profess the Druze religion; such as the question: Are there farmers in your country who plant the seeds of the myrobalan (*Ihlīlag*) plant? *Ta'līm*, Question 41.
100 *Qur'ān,* Chapter 21 (*Sūrat al-Anbiyā'*), verse 23. Compare with Job 9, 12; Ecclesiastes 8, 4.

5 *The Life-Cycle of the Druze Individual*

1 There are also adults who use the *taḫwīṯa* for the same purpose as well as to get rid of pains and so forth.
2 Druze Religious Court on the Golan, files 27/81 and 28/81.
3 *Ibid.*, File 56/79.
4 *Ibid.*, Divorce File 28/80.
5 *Ibid.*, File 35/80.
6 It should be recalled that the Druze show over-sensitivity to three subjects: *'arḏ,* or a woman's honor; *arḏ*, or land; and *farḏ*, or religious commandments.
7 Estimates are that the frequency of the phenomenon is only about 15 percent of all cases.
8 The principal sources are Makārim, Najjār, and the work by Ṯalī' Amīn Muḫammad, *Aṣl al-Muwaḫḫidīn al-Durūz wa-Uṣuluhum* (Beirut, 1961).
9 Najjār contends that he relies on Epistle 67 of the *Rasā'il.* We should recall here what Falāḫ wrote, *ha-Druzim be-Israel*, p. 44: "The soul in one migration cycle may remember what happened to it in its preceding cycle."
10 Najjār, *Mabhhab al-Durūz wal-Tawḫīd*, pp. 63, 120.
11 *Ibid.*, p. 56.
12 *Ibid.*, p. 62.

13 Ṯalī', *Aṣl al-Muwaḥḥidīn al-Durūz*, p. 99.
14 Makārim, *Aḏwa' 'ala Maslak al-Tawḥīd*, p. 122.
15 Ṯalī', *Aṣl al-Muwaḥḥidīn al-Durūz*, p. 100. This phenomenon is known as *al-Ḥulūl* or *al-Nuṭq*.
16 Compare the Jewish epigram, enunciated in the Ethics of the Fathers 3:19, that "everything is foreseen, but freedom of action is given." See Ṯalī', *Aṣl al-Muwaḥḥidīn al-Durūz*, p. 99.
17 Judgment day has several names: *Yawm al-Daynūna, Yawm al-Dīn, Yawm al-Jazā'*, and *Yawm al-ḥisāb.*
18 Compare the last Mishnah in Tractate Sotah of the Babylonian Talmud: "In the footsteps of the Messiah, audacity will grow."
19 *Yawm al-Ma'ād* or *Yawm al-Qiyāma.*
20 Najjār *Mabhhab al-Durūz wal-Tawḥīd*, p. 76, argues that belief in the transmigration of souls leads a Druze to believe that even if he is killed, his soul can return after a while in its new incarnation and take revenge on the murderer of the body in which it was ensconced in its previous migration-cycle.
21 Because the Druze prayer for the dead is said in public, this may be the reason that it is identical to the prayer that is customary among Muslims, as is the custom of having the feet of the deceased point south.
22 Several reasons are advanced for this custom, such as the desire to enable the family to be free to deal with the business of honoring the dead (through such acts as purifying the body, wrapping it in a shroud, etc.). There is also an economic reason: generally many people participate in a funeral, and providing food to all comers would cause the family financial hardship.

6 *The Druze Spiritual Leadership in the Middle East*

1 Wādī al-Taym is a region of Lebanon west of the Hermon Mountain; it contains the towns of Ḥāṣbayyā and Rāshayyā, among others.
2 (Al-)Shūf is one of the districts in Lebanon where, among others, the towns of B'aqlīn, Dīr al-Qamar, and Bayt al-Dīn are located.
3 These shaykhs' livelihood was to a large extent dependent on the members of the community through their donations of material gifts.
4 Compare the story of Bruria in the Babylonian Talmud, Wiesatsky edn. (New York, 5750 [1990]), Chapter 31, pp. 190–2.
5 There are those who attribute the story to al-Amīr al-Sayyid.
6 Compare the prohibition issued by Rabbi Meir of Rottenberg (a thirteenth-century German Talmudist) against his followers' redeeming him from prison in the Oziesheim Fortress.
7 In the beginning there was even a third shaykh serving the Druze leadership. He was Shaykh Abū Ḥusayn Shiblī Abū al-Mina, who was entrusted with the area between Bayt al-Dīn and B'aqlīn.
8 At the time the law was legislated, Lebanese Druze had three religious figures who served as spiritual leaders of the community. According to the law, this situation was exceptional, and a phenomenon that could not serve as a precedent.
9 It is customary in Lebanon today for members of the Druze community to

support their spiritual leaders with cash grants and other donations.

10 See chapter 7, section "*Maddhabi* courts."

11 *Ibid.*

12 See chapter 3.

13 See Regulations of the Religious Communities (Organization) (The Druze Community), 5717–1957, Regulation 695 of April 21, 1957.

14 Article 11a of the Druze Religious Courts Law, 5723–1962, implies that it is possible to have a situation in which a member of the Religious Appeals Court does not serve as a member of the Druze Religious Council. The regulations pertaining to the Religious Council do not make any connection between the members of this institution and the Druze Religious Court of Appeals. Members of the latter, like the *Qādīs* for the first appeal, receive their salary from the State treasury by virtue of their being *Qādīs* and not as members of the Religious Council. See chapter 7.

15 *Al-Akhbār al-Durziyya*, a publication of the Israel Ministry of Religions (hereafter, *Akhbār*), March 1958.

16 *Ibid.*, May 1968.

17 *Ibid.*, August 1959.

18 *Ibid.*, December 1958.

19 *Ibid.*, July 1970; *al-Anbā'*, April 26, 1970.

20 *Akhbār*, April 1958.

21 *Al-Anbā'*, June 24, 1970. Currently both boys and girls study in this high school, though in separate wings.

22 According to a statement published at the conclusion of an assembly held a number of years ago in *Maqām* Nabī Sabalān. In 1953, Salmān Falāḫ acted to set up a Druze Scouts troup, even seeing in this a first step toward establishing a community organization, to the resentment of the spiritual heads of the Druze community and *'uqqāl* circles, who expressed serious reservations about such an activity.

23 According to the statement published at the conclusion of an assembly of religious figures in the *Maqām* al-Khaḏr on January 15, 1969.

24 *Al-Anbā'*, January 16, 1969.

25 These prohibitions were published in a statement at the end of an assembly that took place in *Maqām* Nabī Sabalān in September 1968. See also *al-Anbā'*, September 13, 1969.

26 *Akhbār*, May 1966; *al-Anbā'*, September 13, 1965.

27 *Akhbār*, July 1969; *al-Anbā'*, April 20, 1969. Hundreds of religious figures who participated in this assembly signed the Religious Council's decree.

28 *Akhbār*, May 1966.

29 Aḫmad Khayr, *Akhbār*, April 1958.

30 *Akhbār*, November 1971.

31 *Ibid.*, May 1966.

32 *Ibid.*, July 1969.

33 From a statement published at the conclusion of an assembly at *Maqām* Nabī Sabalān in September 1968.

34 *Ibid.*, July 1970.

35 *Ibid.*, May 1966. See the article on this subject by Ms. ʻAfīfa Saʻb, in Dana, *ha-Druzim*, chapter 8.

36 The resolution is found in the files of the Religious Communities Division of the Ministry of Religions.

37 Included in this group are religious figures, those responsible for Druze houses of prayer (*sā'ises*), heads of local councils, and of course many of the Ṯarīf family themselves, at the head of which is MK Ṣāliḥ Ṯarīf.

38 This second group, consisting of many academics, was led by Adv. Shakīb ʻAlī, Prof. Fāḏil Manṣūr, and former MK Zaydān ʻAtsche; retired senior army officers, headed by former MK Asʻad Asʻad; and not a few religious figures and heads of local authorities.

39 Among the suits filed, the following may be cited: 804/94, 4687 (Tawfīq Ḫalabī *et al.*); 2146/94 (ʻAlī Shakīb *et al.*); 6806/94 (ʻAlī Shakīb *et al.*); 7523/95 (Asʻad Asʻad); 7351/95, 7765, 7649, 365/96, 146 (Association for the Organization of the Druze Community *et al.*), 4779/95 (ʻAlī Shakīb *et al.*), 5687/96 (ʻAlī Shakīb *et al.*) 209/97 (Salīm Muʻaddī *et al.*); 4916/97 (ʻAlī Shakīb *et al.*); 4412/97, 4080 (Yūsuf Nabwānī *et al.*); 4627/97 (ʻAlī Shakīb *et al.*); 4451/97 (Ṣalāḥ Ḫalabī *et al.*); 5050/97 (ʻAlī Shakīb *et al.*); 5082/97 (Zaydān Qāsim *et al.*). These were all filed in the Supreme Court. There were also case 4166/97 (ʻAlī Nā'if *et al.*) in the District Court and case 217/93 (Asʻad Asʻad *et al.*) in the Druze Religious Court.

40 The Israeli Prime Minister at the time, Yitzhak Rabin, was also serving as Minister of Religions; he promised, in writing, that he had no intention of "interfering in the internal decisions of the community" and that he "hopes and believes that in the final analysis, the community will find the strength, the advice, and the wisdom to overcome disputes and to increase internal unity."

41 The appellants mentioned at times their desire to bring it about that the Druze elections would be conducted like the election to the Israeli Chief Rabbinate, which is based on the Chief Rabbinate of Israel Law, 5740–1980.

42 Religious Communities (Organization) (The Druze Community) Regulations, 5756–1995.

43 In actuality, it was none other than the Attorney General who made the original proposal.

44 Article 2(A) of the regulations.

45 Article 7 of the agreement.

46 Article 14(A) of the regulations states that the regulations are valid for five years from the day of the establishment of the Religious Council. The regulations were published on November 7, 1995.

47 Articles 10–11 of the agreement.

48 It has been noted that Article 8 of the agreement contained a recommendation that the Minister of Religions make a certain emendation in the regulations to the effect that the authority to appoint new members to the council will lie with the Religious Council; however, it does not appear that this recommendation will be accepted by governmental parties, and it is doubtful whether it is viable from a legal standpoint.

7 *The Status of the Druze and Their Community Organization*

1 A. Ṯalī ', "Mashyakhat al-'aql wal-qaḏā' al-Madhhabī al-durzī fi 'abr al-ta'rīkh," Beirut, 1971, p. 148.

2 Details about this document from the High Porte are unavailable. The al-Islam Shaykh's letter was published in the Lebanese Druze journal *(al)Ḏuḥa* (October 1957) and reprinted in *Akhbār* (August 1958). For more on this epistle, see Ṯālī', *Aṣl al-Muwaḥḥidīn al-Durūz*, pp. 149–50.

3 This difference in the source of authority that determined the definition of the status of the Druzes in Palestine served as a pretext for Britain not to recognize the Druze as an independent community and not to establish a court system for them.

4 In 1930–1, Shaykh Qāsim Farhūd of the village of Rāma was appointed as an additional officiator of marriages. This came about because of a struggle that had been going on at the time between the Ṯarīf and Khayr families. Most ceremonies, however, were still conducted by Shaykh Salmān Ṯarīf.

5 Ṯalī ', "Mashyakhat," pp. 156–64.

6 This was laid down in legislation from 1947–8. It was also stated that if for any reason it would not be possible to convene the Court of Appeals, the Justice Minister would appoint one or more *Qāḏī-Madhhab*, except that the *Qāḏī* who heard the original suit that led to the appeal would not be one of the new appointees.

7 On the basis of a 1967 regulation. In the previous law of 1960 and also its predecessor of 1947, it was stipulated that the Court of Appeals would be composed of three members: two *shaykhs 'aql* and a Druze advisor. In 1965–7, the appointments of all eight *Qāḏīs* in the lower courts and in the Court of Appeals were made public. A striking phenomenon in regard to these appointments was that in contrast to the existing situation, the spiritual leadership was no longer given any representation in the religious judicial system.

8 Excluding the Khalwāt al-Bayyāḏa, which was left to the supervision and management of the previous religious officials.

9 In Syria, it was known sometimes as *hay'a dīnīyya,* at times as *ri'āsa rūḥīyya,* and at other times as *mashyakhat al-'aql.*

10 Instead of three or more who had served up to then. The court was relocated to al-Suwaydā'.

11 Signs of this tendency are also noticeable in Lebanon. In 1952 – in other words, before this legislation was enacted – a Druze jurist who was not a religious figure was appointed to the position of *Qāḏī-Madhhab.* He was the judge who was to be replaced in 1962.

12 During the British Mandate, the authorities had appointed Shaykh Salmān Ṯarīf to the position of authorized registrar of marriages and divorces after taking into consideration the special community character of the Druze; nevertheless, they were not recognized as a religious community.

13 Currently there are some 50 certified registrars of marriages in the various Druze villages in Israel.

14 Meaning the prevailing local custom among the Druze in Israel on matters of personal status prior to the publication of the Lebanese law.

15 See p. 80: The Druze Religious Council in Israel.
16 Regulations 5717–1957, Articles 2–4.
17 Selections of the speeches that were delivered on that occasion were published in *Akhbār*, 5th year, No. 3, July 1957.
18 See "Minbar al-Muwāṯinīn al-Durūz," *al-Yawm,* Druze edition, July 19, 1961.
19 In accordance with the Women's Equal Rights Law of 5711–1951, Article 8.
20 See proposed law 404 of July 28, 1959.
21 See proposed law 422 of May 23, 1960. The principal differences between the two proposed laws was the erasure of the title "spiritual head" of the Druze community, and its replacement by "senior sage of the religion." The second proposed law was tabled for more than a year in the Knesset but never brought up for discussion in the plenum. In the end, the fourth Knesset removed it from the Knesset agenda.
22 See proposed law 509 of April 4, 1962.
23 The law was amended in 1972, thus: "If the number of *Qāḏīs-Madhhab* serving on it [the Appeals Bench] is fewer than three, or one or two of the judges cannot fulfill their tasks, the court has the right to discuss the matter with one sitting judge."
24 In this case, too, the law was amended (5740–1980), and it now states that "if the number of *Qāḏīs-Madhhab* is reduced to fewer than three . . . the Appeals Court is entitled to hear cases with two sitting members."
25 Except for the head of the Court of Appeals, who on the basis of the amended law serves in this position, along with his position as chairman of the Religious Council, for life.
26 This directive was intended, in effect, for Shaykh Salmān Ṯarīf, who because of his advanced age was unable to serve as *Qāḏī-Madhhab.* The amended law, again, enabled Shaykh Salmān Ṯarīf to serve as *Qāḏī-Madhhab* until January 1971.
27 This abstract definition expresses the inability of many members of the appointments committee to examine fully the candidate's knowledge in the area of the Druze religion, which of course is secret, and also manifests the lack of a religious institution in Israel that could train *Qāḏīs-Madhhab* and prepare Druze religious functionaries. Proposed laws were discussed a number of times that would require a candidate to have legal training or other higher education, but such proposals were not accepted.
28 Shaykh 'Alayān died in December 1967. In January 1970, Shaykh Nūr al-Dīn Ḫalabī was appointed to the position of *Qāḏī-Madhhab.*

8 *The Druze in Israel – Demography, Settlement, Residence*

1 There is a Druze belief that many people around the world are in fact Druze even though they themselves do not know it.
2 The number for Israel includes the Druze on the Golan Heights. When the State of Israel was established, there were only about 13,000 Druze in the country.
3 According to accepted Druze religious criteria, many Druze who live outside the Middle East are not considered Druze, since they are descendants of

mixed marriages. The spiritual leadership of the Druze in Lebanon – *mashyakhat al-'aql* – is active in maintaining contact with these Druze concentrations around the world and providing them with religious guidance and other services.

4 Data supplied by the Israel Central Bureau of Statistics.

5 Dana, *ha-Druzim*, p. 188.

9 *Social and Economic Changes among the Druze in Israel*

1 The very fact that the vast majority of Druze live in hilly villages greatly helps them preserve their uniqueness and holds them together (even though it slows down the pace of their development). Other important contributions to intensifying feelings of solidarity and uniting individuals is the commandment of *hifz al-Ikhwān*, the strict adherence to not marrying outside the community, and the belief in the transmigration of souls. These religious fundamentals impart the feeling that the members of this community are in effect one large family.

2 In a comprehensive study conducted by Sālih al-Shaykh, "The Druze Identity," MA thesis (Department of Educational Sciences, Tel Aviv University, 1978), the Druze researcher concluded that the Druze see themselves primarily as Druze because this concept underlies their thoughts and feelings. They preserve their uniqueness, they have a strong religious identification, and they take great care to maintain their community identity – not assimilating and laboriously safeguarding their unique character from what has happened to other groups; their religion is the foundation of their collective identity. He also remarks that their Arab identity emanates in the main from the common language and their socio-cultural background, but is detached from any national political conception. It is not directed at Arab countries or Arab nationality or the Palestinian people, and it does not express sharing any fate with them. From this point of view, their identity is Israeli, and this identity is stronger than their Arab identity. In the researcher's opinion, "the fact that the Jews and the Druze were religious and ethnic minorities for many hundreds of years and were persecuted and attacked by the oppressive majority; that and the feeling of identification and a shared fate, accompanied by mutual trust, understanding, and empathy between the two peoples right from their initial contacts, all led to the creation of a strong Israeli identity, which precedes the Arab one. Furthermore, the community's involvement in the life of the State contributes to its laying stress on its Israeli identity.

3 "The Druze Community in Israel Toward the 21st Century," 1996, p. 42.

4 *Ibid.*, p. 34.

10 *Strayers and Those who Return to the Fold*

1 The information for this chapter originates principally in the case files of the Druze Religious Courts and various publications (scholarly and general – as well as in interviews initiated by the author with several of the community's leaders and several of those who "went astray" themselves.

2 The study for this chapter was carried out in the full knowledge that the basic

data are relatively small. It should be remembered, however, that these statistics form the entire corpus of "straying" that occurred in this period; therefore, they definitely enable an exhaustive study of the characteristics of the phenomenon.

3 This refers both to the new religion to which the individual chose to belong by formal act and to the religion of the non-Druze spouse, for in the latter case there is a tendency for the couple and their children to assume a non-Druze way of life and to adopt the tradition of the non-Druze partner.

4 See the section, "Straying in the Direction of Islam."

5 The village of Rāma is a very developed settlement and is active politically. See *ha-Mizrah he-Hadash,* 11 (1961), p. 252.

6 In order to strengthen their argument, the appellants presented declarations of support for their position from Shaykh Farhūd Farhūd of Rāma, who for a time had served as chairman of the "Druze Initiative Committee" (see below, section "Becoming Muslim from political motives"); the poet Samīḫ al-Qāsim; Dr. Sulaymān Bashīr; and Aharon Cohen.

7 High Court of Justice 436/77, Kayyūf v. Minister of the Interior; also, Case no. 318/78/3 in the Haifa District Court.

8 The significance of the rejection of the Kayyūf brothers' appeal lay in the fact that they, along with a group of young Druze who were backing them, were disappointed in their attempt to escape IDF service. This seems to be the explanation for the wave of conversions and its drop to a "normal level" after a few years.

9 Druze Religious Court Case 64/88. It should be noted that the appellant had declared at the time of his becoming a Muslim in the *Shar'ī* Court in Haifa that his request to convert was being done "of his own free will and that he had taken it upon himself to be a Muslim in every sense of the word." After less than a month, however, he appealed to the Druze Religious Court to come back to his community. Similarly, see Case 175/88.

10 Case 113/89. For a similar situation, see the verdicts of Druze Religious Court Cases 156/81, 110/82, 169/82, 63/83, 64/83, 131/83, 146/83, 194/83, 191/86, 175/88, and 208/88.

11 *Ittiḫād,* May 16, 1989, and February 6, 1989.

12 *Ibid.* Jamāl Mu'addī also demanded revocation of the compulsory conscription law for Druze and making military service a matter of choice to be determined by each young Druze himself.

13 *Ittiḫād*, December 6, 1989, and January 24, 1990. At this convocation, MK Hāshim Maḫāmīd also took part and praised the role that the Druze Initiative Committee was fulfilling in its efforts to spoil "the government's attempts to split the ranks of the Palestinian Arab people in Israel." Maḫāmīd also condemned "the compulsory service coercion of Druze youngsters" and demanded its abolition.

14 *Ittiḫād*, supplement on the third anniversary of the *intifāḏa*, December 7, 1990.

15 *Ittiḫād*, September 10, 1990, Mu'addī repeated this idea over and over again even after the war. See *Midān*, January 25, 1991, which reported Mu'addī's appeal to Israel to "exploit the opportunities and announce its agreement to

convene an international conference that will lead to the establishment of an independent Palestinian state in the territories, as such a step would help in stopping the war."

16 Mu'addī was quoted as seeing the demonstration as an expression of rejection, for the Druze were rejecting "the distortion of their identity and will." He stressed that they were refusing "to serve as a whip in the hands of the oppressor." See *Ittiḫād,* December 26, 1990.

17 *Ittiḫād,* December 31, 1990. At the demonstration, a promise was made that the next step would be a demonstration to strike the word "Druze" from the Nationality item on Israeli identity cards and to substitute "Arab" in its place.

18 See, for example, *Ittiḫād,* September 11, 1991.

19 Case 136/83. See also Cases 188/84 and 5/86.

20 Case 171/91.

21 The remaining cases of returning to the fold involved youth who converted to Islam for political motives, as discussed above in section "Becoming Muslim from political motives."

22 From the remarks of *Qāḏī* Na'īm Hinū, Case 207/89. See also Cases 60/88, 208/88, 113/89. *Qāḏī* Labīb Abū Rukn analogized the Druze faith to iron: a change in the Druze religion is like external rust, which cannot at all harm the strength of the iron itself.

23 Contrary to this assertion, Salmān Falāḫ, *Toldot,* pp. 110–11, contends that "the woman [non-Druze married to a Druze man] cannot become a Druze; but her children are indeed Druze. According to Druze law, the children follow the father [and not the mother]. So long as the father is a Druze, his children are Druze in the eyes of Druze law." Salmān Falāḫ adds that all the children of mixed marriages with Jewish women are considered Druze according to Druze law, and Jewish according to Jewish law. The writer of this chapter does not agree with Falāḫ and is of the opinion, according to Druze religious law, that the offspring of a mixed marriage are not considered Druze.

24 Case 56/79.

25 *Ibid.*

26 *Ibid.*

27 *Shahwa bahīmiyya . . . ghaẓīra ḫayawāniyya.*

28 Cases 232/86, 222/87.

29 Case 131/89. See Article 43 of the Law of the Status of the Druze Man.

30 The father of the family came from Syria in 1949 and in a civil marriage wed a woman who was not Druze; all his life, however, he educated his children to maintain their Druze religious and national heritage. It should be mentioned here that the few Druze who set up a family framework with a non-Druze wife came from either Syria or Lebanon.

31 This resolution carried great weight because the head of the Druze Religious Court of Appeals and his associates, who also signed the verdict, also served in the role of chairman and members of the Druze Religious Council, which is the highest spiritual authority of the Druze community in Israel.

32 Signing this decision were Shaykh Amīn Ṭarīf, spiritual head of the Druze community and head of the Druze Religious Court of Appeals; Shaykhs

Aḫmad Khayr and Kamāl Mu'addī, members of the Druze Religious Court of Appeals; the *Qāḏīs* Labīb Abū Rukn and Nūr al-Dīn Ḫalabī; and also Adv. Z. Kamāl, at the time director of the Druze Religious Courts. See Appeals Case 118/77.

33 Case 408/78 of the *Shar'ī* Court in Acre.

34 Among others, a declaration was submitted in his name on the matter of changing the "Nationality" item in the identity card (Case 318/78/3). The matter was discussed in the Haifa District Court; see notes 7 and 8 above. This declaration stated forcefully that "the Druze are a Muslim religious sect of Shī'īte–Ismā'īlite roots, and they are also Arabs culturally–nationally."

35 Case 207/89. For similar cases, see Cases 60/88 and 208/88.

11 *Laws of Personal Status of the Druze in Israel, Lebanon, and Syria: Implementation in Practice*

1 *Qāḏī-madhhab* is the term for a Druze *Qāḏī*, or judge, as distinct from *Qāḏī Shar'ī*, a Muslim *Qāḏī*.

2 Personal Status Law, Articles 37–38. The amendment was passed on February 16, 1979 (see below, section 6).

3 *Ibid.*, Articles 157, 167–71, and others.

4 *Ibid.*, Article 1.

5 *Ibid.*, Article 10.

6 *Ibid.*, Article 11.

7 *Ibid.*, Article 43ff.

8 *Ibid.*, Article 50.

9 *Ibid.*, Section 18.

10 Israeli legislation improved in certain areas the status of the Muslim woman, especially when it came to the marriageable age law of 5710–1950 and the Equal Rights for Women Law of 5711–1951. This legislation had almost no effect on the Druze woman, since her status was very good to begin with in those areas dealt with by the legislation. See Dana, *ha-Druzim*, pp. 47, 156, etc. The *Qāḏī-madhhab*, Shaykh Na'īm Hinū, discussed this matter on several occasions, arguing that the basis for this is found in the idea of Druze solidarity (*ḫifẓ-al-ikhwān*). See Druze Religious Court files, especially 31/95 and 123/96. On the matter of Druze solidarity, see Dana, *ha-Druzim*, p. 41.

11 This is the place to thank the many persons who contributed to the writing of this monograph. Appreciation is extended in particular to Rabbi Nissim Cohen; Shaykh Na'īm Hinū, *Qāḏī* of the Druze Religious Court; Shaykh Ziyād 'Asaliyya, *Qāḏī Shar'ī* of Jerusalem; Shaykh Salmān Badr, director of the Druze Religious Courts; and Shaykh 'Imād Abū Rīsh, Secretary of the Druze Religious Courts.

12 Druze Personal Status Law, Article 1. It should be noted that Muslim religious law does not state a minimum age for marriage. Ottoman Family Law, Article 4, however, sets down as a condition of legal competence for the purpose of marriage that the bridegroom should be at least 18 years old and the bride at least 17. Jewish law states that the marriage of a minor male (below the age of 13) is not valid while that of a minor female takes effect, through her father,

even from birth. See Shulhan 'Aroukh, Even ha-Ezer, §43 and §37. The marriage of a young girl (age 12) is valid; *ibid.*, §2.

13 Personal Status Law, Article 3. An important condition demanded of the guardian is to be *mukallaf*, or being legally accountable; see Article 7. In Jewish law, nothing stands in the way of anyone marrying, and the marriage is valid, except for a deaf and an insane person, the main problem for whom is the lack of knowledge; see Shulhan 'Aroukh, Even ha-Ezer, §44.

14 The Knesset was also unwilling to accept parental consent as a test of a girl's competence for marriage out of concern that considerations not to the girl's well being would dictate the parents' behavior. On the other hand, the District Court was authorized to permit the marriage of a girl who had not turned 17 if there were special circumstances for doing so. This court was granted authority to permit the marriage of a minor below this age to a man who had fathered her child or had made her pregnant.

15 Personal Status Law, Article 15.

16 The waiting period is a prolonged period of four months in which the divorcee or widow needs to wait following her divorce or on becoming a widow before being able to re-marry. This waiting period is important in order to enable a determination of the baby's lineage (father) if it becomes clear that the divorced woman or widow is pregnant. See Section 8 below and also the Personal Status Law, Articles 50–53.

17 *Ibid.*, Article 9; Ottoman Family Law, Article 13. On the prohibition of marriage to a married woman in Jewish law, see Shulhan 'Aroukh, Even ha-Ezer, §17.

18 *Ibid.*, Article 10. Polygamy is not forbidden in either Islam or Judaism. See *Qur'ān*, Chapter 4 (*Sūrat al-Nisā'*), verse 3; Talmud Bavli, Tractate Yevamoth 44a; and Shulhan 'Aroukh, Even ha-Ezer, §1; later, in §11, there is a recommendation not to marry two women. In contrast to the Equal Rights for Women Law of 5711–1951, which forbids polygamy but does not declare invalid polygamous marriages, Druze religious law states that a second marriage is ipso facto null and void.

19 Included in this prohibition are the daughters of his brothers and of his sisters of any kind, and their granddaughters, as well as his aunts of any kind on both sides of the family. Personal Status Law, Article 12; *Qur'ān*, Chapter 4, (*Sūrat al-Nisā'*), verse 23; Ottoman Family Law, Article 17. It should be stressed that marriage with a niece in Judaism is not only not proscribed, but it is also considered a *mitzvah* (positive religious commandment), see Talmud Bavli, Tractate Yevamoth 62–63. Noteworthy is that according to Islamic doctrine, marriages between a man and his wet nurse or her close relatives are also forbidden. This prohibition is based on the opinion in ancient Arab tradition that a child who nurses from a woman is considered like her son even if she did not give birth to him, for a mother's milk, like the child, is like an integral part of a woman's body. See *Qur'ān*, Chapter 4, (*Sūrat al-Nisā'*), verse 23; and Ottoman Family Law, Article 18. In Judaism, there is no such prohibition, but see Talmud Bavli, Tractate Ketuboth 60a ff.

20 Included in this prohibition are the wives of his sons and his grandsons, the daughters of his wives, and others. Personal Status Law, Article 13. On inces-

tuous marriages in Jewish law, see Shulhan ʻAroukh, Even ha-Ezer, §15.

21 *Ibid.*, Articles 14–15. The need to register the marriage is not obligatory in Islam. See Ottoman Family Law, Article 35. This is not the case according to Jewish law, according to which a man may not stay alone with a woman even one day without a *ketuba*, or marriage contract. See also Ottoman Family Law, Article 37. As for the need for witnesses, see idem, Article 56, which states that a wedding that is conducted without witnesses is nullified. In Jewish law, the agreement of the female partner to the marriage is required; however, see note 12 above and Shulhan ʻAroukh, Even ha-Ezer, §27.

22 Personal Status Law, Articles 16–18. Conducting a wedding without the marriage registrar is very rare, except for the Golan Heights region. Every year, there are a number of such cases, especially when the girl is below the legal marriageable age. Registration of the marriage is postponed until she reaches age 17 or the couple goes to court to obtain a declarative judgment as to their being married retroactive to the date of the ceremony (*taṣdīq zawāj* or *ithbāt zawāj*).

23 In most cases, the gap in time between the engagement and the wedding is shortened or the two events are unified. On this phenomenon and its implications, see Section 7 below. For more on the marriage stages among Druze, see Dana, *ha-Druzim*, pp. 125ff. On the marriage bond in Jewish law, see Shulhan ʻAroukh, Even ha-Ezer, §27, 32–33, and 41–42. On the stages of marriage in Jewish law, see *ibid.*, §56–66. Nowadays, the engagement and marriage stages are integrated, but when they were separate, the bride would live in her father's house until the wedding.

24 *Qāḏī madhhab* Shaykh Naʻīm Hinū tends to disregard this possibility, especially since the marriage of the couple is generally performed at the same time and with the same standing.

25 For an expanded discussion on the issue of bridal price, see the following section.

26 Personal Status Law, Article 20; cf. *Qur'ān*, Chapt. 4 (*Sūrat al-Nisā'*), verse 34, which says: "Men rule over women, since God prefers them over the other." See also Dana, *ha-Druzim,* p. 132.

27 Personal Status Law, Articles 22–23. A "legal dwelling" is a place of residence where there are at least minimal conditions for a proper family life and also the husband's family doesn't live there, except for a very small child who cannot discern things.

28 The *Qāḏī* of the Druze Religious Court explained that a "legal motive" includes, among others, a move to a residence in a problematic area in regard to the people living there (criminals, violence, use of drugs, etc.) or to a residence with a serious health risk or which is located in a settlement that does not have a Druze house of worship (*khalwa*) while the wife belongs to the elite religious grouping (*ʻuqqāl*). Jewish law enumerates 10 things that the husband is obligated to do in a marriage but four things that he is not obliged to do; see Shulhan ʻAroukh, Even ha-Ezer, §§69ff. Among others, it states that the woman must live in her husband's house; *ibid.*, §75.

29 Personal Status Law, Article 21. Here is the place to note that in the marriage contract form, the woman has the apparent right to include terms beyond the

customary relationship between a Druze husband and his wife; however, in practice, the use of this mechanism is quite rare. In the hundreds of marriage documents that were examined, it was clearly discerned that the paragraph meant to detail special terms of this sort had been systematically filled in just as those who conducted the marriage ceremony desired, each according to his own set version, but without giving any expression whatsoever to what the bride wanted. Thus, for instance, every marriage certificate of a wedding conducted in Bayt Jann had the words "No conditions" written in; in Dāliyat al-Karmil, one who conducted the ceremony used the phrase, "amount of bridal price not set"; another consistently wrote, "supply of clothing and household furniture to the woman"; a marriage "conductor" from Buq'āthā recorded "ten gold coins in case of divorce or break-up of the marriage." The non-use of this mechanism on the part of the Druze woman possibly stems from her better-off condition in any case – the source of which is the religion itself – such that she is exempt from having to seek alternative means to assure her status.

30 Personal Status Law, Articles 24–25. For more details on the issue of bridal price, see Dana, *ha-Druzim*, especially pp. 125 and 132. The *ketuba* amount in Jewish law is collected at the time of a divorce or the husband's death. On this subject and the final obligations between husband and wife, see Shulhan 'Aroukh, Even ha-Ezer, §55, 88, 96, and 100.

31 See Exodus 25: 15–16; Genesis 34: 12; Mishna Tractate Sanhedrin, Chapter 1, Mishna 5.

32 Personal Status Law, Article 27.

33 *Ibid.*, Article 26.

34 *Ibid.*, Article 29. On alimony for the wife and children in Jewish law, see Shulhan 'Aroukh, Even ha-Ezer, §70 and 78; on medical treatment, see §79; on houshold help if the woman is wealthy, see §80.

35 *Ibid.*, Articles 30–31.

36 *Ibid.*, Articles 32–34.

37 *Ibid.*, Articles 35–36.

38 The original Lebanese law reads as follows: *La yanḫallu 'aqd al-zawāj illā bi-ḫukm qāḏī al-madhhab bil-ṯalāq;* meaning: The marriage bond is no longer through *ṯalāq* [unilateral divorce on the part of the husband], but after (the approval of) the judgment of the *Qāḏī-madhhab*. Personal Status Law, Article 37.

39 The amended version of the Article, as set down by members of the Druze Religious Council is this: *Yanḫallu 'aqd al-zawāj bil-ṯalāq ḫālan amām shuhūd thiqāt;* which means: In a divorce conducted before reliable witnesses, the bond of marriage immediately comes to an end. The decision of the Religious Council was accepted on February 16, 1979, and is on file in the Ministry of Religions. This amendment appears to contradict Article 8(b) of the Equal Rights for Women Law, according to which the dissolution of a marriage against a woman's will if the court's verdict obliges her to undo the marriage bond – is considered a criminal offense and its perpetrator can expect a punishment of up to five years in jail. The need for reliable witnesses to make a divorce valid in Islam is based on the *Qur'ān*, Chapter 65 (*sūrat al-ṯalāq*), verse 2. On the surface, the *Qāḏī's* status in matters of divorce is marginal. See Ottoman

Family Law, Article 110. For more on the immediate need to separate after the divorce, see Kamāl Mu'addī, "The Druze Woman," in Dana, *ha-Druzim*, p. 116, which mentions that divorce is for life and that it is valid even if done without witnesses.

40 Personal Status Law, Article 38. Even in this case, the Religious Council was of the opinion that the validity of the prohibition of the husband's taking back his divorced wife begins immediately with the husband's announcement in front of reliable witnesses of his divorce from his wife, and not from when the *Qāḏī-madhhab* gives his judgment about the divorce. It should be noted that according to Islam, an oral divorce statement is sufficient, whereas in Judaism there is need of a written document. See Deuteronomy 24: 1. Examination of the Druze Religious Court files shows that despite this article, the court itself tries to instill harmony between the couple, and this is done after the husband has divorced his wife. See, for instance, file no. 240/97. *Qāḏī* Shaykh Na'īm Hinū approved this trend, particularly when the couple has offspring and provided that the divorce has not been declared before witnesses. It might be noted here that *Qāḏīs* are divided on the matter of the inheritance rights of such a divorced woman in a case in which the husband passes away in the interim period between his announcement of his divorce and the court's validating this act. On taking back one's divorced wife in Jewish law, see Shulhan 'Aroukh, Even ha-Ezer, §149.

41 See below, Section 8. The idea of *taḫlīl* is based on the *Qur'ān,* Chapter 2 (*Sūrat al-Baqara*), verses 229–30. See also S. D. Goitein and A. Ben-Shemesh, *Muslim Law in the State of Israel*, 1957, p. 137. In Judaism, a man may not take back his divorced wife if she has married someone else in the meantime. See Deuteronomy 24: 3–4.

42 The idea of mediators (*ḫakam*) exists in Islam and is based on the *Qur'ān*, Chapter 4 (*Sūrat al-Nisā'*), verse 35.

43 Personal Status Law, Articles 47–49.

44 *Ibid.*, Articles 39–41, 43–45. The *Qur'ān* speaks of the woman's putting an end to the marriage in a certain way (*khul'*), but in practice this is not possible. See *Qur'ān*, Chapter 2 (*Sūrat al-Baqara*), verse 229. For more on the right of a woman to initiate a divorce, see Kamāl Mu'addī, "The Druze Woman," in Dana, *ha-Druzim*, p. 111ff. According to Jewish law, forcing a husband to give a bill of divorcement (a *get*) abrogates the divorce; see Shulhan 'Aroukh, Even ha-Ezer, §134.

45 Druze Religious Court files 3/83, 92/83, 108/83, and 134/83.

46 *Ibid.*, file 123/96.

47 *Ibid.*, file 93/97.

48 *Ibid.*, file 323/97.

49 *Ibid.*, 141/97.

50 Other files of divorces initiated by the husband: 131/87, 180/97, 251/97, 166/98.

51 *Ibid.*, 31/95 and 205/96.

52 *Ibid.*, 31/95. This file relates that the husband was examined in accordance with the woman's demand, and it turned out that he was not impotent; nevertheless, the *Qāḏī* acceded to the woman's request for a divorce by making a

distinction between the husband's physiological ability to have marital relations and his inability to realize the act, apparently because of some psychological obstacle.

53 *Ibid.*, 142/98.

54 *Ibid.*, 76/98.

55 Other cases of divorce initiated by the woman, files 99/97, 215/97, 246/97, 275/97, 329/97, 85/98, 143/98, 184/98.

56 *Ibid.*, 31/95, 131/97, 275/97, and 166/98.

57 Generally this involves an engagement and the *'aqd* being conducted at the same event or very close in time to each other.

58 *Ibid.*, 31/95.

59 Personal Status Law, Articles 50, 52. In contrast to Druze law, Islamic law distinguishes between the waiting period after a divorce or after a marriage break-up, a period lasting three months, and the waiting period after a death, which lasts four months and 10 days. There are those who explain this expanded waiting time as stemming from the obligation placed on the Muslim wife to mourn 40 days for her deceased husband plus a waiting period of three months. The *Qur'ān,* Chapter 65 (*Sūrat al-ṯalāq*), verse 4, states: Divorced women will wait three cycles [months]. The Mishna, Tractate Yevamoth, Chapter 4, Mishna 10, reads: Divorced women will not marry until they have passed three months. Unlike Druze religious law, the divorced wife in Islam continues to reside in her husband's home during this period, and he has an opportunity to reconsider his action; see *Qur'ān*, Chapter 65 (*Sūrat al-ṯalāq*), verse 6. In Jewish law, a waiting period of 90 days is set for a divorced and a widow; see Shulhan 'Aroukh, Even ha-Ezer, §13.

60 Personal Status Law, Article 51.

61 *Ibid.*, Article 50. According to Jewish law, a pregnant woman has to wait until after she gives birth; see Shulhan 'Aroukh, Even ha-Ezer, §13.

62 *Ibid.*, Article 53. This is also the situation in Islamic law; it stems from the fact that according to both Islam and Druze law, the widow is entitled to share in her deceased husband's estate.

63 *Ibid.*, Article 51; see also above, Section 7, on tying the marriage bond. In Jewish law, too, there is no alimony for a divorced woman, except for her collecting the amount cited in the *ketuba;* see Shulhan 'Aroukh, Even ha-Ezer, §93. As for a widow, she receives maintenance support so long as she does not demand her *ketuba*; *ibid.*

64 *Qāḏī* Shaykh Na'īm Hinū explained that he gives important, even at times decisive, weight to the woman's declaration, for if she risks a false declaration in regard to pregnancy, she might find herself bearing the expense of raising her offspring alone; her son might find himself suspected of being the child of an illicit union. See Ottoman Family Law, Article 139, according to which one does not listen to a divorced woman who claims that her period of *'idda* terminated before three months had passed (since the divorce).

65 Personal Status Law, Articles 54–55.

66 *Ibid.*, Articles 56–57.

67 *Ibid.*, Article 60.

68 *Ibid.*, Article 64. In Jewish law, the girl stays with the mother forever, with the

latter's consent, even if the mother is remarried; a boy, on the other hand, stays with the mother only until the age of six, after which he goes to live with the father. See Shulhan 'Aroukh, Even ha-Ezer, §82.

69 *Ibid.*, Articles 65–66.
70 Court file 118/83.
71 *Ibid.*, file 220/87.
72 *Ibid.*, file 364/98.
73 This involved a case in which the divorced man demanded the return of his 8-year-old daughter, since his ex-wife married a man who is not *maḫram* to his daughter. Religious Court file 295/98.
74 Personal Status Law, Article 67. On maintenance support in Jewish law, see Shulhan 'Aroukh, Even ha-Ezer, §68, 71, and 82, which state, among other things, that no obligation is placed on the mother to support them at all; see also §112, 186, and 240.
75 *Ibid.*, Article 70.
76 *Ibid.*, Article 73.
77 *Ibid.*, Article 75.
78 *Ibid.*, Article 77.
79 *Ibid.*, Article 79.
80 *Ibid.*, Articles 81–84.
81 *Ibid.*, Article 89.
82 *Ibid.*, Article 90.
83 *Ibid.*, Article 116.
84 *Ibid.*, Articles 119–121.
85 *Ibid.*, Article 126.
86 *Ibid.*, Article 127.
87 *Ibid.*, Article 128.
88 *Ibid.*, Articles 134–135.
89 *Ibid.*, Article 136.
90 *Ibid.*, Article 137.
91 *Ibid.*, Article 138.
92 Religious Court file 138/98. *Qāḏī* Shaykh Na'īm Hinū did approve this view when he explained that the child should be assigned no guilt for the sins of his parents. In this context, note should be made that in Judaism, the *mamzer,* or bastard child, is not disqualified in matters of inheritance. See Rambam, *Mishne Tora,* Nahalot A. G. Islam directs that the child born from a forbidden union will inherit his father only, and not his mother.
93 Personal Status Law, Article 145.
94 *Ibid.*, Article 153.
95 *Ibid.*, Article 146.
96 *Ibid.*, Article 148. This directive contradicts Muslim law, according to which the Muslim man is entitled to name a foreigner in his will, but to leave him no more than a third of the estate.
97 *Ibid.*, Article 151. In actual fact, there has been no such case in regard to wills registered in the courts in 1983, 1988, and 1998. Even in Judaism, this is possible: an apostate Jew can inherit his Jewish father. See Rambam, *Mishne Tora*, Nahalot, Chapter 6, Law 12.

98 *Ibid.*, Articles 155–157. This statement in Druze law contrasts with Muslim law, according to which the man's share in such cases goes to those who inherit the heir or the testator, and not to the deceased person. Druze Religious Courts have recorded many cases of this sort. S. D. Goitein, *Ha-Mishpat ha-Muslemi bi-Medinat Israel* (Jerusalem, 1957), advances the hypothesis that skipping over these twins is proof that inheritance is a kind of distribution of spoils: the deceased cannot go to war and, therefore, cannot take part in the division of the estate. Jewish law on this issue is close to Druze law; see Mishna, Tractate Bava Batra, Chapter 8, Mishna B.

99 Personal Status Law, Article 169.

100 Court files 39/88 and 65/88 even mention granddaughters who were entitled to inherit (instead of their fathers, who had died), but who conceded their share in favor of their cousin or brothers.

101 This trend of women giving up inheritance rights is actually on the increase as is shown not only by a comparison of 1998 and 1988 data but also by a comparison with 1983 statistics. Of 16 cases investigated for 1983, there was only one concession by a female in favor of a male.

102 Court cases, files: 132/86, 22/88, 55/88, 74/88, 113/88, and 117/88. It should be mentioned that in 'Afifa Sa'b's article, "The Impetus to Change the Current Standing of the Druze Woman," in Dana, p. 119, the author claims that a large gap exists between Druze religious law in regard to wills and inheritances for women and its actual implementation in the Druze courts in Lebanon. See also A. Layish, "The Druze Family in Israel – Continuity and Change," in Dana, *ha-Druzim*, p. 131ff.

103 Personal Status Law, Articles 170–171.

104 See above, Law of the Personal Status of the Druze Community in Israel and Lebanon, Articles 2, 3, and 5.

105 *Ibid.*, Article 10.

106 *Li'ān* is one of the ways of ending the marital state in Islam: In the event that a man suspects his wife of being unfaithful, the two are made to swear that their claim is truthful and will curse themselves if it is not so. See *Qur'ān,* Chapter 24, (*Sūrat al-Nūr*), from verse 6 on; also, Gottein, *Ha-Mishpat ha-Muslemi*, p. 139.

107 According to Islam, nursing from one source creates a blood relationship, and therefore marriage is forbidden between two who nurse from that source. See *Qur'ān,* Chapter 4, (*Sūrat-al-Nisā'*), from verse 22 on; also Gottein, *Ha-Mishpat ha-Muslemi*, p. 127.

108 See above, Law of the Personal Status of the Druze Community in Israel and Lebanon, Article 43.

109 *Ibid.*, Articles 37–38, especially notes 8–9.

110 In other words, there are no limitations neither in the identity of the heirs nor in the size of their inheritance.

Afterword

1 H. Blank, *The Druze* (Jerusalem, 1958), p. 31.

2 *Kol-bo* (Haifa), October 25, 1991.

Bibliography

English and French

Anderson, J. N. D., "The Personal Law of the Druze Community," *Die Welt des Islams*, NS II (1952), pp. 1–9, 83–94.

——, "The Syrian Law of Personal Status," *Bulletin of the School of Oriental and African Studies*, xvii (1955).

Atashi, Z., *Druze and Jews in Israel – A Shared Destiny*, Brighton and Portland,1995.

Atrache, J., *La Religion des Druzes*, Cahiers de l'Est, 2nd Series, Vol. I, Beyrut 1947, pp. 16–36.

'Azzām, F., "Druze Identity – A Problem Demanding Solution," in N. Dana (ed.), *The Druze, a Religious Community in Transition*, Jerusalem, 1980.

Ben-Dor, G., *The Druzes in Israel. A Political Study*, Jerusalem, 1979.

Ben-Zvi, Y., *The Druze Community in Israel*, Jerusalem, 1954.

Blanc, H., "Druze Particularism: Modern Aspects of an Old Problem," *Middle East Affairs*, 3 (November 1952), pp. 315–21.

Bouron, N., *Les Druzes, Histoire du Liban et de la Montagne Hauranaise*, Paris, 1930.

Bryer, D., "The Origins of the Druze Religion," *Der Islam*, Vol. 52 (1975), pp. 48–84, 239–62; Vol. 53 (1976), pp. 5–27.

Burckhardt, J. L., *Travels in Syria and the Holy Land*, London, 1822.

Churchill, C. H., *Mount Lebanon, A Ten Years' Residence*, 3 vols, London, 1853.

——, *The Druzes and Maronites under Turkish Rule – from 1840 to 1860*, London, 1862.

Conder, C. R., *Tent Work in Palestine*, Vols I–II, London, 1878.

——, and H. H. Kitchener, *Memories of the Survey of Western Palestine*, Vol. I, London, 1881.

——, *Heth & Moab, Explorations in Syria in 1881 and 1882*, London, 1883.

——, *Palestine*, London 1889.

Dana, N. (ed.), *The Druze: A Religious Community in Transition*, Jerusalem, 1980.

De Sacy, S., *Exposé de la Religion* des *Druzes*, Paris, 1836.

Falah, S. H., "Kafr Sumay' – A Druze Village in Upper Galilee," *The Israel Exploration Journal*, Vol. 18, No. 1 (1968), pp. 27–44.

Firro, K., *A History of the Druzes*, Leiden, 1992.

——, *The Druzes in the Jewish State*, Brill, 1999.

Friendly, A., *Israel Oriental Immigrants and Druzes*, London, 1972.

Gelber, Y., "Druze and Jews in the War of 1948," *Middle Eastern Studies*, 31/2 (April 1995).

Guys, H., *La Nation Druze, son Histoire, sa Religion, ses Mouers et son Etat Politique*, Paris, 1863.

Hirschberg, H. Z., "The Druzes," in J. A. Arberry (general ed.), *Religion in the Middle East*, Vol. 2, Cambridge, 1966, pp. 330–48.

Hitti, Ph. K., *The Origins of the Druze People and Religion*, New York, 1928.

Hodgson, M. G. S., "Duruz," *The Encyclopaedia of Islam*, New Edition, Leiden and London, 1960 ff., pp. 631–4.

——, "Al-Daraz" and Ḥamza in the Origin of the Druze Religion," *Journal of the American Oriental Society*, 82/1 (1962).

Hourani, A., *Minorities in the Arab World*, Oxford, 1947.

Izzedin, N., *The Druzes, A New Study of Their History, Faith and Society*, Leiden, 1984.

Kasdan, L., "Isfiya Social Structure, Fission and Faction in Druze Community," Ph.D. thesis, University of Chicago, 1961.

Kohlberg, E., "Some Imām" Shīʿī Views on Taqiyya," *Journal of the American Oriental Society*, 95, 3 (1975), pp. 395–402.

Layish, A., "Women and Succession in the Druze Family in Israel," *Asian and African Studies*, Vol. 11, no. 1 (1976), pp. 101–19.

——, "Compensation to the Divorced Women in the Israeli Druze Family," *Israeli Law Review*, Vol. 12, No. 3 (1977), pp. 330–43.

——, "The Prohibition of Reinstating a Divorced Wife in the Druze Family," *Bulletin of the School of Oriental and African Studies* (1978), pp. 258–71.

______, *Marriage, Divorce and Succession in the Druze Family*, Leiden, 1982.

______, "Taqiyya among the Druzes," *Asian and African Studies*, 19 (1985), pp. 245–81.

——, and N. Dana, "The Law of Personal Status of the Druze Community in Israel," in N. Dana (ed.), *The Druze: A Religious Community in Transition*, Jerusalem, 1980, pp. 147–75.

Lewis, B., "An Arabic Account of the Province of Safad," *Bulletin of the School of Oriental and African Studies*, Vol. XV (1953), pp. 477 ff.

Oliphant, L., *The Land of Gilead*, London, 1880.

——, *Haifa or Modern Life in the Holy Land 1882–1885*, London, 1887; New Edn., Jerusalem, 1976.

Oliva, Y., "Political Involvement of the Druze in Israel," in N. Dana (ed.), *The Druze: A Religious Community in Transition*, Jerusalem, 1980.

Oppenheimer, J. W. S., *The Social Organization of Druze Villages in Israel*, London, 1985.

Parfit, J. T., *Among the Druzes of Lebanon & Bashan*, London, 1917.

Parsons, L., "The Druze in the Arab–Israeli Conflict, 1947–1949," D. Phil., St Antony's College, Oxford University, 1995.

P. E. F., *Palestine Exploration Fund, Quarterly Statement*, Vols 1874, 1886, 1889, 1894, 1896, 1901, 1930.

Pococke, R., *Description of the East and Other Countries*, 2 vols, London, 1745.

Polk, W. R., "The British Connections with the Druzes," *Middle East Journal*, xvii (Winter–Spring 1963).

Ray, A., "The Strange World of the Druzes," *Commentary*, January 21/1, 1965.

Robinson, J. M. (ed.), *The Nag Hammadi Library*, San Francisco, 1978.

Saleh, S., "The British-Druze Connection and the Druze Rising of 1896 in the Ḫawrān," *Middle Eastern Studies*, 13/2 (May 1977).

——, "The Anglo–Druze Connection 1841," in P. Artzi (ed.), *Bar-Ilan Studies in History*, Ramat-Gan, 1978.

——, "Relations between Jews and Druze between the Two World Wars," in P. Artzi (ed.), *Bar-Ilan Studies in History* II, Ramat-Gan, 1984.

Sherman, A., *The Druze*, Tel-Aviv, 1975.

Sprengling, M., "The Berlin Druze Lexicon," *Journal of Semitic Languages and Literatures*, LVI (1939), 338–414.

Springett, H. B., *Secret Sects of Syria and the Lebanon*, London, 1922.

Teitelbaum, J. "Ideology and Conflict in the Middle East Minority: The Case of the Druze Initiative Committee in Israel," *Orient* 3/26 (1985).

Tshelbe, E., "Travels in Palestine," *Quarterly of the Department of Antiquities in Palestine*, 4 (1935).

Vatikiotis, P. J., "Al-Ḫākin bi'Amr Allāh: The God King Idea Realized," *Islamic Culture*, 29 (1995).

Velde, Van de, C. W. M., *Narrative of a Journey through Syria and Palestine in 1851 and 1852*, London, 1854.

Volney, M. C. F., *Travels through Syria and Egypt, in the Years 1783, 1784 and 1785*, London, 1786.

Arabic and Hebrew

'Anān, M., *Al-Ḫākim bi-Amr Allāh wa-Asrār al-Da'wa al-Fāṯimiyya*, Cairo, 1937.

'Azzām, F., *Fuṣūl fi al-Turāth al-Durzī*, Shafā'amr, 1982.

'Azzām, F. and S. Falāḫ, *Durūs fi al-ādāb al-Durziyya, al-A'yād*, Jerusalem, 1979.

——, *Durūs fi al-ādāb al-Durziyya, Qiyam wa-Taqālīd*, Jerusalem, 1978.

Abū Ismā'īl, S., *Al-Durūz, Taḫrīf wa-Ta'līf wa-Taṣnīf*, Beirut, 1955.

Abū 'Izz al-Dīn, S., *Aṣl al-Durūz, al-Muqtaṯaf*, Beirut, 1930.

Abū Muṣliḫ, G.H., *Al-Durūz fī ẕill al-Iḫtilāl al-Isrā'īlī*, Beirut, 1975.

Abū Muṣliḫ, H., *Wāqi' al-Durūz*, Beirut, 1978.

Abū Rashīd, H., *Jabal al-Durūz*, Cairo, 1925.

Abū Rukn, L., "Ḫawla al-Zawāj al-Mukhṯalaṯ," *Majallat al-Akhbār al-Durziyya* (*MAD*), Jerusalem, 1966.

——, "Ḫurriyyat al-Mar'a al-Durziyya," *MAD*, 1981.

Abū Shaqrā, 'A., *Thalāthat 'Ulamā' min Shuyūkh Banī Ma'rūf*, Beirut, 1957.

Al-Anṯakī, Y., *Ta'rīkh*, Beirut, 1905–9.

Al-Aṯrash, F., *Al-Durūz, Mu'āmarāt wa-Ta'rīkh wa-Ḫaqā'iq*, Beirut, 1975.

Al-A'war, Y., *Al-Aḫwāl al-Shakhṣiyya al-Durziyya ḫilman wa-Ijtihādan*, Beirut, 1983.

Al-Bāshā, M., *Mu'jam A'lām al-Durūz*, Beirut, 1990.

Al-Shaykh, S. *Ha-Zehut Ha-Druzit*, MA Thesis, Tel Aviv University, 1978.

Al-Tanūkhī, J. D., "Risālat Kashf al-Ḫaqā'iq" (fi) Al-*'Aqīda al-Durziyya*, Yāsīn, A., Paris, 1985.

Azrieli, Y. and Abu Rukn, J., *Ahava She-'Amda be-Mivhan*, Jerusalem, 1989.

B'ayni, H., *Durūz Suriya wa-Lubnān fī 'Ahd al-Intidāb al-Faransī, 1920–1943*, Beirut, 1993.

——, *Sulṯān al-Aṯrash*, al-Suwayda', 1985.

Blanc, H., *Ha-Druzim*, Jerusalem, 1971.
Bustānī, N., "Durūz," *Kitāb Dā'irat al-Ma'ārif*, Beirut, 1983.
Dana, N., "Al-Amākin al-Muqaddasa wal-A'yād wal-Munāsabāt 'inda al-*Durūz*," *MAD*, Jerusalem, 1981.
——, *Ha-Druzim – 'Eda U-Massoret*, Jerusalem, 1974.
Falāḩ, F., "Al-Marāḩil allatī Marra bihā al-Ḩukm al-Ṯā'ifī 'inda al-Ṯā'ifa al-Durziyya," *MAD*, 3, 1966, 1–2, pp. 4–11.
——, "Taṯawwur al-Maḩākim al-Dīniyya al-Durziyya fī al-Sanatayn al-Māḏiyatayn," *MAD*, 3, 1968, 3–4, pp. 45–8.
Falāḩ, S., *Ha-Druzim Be-Israel*, MA thesis, The Hebrew University, Jerusalem, 1962.
——, *Toldot ha-Druzim be-Yisra'el*, Jerusalem, 1974.
——, *Durūs fī al-Turāth al-Durzī ,al-Turāth al-Sha'bī*, Jerusalem, 1979.
——, (ed.) *Fuṣūl fī Ta'rīkh al-Durūz*, Jerusalem, 1980.
—— and F. 'Azzām, *Durūs fī al-ādāb al-Durziyya*, Jerusalem, 1979.
—— and N. Khayr, *Durūs fī al-Turāth al-Durzī, Qiṣaṣ min Qurāna*, Jerusalem, 1982.
—— and A. Shenhar, *Sippure 'Am Druziyyim*, Jerusalem, 1978.
Faraj, R., "Ha-Qhsharim ben ha-Druzim ve-ha-Yehudim betqufat ha-Mandat ha-Briti, 1918–1948," MA thesis, University of Haifa, 1990.
——, *Durūz Falasṯīn fī Fatrat al-Intidāb al-Bariṯānī, 1918–1948*, Israel, 1991.
Faraj, S., *Marāḩil Taṯawwur al-Mujtama' al-Durzī fī Isrā'īl*, Israel, 1992.
Firu, K., *al-Durūz, Man hum wa-mā qīla fihum Bil-Qarn al-'Ishrīn*, Jizzīn, 1978.
Har'el, M., *Yānūḩ*, Jerusalem, 1959.
Hariz, S., "Al-Shar' al-Durzī," *Al-Wāqi' al-Durzī wa-Ḩatmiyyat al-Taṯawwur*, Beirut, 1962, pp. 71–110.
——, "Tanẕīm al-Qaḏā' al-Madhhabī fī Lubnān," *MAD*, 6 (1973), pp. 56–63.
Hasan, Y., "Tmurot ba-Yishuvim ha-Druziyim ke-Totza'a mi-Shiluvam ba-Ma'arekhet ha-Bithonit ha-Isra'elit," MA thesis, University of Haifa, 1992.
Husein, M., *Ṯā'ifat al-Durūz wa-Ta'rīkhuhā wa-'Aqā'iduhā*, Egypt, 1962.
Junblāṯ, K., *Hāẕihi waṣiyyatī*, Beirut, 1978.
Kamāl, Z., "Al-Waṣiyya fī al-Aḩkām al-Durziyya," *MAD*, Jerusalem, 1981.
——, "Al-Qaḏā' al-Ṯā'ifī al-Durzī fī Isrā'īl," *MAD*, Jerusalem, 1970.
——, "Al-Qaḏā' fī al-Maḩākim al-Dīnīyya al-Durziyya," *MAD*, Jerusalem, 1971.
Layish, A., "Al-Ṯalāq lada al-Ṯā'ifa al-Durziyya," *MAD*, 1981.
——, "Ma'amad ha-Islam ba-Mishpaha ha-Druzit be-Yisra'el," *Ha-Mizrah He-Hadash* (*MH*), 26, 1976, 3–4, pp. 149–61.
——, "Ha-Shiput ha-Adati shel ha-Druzim be-Yisra'el," *MH*, 11 (1961), 4, pp. 258–62.
——, "He'arot le-Hoq Batei ha-Din ha-Datiyyim ha-Druziyim," 5723–1962, *MH*, 15, 1965, 1–2, pp. 102–3.
Lazarus-Yafeh, H., *Peraqim Be-Toldot ha-Aravim ve-ha-Islam*, Tel-Aviv, 1970.
Majid, 'A. M., *Al-Ḩākim bi-Amr Allāh, al-Khalīfa al-Muftara 'alayhi*, Cairo, 1959.
Makārim, S., *Aḏwā' 'ala Maslak al-Tawḩīd al-Durziyya*, Beirut, 1966.
(Al-)Maqrīzī, T. D., *Kitāb al-Sulūk Lima'rifat al-Mulūk*, Cairo, 1979.
Mu'addī, K., "Al-Mar'a al-Durziyya Ḩuqūquha Wājibātuhā Zawājuhā wa-Ṯalāquhā," *MAD*, 6, 1973, pp. 9–25.
——, "Al-Durūz qabla Isrā'īl," *MAD*, 1, 1958, pp. 1–4.

Najjār, 'A., *Banū Ma'rūf fī Jabal Ḫawrān*, Damascus, 1914.

——, *Madhhab al-Durūz wal-Tawḫīd*, Cairo, 1965.

Nuwayhid, 'A., *Sīrat al-Amīr al-Sayyid Jamāl al-Dīn 'Abd Allāh al-Tanūkhī wal-Shaykh Muḫammad Abī-Hilāl al-Ma'rūf Bil-Shaykh al-Fāḏil*, Beirut, 1975.

Oliva, Y., "Ha-Druzim be-Isra'el. Ba'ayat Zehut 'Atzmit ve-Hishtaykhut Politit," *Medina U-Mimshal* 2/1 (1972).

Qāsim, N., *Wāqi'al-Durūz fī Isrā'īl*, Jerusalem, 1976.

Qays, F. N., *Majmū'āt Ijtihādāt al-Maḫākim al-Madhhabiyya al-Durziyya 1968–1972*, Beirut, 1972.

S̱a'b, 'A., "Al-Mar'a al-Durziyya," *Al-Wāqi' al-Durzī wa-Ḫatmiyyat al-Taṯawwur*, Beirut, 1962.

S̱āleḫ, Sh., *Toldot ha-Druzim*, Tel Aviv, 1989.

Salmān, T., *Aḏwā' 'ala Madhhab al-Tawḫīd*, Beirut, 1963.

S̱ghayar, S., *Banū Ma'rūf fī al-Tā'rīkh,* al-Qraya, Lebanon, 1984.

Ṯalī ', A., *As̱l al-Muwaḫḫidīn al-Durūz wa-Us̱ūluhum*, Beirut, 1961.

_____, *Mashyakhat al-'Aql wal-Qaḏā' al-Madhhabī al-Durzī 'abra al-Tā'rīkh*, Beirut, 1971, 1979.

_____, "Nash'at al-Durūz, *Al-Wāqi'al-Durzī wa-Ḫatmiyyat al-Taṯawwur*, Beirut, 1962.

Taqī, al-Dīn, 'A., *Kitāb al-Nuqaṯ wal-Dawā'ir*, Germany, 1902.

Taqī al-Dīn, Kh., *Al-Aḫwāl al-Shakhs̱iyya 'inda al-Durūz wa-Awjah al-Tabāyun ma'a al-Sunna wal-Shī 'a Mas̱daran wa-'jtihādan*, Beirut, 1981.

——, *Quḏāt al-Muwaḫḫidīn al-Durūz*, Beirut, 1979.

Ṯarīf, 'A., *S̱īrat Faḏīlat al-Shaykh Amīn Ṯarīf*, Jerusalem, 1987.

Yāsīn, A. (pseudonym), *Bayna al-'Aql wal-Nabī*, Paris, 1981.

——, *Al-'Aqīda al-Durziyya*, Paris, 1985.

——, "Ta'līm al-Dīn al-Durzī," *Al-'Aqīda al-Durziyya*, Paris, 1985.

Zbeida, A., *Ha-Druzim be-Ramat ha-Golan 1968–1982*, Tel Aviv, 1988.

Zu 'bī, M., *Al-Durūz Ẕahiruhum wa-Bāṯinuhum*, Beirut, 1972.

Index